Industrial Democracy: Yugoslav Style

Industrial Democracy: Yugoslav Style

The Effect of Decentralization on Organizational Behavior

by ICHAK ADIZES

Assistant Professor of Administrative Studies
The University of California at Los Angeles

The Free Press, New York
Collier-Macmillan Ltd., London

To my parents
Salamon and Diamanta Adižes

Contents

I

Introduction

III

The Environment and the Organizational Structure

List of Charts

List of Tables

Preface

This book deals with industrial democracy in Yugoslavia or with, as the Yugoslavs call it, self-management. The book presents case studies of two Yugoslav companies, ABC and XYZ (disguised names), which were observed in operation during the spring of 1967. In an attempt to analyze several aspects of organizational behavior by studying its relationship to a dynamic environment, the study describes the process of decision-making on the company level after the Yugoslav economic reform of 1965 (which consisted of further decentralization).

The study claims that both an increase in uncertainty and a change in the character of uncertainty under which the companies operated evolved from developments in the economic and political environment (i.e., the economic decentralization and its political repercussions) after 1965. However, the constraints of the organizational structure remained unchanged to a great extent and were based on ideological premises which assumed certainty. Thus, while the organization was structured on one set of premises, changing environmental forces required different structures, and pressure was introduced for organizational adaptation. A comparison of the environmental forces and their effect on organizational structures is made at the end of the book.

In a broader view, the study deals with the post-reform managerial difficulties encountered by the two companies, difficulties which other decentralizing countries may encounter in their efforts to stimulate higher productivity through competition, while still adhering to the egalitarian principles which are the basis of the Communist doctrine. These conflicts will become evident as the study progresses.

This study is organized into three major parts. Part I contains three introductory chapters: Chapter 1 explains the goals, significance, and methodology of the study; Chapter 2 describes and analyzes the changing environment by offering a description of the economic and socio-political background, the ideological concepts of self-management and the legal constraints imposed on decision-making, and the organizational structure created by this ideology. This chapter includes also a discussion of the various groups, operating within and outside of the companies, which are formal but are not a part of the organizational chart as it is commonly designed. Finally, Chapter 2 offers a description of the unique reward system in Yugoslav industrial organizations. Chapter 3 describes the histories of the two companies studied and the differences in their economic efficiency. Part II is composed of Chapters 4-6 which describe and analyze the two companies' organizational behavior; it describes and analyzes the various decisions made within each organization: Chapter 4 describes the process of modernization; Chapter 5, the process of preparing the annual plan; Chapter 6, the process of hiring, firing, and disciplining. This last chapter includes a description and analysis of a wildcat strike in one of the companies observed by the researcher, as well as a comparison with findings on this phenomenon made by other Yugoslav social scientists.

Part III attempts to relate environmental changes described in Part I to organizational behavior described in Part II. Part III is composed of two chapters: Chapter 7, which analyzes the self-management system and attempts some predictions as to its further development and adequacy for other centrally planned economies contemplating decentralization; and Chapter 8, which focuses on organizational theory and the insights which may be gained from this study. In this last chapter, the changing American environment is compared to the Yugoslav environment, and the organizational, structural adaptations taking place in both countries are analyzed. This chapter attempts to add new dimensions to existent organizational participative theories by pinpointing some of their limitations, and adds as well to the existent body of knowledge on open systems whose theoretical framework the researcher utilized.

Acknowledgements

This book is a revision of a major part of my doctoral thesis submitted to Columbia University in 1968 under the title: *The Effect of Decentralization on Organizational Behavior: An Exploratory Study of the Yugoslav Self-Management System.* I want to thank all those people who made my doctoral dissertation possible. This includes the innumerable people who assisted me in Yugoslavia, members of the organizations I studied who spent nights telling me "the story of the company," who at any time were willing to explain, clarify, provide data, and assist in any manner. To the Department of International Cooperation of the Yugoslav Federal Government and the Department of Information of the Republic of Serbia go my thanks for the full cooperation they extended to me in my research efforts. Especially I extend my thanks to the *Centar za Stručno Osposobljavanje Rukovodećih Kadrova u Privredi* (The Center for Executive Training) in Belgrade and to its (at that time) director, Ing. Vlastimir Matejic, who provided me with the necessary introduction to the industry in order to carry out this research.

This undertaking, the doctoral thesis and later its reediting into book form, was a costly endeavor. The Samuel Bronfman Foundation was most kind in its generous financial support of this study through a series of scholarships and fellowships awarded to me

xix

during my doctoral candidacy at the Columbia Graduate School of Business. At UCLA, where I am currently teaching, the Division of Research at the Graduate School of Business and the Senate Research Committee granted financial support to finish the study and prepare it in its present form.

To the members of my doctoral thesis committee, Professors Boris Yavitz, Margaret Chandler, Jean J. Boddewyn, Robert Richards, and its chairman, William H. Newman, Samuel Bronfman Professor of Democratic Business Enterprise, go my sincerest thanks for the hard work they undertook in guiding my efforts and reviewing my endless drafts and for the encouragement they provided me while working on this project.

To the members of the Publications Committee of the Graduate School of Business at Columbia University, Professors Neil Chamberlain, Margaret Chandler, and Nathaniel Leff, go my thanks for their work in reviewing this book. Professors William McWhinney, Barry Richman, and Eric Trist, from the UCLA Graduate School of Business, and Professor Josip Županov from the University of Zagreb, Mr. Jan Vanek from the I.L.O., Geneva, Switzerland, and Professor Robert Kahn from the University of Michigan at Ann Arbor, were very helpful in various suggestions for improving my arguments and presentations.

To Professor Leonard Sayles, from Columbia University, go my thanks for his encouragement to undertake this project and for his excellent advice on methodology. To Professor Samuel Richmond, also from Columbia, and Mrs. Richmond, goes my gratitude for the continued support and trust they gave at times when it was most needed.

Every book has endless drafts which have to be typed, edited, worked on until an acceptable document is produced. I was very fortunate in obtaining excellent support, and I am most grateful to my secretaries who loyally, conscientiously, and with patience worked with me, whose usual working habits are of the "management by crisis" school. Miss Alice Bloch labored on the thesis, Mrs. Margaret Tisa on its conversion to the present book form, and Miss Mirta Bezjak on the bibliography. Miss Karen Paulson worked on the final editing, and Mr. M. Harlev on the latest research.

Dr. Irwin Pincus and his wife, Lena, were most kind in providing me with their beautiful home in Malibu, California, where I could work peacefully, interrupted only by the waves on the shore.

To Professor William Newman, previously mentioned, go thanks for more than being just the chairman of my doctoral committee. I feel grateful to Professor Newman because he was more than a committee chairman. To him I am indebted for building my love for the field of management, for the confidence he gave me, and for the endless encouragement and understanding without which this study would never have been completed.

With such quality of support this book should not contain errors. However, if there are any, they are all mine.

Ichak Adizes
Pincus Estate, Malibu
December, 1970

PART I

Introduction

1.

The Goals, Significance, and Methodology of the Study

Goals and Significance

What would happen if the law required that industrial organizations be managed "democratically"? Directors, as well as those in administrative positions, would be elected for a stipulated term by the members of each organization. Administration would not be allowed to hire, fire, or discipline anyone. Instead, these functions would be performed only at the discretion of the general membership or its elected committee. Furthermore, salaries, bonuses, and production norms would be established by the general membership through a democratic vote.

A similar system is in operation in Yugoslav industry; it is called "self-management." According to this system, organizations are supposed to manage themselves through elected governing bodies and nominated administrators. It is the goal of this book to describe and analyze how the Yugoslav system works, and to derive from this study some insights on the managerial processes in democratic organizations and how they differ from other organizations.

This study is important for several reasons. It deals with organizational behavior within an organizational structure and an environment, both of which are different from those usually explored. Specifically, the study analyzes developments in Yugoslavia, the pathfinder in decentralization. Analyzing these developments may assist interested researchers in understanding developments in other centrally planned, decentralization-oriented countries. Finally, the self-management system developed in Yugoslavia has attracted interest from developing countries in Africa and Asia.

Professional managerial literature has utilized existing studies of behavior in industrial organizations with vertical organizational structures where status, prestige, rewards, and power increase as the pyramid is ascended, and their maximum is at the pinnacle of the organization, the position of president. This is a familiar organizational structure, especially in today's business institutions. Furthermore, the business organizations studied in the United States have one main characteristic in common in addition to being vertically structured: they operate within environments of differing degrees of competition.

Studies which deal with horizontally structured industrial organizations operating in a changing but regulated environment are scarce.[1] Thus, this case study of two Yugoslav companies offers an added dimension for comparative studies of complex organizations.

In a horizontal structure: (1) power distribution is effected by distinguishing between administrative and legislative power (in the vertical model these functions are united into "management"); (2) the veto power, instead of being entrusted to the chief executive, is rendered to the general membership or its representatives; (3) tenure, selection, and dismissal, especially for key executive positions, are decided by the general membership or its representa-

---

1. A. Sturmthal, *Workers' Council* (Cambridge, Mass.: Harvard University Press, 1964); Jiri Kolaja, *Workers' Councils, The Yugoslav Experience* (London: Tavistock Publication, 1964). However, neither study related environment to organizational changes. Thus, the focus of our study has not been covered.

4

tives. Administrators are reelected or recalled, depending on how successful they are in the judgment of their constituents.[2]

A move toward a more horizontal, "participative" structure in organizations is being advocated by most contemporary management theoreticians.[3] The Yugoslav self-management system possesses several of the characteristics of organizational systems advocated by these theoreticians. In addition to being horizontally structured (Katz and Kahn's democratic structure), the Yugoslav system has instituted groups ("task forces") in their organizations which have common goals and in which social structures are fostered (as suggested by Likert). Management has to be worker-oriented if it wants to be reelected, and an atmosphere with a high level of openness prevails when the leadership encourages it, since the self-management ideology encourages workers to take a stand. These conditions fulfill some of Argyris' and Bennis' recommendations.

Although the Yugoslav self-management system represents the extreme in the spectrum of horizontal-vertical structures, a study of the system is worthwhile in that it may act as a point of comparison for evaluating various participative, democratic theories of management. In addition, this study examines the changes imposed by decentralization on organizational behavior and thus offers a critical evaluation of the path other centrally planned decentralizing countries may be taking,[4] if we allow for political

---

2. The distinctive characteristics of vertical and horizontal structures were taken from D. Katz and R. Kahn, *The Social Psychology of Organizations* (New York: Wiley, 1967), pp. 221-223. We use the terms horizontal and vertical structures, instead of "democratic" and "hierarchical" structures as they do, in order to avoid unfavorable connotations.

3. W. Bennis, *Changing Organizations* (New York: McGraw-Hill, 1968); C. Argyris, *Integrating the Individual and the Organization* (New York: Wiley, 1967); R. Likert, *The Human Organization* (New York: McGraw-Hill, 1967).

4. "Pebble in Water, Freedom in Yugoslavia Makes Waves for East Bloc," *Christian Science Monitor*, November 18, 1967. See "Central Planning in a Guided Market Model," *Acta Oeconomica Academiae Scientiarum Hungaricae*, 1, 1966,

interventions whose magnitude and character are hard to predict.[5] The developments in Yugoslavia are of importance because they seem to be several steps ahead of the other Communist countries.[6] Yugoslavia appears to be tackling problems now with which other Communist countries may have to cope later: the conflicts produced by decentralization, the drift towards a market economy while still attempting to preserve communistic social values. In addition to being a leader in decentralization policies, Yugoslavia has been serving as a model to emerging nations which are coping with similar socio-political problems.[7]

Methodology

The study is limited to two Yugoslav companies observed in depth by the researcher during the spring of 1967, and to a dozen others investigated and analyzed during the same period. The

and the talk of the Minister of Justice of Hungary, "Legal Status of Enterprises in Hungary's New Economic Mechanism Defined," printed in *Figgelo*, May 24, 1967 (Budapest); also, "New Leaf, Hungary Ushers in Profit Basis," *Christian Science Monitor*, January 2, 1968. See "Profit Plan," *Christian Science Monitor*, February 2, 1968; also "Stymied Soviets," *The Wall Street Journal*, December 27, 1967. "Rumania Promises Consumer Gains," *Christian Science Monitor*, January 10, 1968; "Rumania Decentralizes," *Christian Science Monitor*, January 20, 1968; "Czechs Welcome Signs of Break With Past," *Christian Science Monitor*, February 5, 1968. Todor Zhivkov, *The New Systems of Economic Management* (Sofia: Foreign Languages Press, 1966); Todor Zhivkov, *Ninth Congress of the Bulgarian Communist Party Report and Concluding Speech* (Sofia: Foreign Languages Press, 1967).

5. As to the dangers, as perceived by the Russians, of decentralization of economic and political powers simultaneously, the Czechoslovak-USSR confrontation of 1968 may serve as an example.

6. It should be noted, however, that the Workers' Council, the self-management style in its extreme form, is shunned.

7. *Tekariv an Muhemet El-Wafd El Arabi Fi Zeyaratehy Li Yugoslavia* (Reports on the mission of the Arab delegation on its visit to Yugoslavia). (Ministry of Planning, Permanent Secretariat of the two permanent committees for technical staff and manpower, Cairo, Egypt: 1966.)

researcher visited Yugoslavia during the summer of 1966 in order to prepare the ground for the study and visited the two companies again in the fall of 1968 to discover what further developments had taken place. The analysis is based on an evaluation of the environmental changes and their relation to changes occurring in the organization (an open systems approach).[8]

Two companies which were similar in eleven factors but different in one key independent variable, the leadership pattern, were selected for the study in order to obtain a general view of organizational behavior as it varies with this independent variable.

The two companies chosen for the study were alike in the following characteristics:[9]

1. Technology employed.

2. Size (2,800 vs. 2,600 employees on the average).

3. Cultural basin from which the companies drew their manpower (villages around Belgrade).

4. The ratio of male/female workers.

5. The markets to which the companies sold, and the distribution channels they employed.

6. The government economic instruments (regulating policies) applied.

7. The external laws determining the formal organizational structure and the manner by which self-management philosophy was applied.

8. The geographical dispersion of plants (a distance of several miles from company headquarters).

9. The age of the companies as measured by the approximate date the company was established.

10. Approximately the same formal organizational structure.

11. The composition of membership in decision-making bodies as measured by education, training, and job position held by the members of those bodies.

---

8. For a detailed discussion of the methodology, see Appendix A of this book.
9. For a detailed description, see Chapter 3.

The leadership patterns of each company were at opposite ends of the authoritarian-permissive spectrum.[10] Since this study presents organizational behavior at the ends of this spectrum, it seems probable that other organizational behavior which might be attributed to differing leadership patterns will fall between these described extremes, thus increasing the value of the study.

Changes in the environment were studied by analyzing changes in economic, political, and social conditions. Organizational constraints were analyzed by studying the laws that determine the formal organization and regulate the way it should operate.[11]

The ideology of the self-management system as a part of the environment is presented in this book in order to familiarize the reader with the political establishment and the goals (anticipated results) it sets for the industrial organization. We tend to believe that expectations had great influence on behavior observed.

In order to discern the way these organizations operated within the given environment, three types of decisions were examined from their initiation to their implementation: (1) modernization of the firm, (2) preparing annual plans, (3) disciplinary actions; among others, hiring and firing.

The three decisions varied by:

a. The *amount* of information that had to be handled in order to make a decision.

b. The *complexity* of the data that had to be handled in making a decision, and thus the amount of *professional knowledge* required.

c. The effect the decision would have on the organization in terms of financial expenses and probable revenue (the principle of commitment).

By maintaining the leadership style as the independent variable

---

10. See Chapter 3.

11. Late changes in the legal environment that dictate organizational structures, like the Fifteenth Amendment to the Constitution and subsequent legislation (1968-69), are not presented here since they did not exist at the time of the study and therefore did not affect the behavior observed.

and by analyzing the same three decisions in two nearly identical companies, we were able to identify a range of differences in managerial processes:

1. Compare different decisions in the same company (i.e., company constant, varied decisions).

2. Compare the same decision between the two companies (i.e., decision constant, varied companies).

3. Compare the participation in decision-making among various decision-making bodies in the same company (i.e., company constant, decision-making bodies varied).

4. Compare the decision-making process in the same decision-making body between the two companies (i.e., the decision-making body constant, varied companies).

Changes in organizational structure were analyzed by following the changes in authority, duties, and responsibilities of various organizational bodies.

In order to obtain some comparison of the efficiency of these two companies, output measurements of economic results and human capital were obtained and compared. Measurement of economic results was achieved through calculating uniform indicators, *jedinstveni pokazatelji*.[12] Human capital figures were established by measuring absenteeism, lateness to work, punishments inflicted (magnitude of disciplinary measures taken), and turnover of labor force. Furthermore, a wildcat strike in one of the companies offered a special opportunity to analyze human relations problems.

The method of conducting research was primarily one of participative observation. (Records and documents also were analyzed.) However, the classical participative observation method had to be altered in this case. Participative observations require that (1) the observer be unobtrusive, that he record his observa-

---

12. *Jedinstveni pokazatelji* is a Yugoslav system of measuring the economic efficiency of a firm. For the approach used in this system, see *Metodologija Koriščenja Jedinstvenih Pokazatelja i Uporedivanja Poslovnih Rezultata Privrednih Organizacija* (Belgrade: Jugoslovenski Zavod za Produktivnost Rada, 1963).

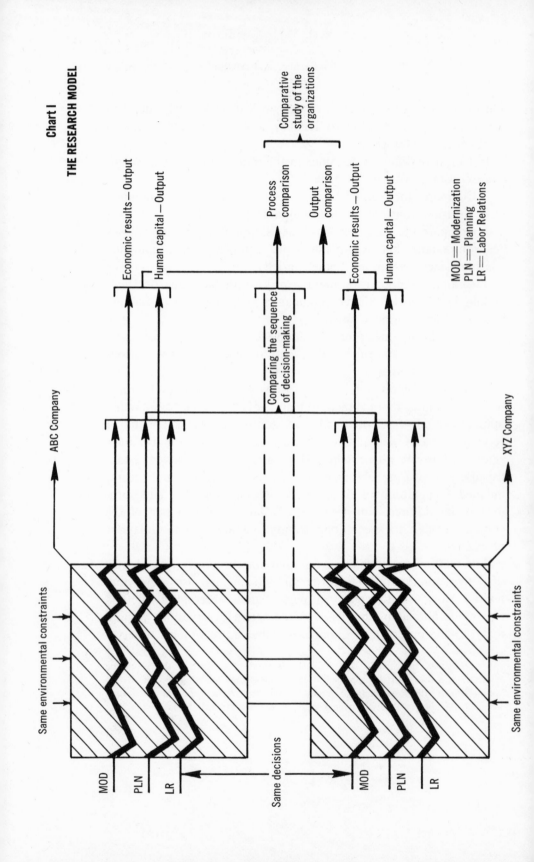

Chart I

THE RESEARCH MODEL

Comparative study of the organizations

Process comparison

Output comparison

Economic results — Output

Human capital — Output

Comparing the sequence of decision-making

Economic results — Output

Human capital — Output

ABC Company

XYZ Company

Same environmental constraints

Same environmental constraints

Same decisions

MOD

PLN

LR

MOD

PLN

LR

MOD = Modernization
PLN = Planning
LR = Labor Relations

tions without interacting with, and thus influencing, the behavior of the observed; and (2) as stated by Madge:

When the heart of the observer is made to beat as the heart of any other member of the group under observation, rather than as that of a detached emissary from some distant laboratory, then he has the title of participate-observer.[13]

The researcher could make "his heart beat as the heart of any other member of the group" by his daily presence in the factory, his knowledge of the language, and his close familiarity with the culture. However, he found it impossible to conduct the study without interaction with the observed, although every attempt was made to minimize the effect of such interaction. Not interacting and simply recording his observations would have made the researcher conspicuous and would have affected the behavior of the observed. Three occurrences could have made the researcher suspected by the observed:

1. During January, 1967, a month before the researcher left for Belgrade, the United States stopped shipping wheat to Yugoslavia—a political act which aroused some anti-American sentiment.

2. During the week in which he left for his research site (the third week of February, 1967), a group of terrorists bombed Yugoslav embassies in the United States and Canada. This event received extensive coverage in Yugoslav newspapers, and, as a result, some of the people the researcher had contacted before beginning this study withdrew their support and aid.

3. When the researcher arrived in Yugoslavia, American newspapers reported that the CIA was financing the National Association of Students and paying foreign students to conduct anti-Communist activities.[14]

---

13. John Madge, *The Tools of Social Science* (Garden City, N.Y.: Doubleday, 1953), p. 137.

14. *Politika Express,* March 31, 1967, claimed that the CIA had been paying $10,000 to foreign students in order to persuade them to become traitors. (The researcher is Yugoslav by birth.)

In addition, the researcher is an Israeli and this factor affected the length of his stay in Yugoslavia. Toward the end of May, 1967, the political situation in the Middle East became extremely tense (on the fifth of June the war started), and there was danger of his being detained and/or deported without his research notes.

All of the above-mentioned political constraints complicated the design of a research methodology and thus required some changes in the classical approach to participative observations. (For a detailed description of the method of collecting data, see Appendix A).

During the summer of 1966, the researcher visited Belgrade, developed contacts for future cooperation, and obtained some idea of what the methodological problems would be. During the first weeks in February, 1967, ten companies in and around Belgrade were visited. Two textile industries were finally chosen, and a permit to conduct the study was obtained from the Ministry of Information. As a matter of fact, the companies in question were not obliged to adhere to the Ministry's request. However, the researcher established firm contacts with the companies by becoming acquainted with the decision-makers during noncommittal interviews in the two weeks of the initial inquiry. Once a trusting, personal relationship had been established, permission was asked to visit the companies more frequently.

In Company ABC, no one would accept the researcher until the Director had approved the study. Permission to conduct a study was given once the Ministry of Information had sent a letter of support, and the researcher was allowed access to all meetings and to all documents of the company. In Company XYZ, the Director preferred not to make the final decision and referred the entire matter to the company's Governing Board, to whom the researcher made a personal appeal. A vote was taken, and he was permitted to stay as long as he wanted and to attend any meetings he wished. During the six months of observations, he attended all meetings and, speaking the language fluently, recorded the discussions without the aid of an interpreter. In both com-

1 2

panies, people were extremely willing to talk to the researcher, to provide him with the data he needed, and to offer their best to make him comfortable.

Toward the end of his stay, the researcher offered his analyses to the executives of the companies and found that in part they had arrived at similar conclusions. During the last three weeks of his stay, he reduced his visits in the companies, except for attendance at meetings, and began interviewing authorities on the Yugoslav self-management system, professors of management, economists, directors and members of research institutes (twenty-eight altogether). During this phase of the study, he offered his findings for critical analysis. In most cases, all persons interviewed concurred that the researcher's findings were similar to their own. For one day, the researcher described his research and analyses to thirty-five directors of Yugoslav companies. Most of the researcher's observations on organizational behavior were shared by these companies. Thus, both practitioners in the field and theoreticians affirmed that the researcher's findings were valid for more than just these two companies, the implication being that the findings extended beyond the scope of case studies.

During the last week of his stay, the researcher traveled to Zagreb and Ljubljana to interview four respected authorities on the subject of self-management in Yugoslavia. He presented his observations to them and all but one person agreed with most of his conclusions.

It should be noted that the timing of the research may have biased the findings. The two textile companies were studied during the spring of 1967, when the 1965 reform hit those industries the hardest. Therefore, they were observed at the peak of their crisis. The reader should bear this fact in mind, since it is claimed that the conditions described in the book were not normal. However, studying an organization at a time of crisis had its methodological advantages. It enabled the researcher to identify "the weak links" of the system, those weaknesses which are not fully apparent when an organization operates under normal conditions. If this methodological point is taken into account by the reader when he makes his own conclusions as to what are the advantages and disadvantages of the system, when he advances from diagnosis to prognosis, the methodological disadvantage of studying an organization in time of crisis will be limited.

Definition of Key Terms Used in This Book

Authority is defined as the legal right to determine or otherwise settle issues and make decisions. A person derives authority by holding a position in a hierarchy, and this authority is independent of the personality holding the position.[15]

Professional authority is defined as a perceived right to determine and decide, which is derived from professional knowledge of a topic on which a determination or decision is made. Professional authority depends on the person and, in certain cases, on the position that he holds. A person has professional authority from his position only if those who receive orders and information from him interpret his position as one that must be filled by someone with professional knowledge. Professional authority does not necessarily include legal authority.

Authority by acceptance is a variation of professional authority. It may be defined as *pure* professional authority wherein the recipient ignores hierarchical position and bases his acceptance of the command *only* on the personality and/or trust of the person making the decision.

Power is defined as the possession or control over sources of reward and/or punishment. Legal authority can be a source of power.

Leadership is defined by Tannenbaum et al., as "interpersonal

---

15. This is usually known as "legal authority." See R. Carzo and J. Yanouzas, *Formal Organization, a Systems Approach* (Homewood, Ill.: Richard D. Irwin and Dorsey Press, 1967), p. 50.

1 4

influence, exercised in situation and directed, through the communication process, toward the attainment . . . of goals."[16] Tannenbaum's definition includes the attainment "of a specified goal or goals." In order to include entrepreneurial spirit in our definition of leadership, we omitted the existence of specified goals. Part of the entrepreneur's role is to specify goals.

Management is defined as a social process, composed of a series of decision-making acts, which leads to the identification and accomplishment of objectives. Management includes leading as well as commanding, coordinating, organizing, planning, and controlling. (It should be noted that this definition encompasses more than the mere decision-making process which leads to accomplishment of given goals. It includes processes of identification of goals, and the characteristics of entrepreneurship as well.)

It should be noted that these terms are interrelated; furthermore, there exists dispute on their definition. However, the definitions as presented above were chosen without regard to the dispute (which would have required a separate book), since they contribute to a clear presentation of the findings to the reader.

---

16. R. Tannenbaum, I. Weschler, and F. Massarik, *Leadership and Organization: A Behavioral Science Approach* (New York: McGraw-Hill, 1961), p. 24.

2.

The Environment and the Yugoslav Industrial Organizational Structure

The first part of this chapter deals with three general areas: (1) economic conditions in Yugoslavia and, more specifically, the processes and repercussions of decentralization; (2) socio-political conditions which may be reinforcing or retarding the process of self-management; and (3) the self-management ideology which has created various expectations and has posed certain goals which appear to have affected organizational structure and behavior to a great extent.

The second part of this chapter deals with the legal regulations which are meant to assure the correct exercise of self-management, and with the reward structure which is intended to motivate organizations toward desired behavior and the fulfillment of the ideals behind the system.

The Environment

THE ECONOMIC ENVIRONMENT

In the last thirty years, Yugoslavia has undergone a complex of revolutionary processes. Within one generation, the country

1 6

has moved at an accelerated pace from the pre-industrial era into the industrial period, and is now fostering the values of a post-industrial society. In addition, Yugoslavia is undergoing a socio-political revolution, and it should be noted as well that this period includes a tragic and destructive World War in which every ninth Yugoslav was killed. On the one hand, an attempt is being made to unite nationalities which have been hostile to one another for generations, and on the other hand, to decentralize the power for economic decision. Since economic and political powers are highly interrelated, the decentralization of economic powers could reinforce nationalistic rivalry. Thus, the desire to decentralize economic powers and, at the same time, unite various nationalities has introduced additional difficulties in policy-making decisions.

To gain an understanding of the setting in which the industrial organizations observed in this study had to operate, an analysis must be made of each element of this extremely turbulent environment.

Before the Second World War, Yugoslavia's economy was based on its agrarian and largely illiterate population. Industrial enterprises were on a small scale, and the level of international trade was low. In 1921, 78.7 percent of the population was agrarian and, all together, there were only 2,000 enterprises with an average of 83 workers in each. National income *per capita* was $70.[1] In 1939, the ratio between agricultural and non-agricultural population changed to 74:26, and, by 1960, was 50:50.[2] The shift in importance from agriculture to industry was expressed in the national income accounts.

Table 1—Contribution to National Income According to Sectors*

Year	Industry	Agriculture	Other
1939	26.8	44.3	28.9
1960	43.5	23.9	32.6

*V. Zeković and S. Novaković, Ekonomika Jugoslavije, 2d ed. (Belgrade: Rad, 1964), p. 164.

---

1. V. Zeković and S. Novaković, *Ekonomika Jugoslavije*, 2d ed. (Belgrade: Rad, 1964), pp. 24, 31.
2. *Ibid.*, p. 71.

Yugoslavia's rapid · industrialization involved demographic changes. Peasants moved to the cities or commuted to the factories from their villages, continuing in their free time to labor on their fields. Illiterates (a phenomenon not uncommon in agricultural societies) had to be taught to read and write, a necessity in an industrial society.

Table 2—Percentage of Illiterates in Working-Age Population*

Age Group	1953	1961
15-19	12.8	6.4
20-34	16.3	13.9
35-49	33.3	24.1
50-64	41.5	39.1

*Yugoslav Survey, Belgrade: Yugoslav Federal Secretary of Information (July-September, 1966), Volume II, p. 3727.

Before World War II, about 90 percent of Yugoslavia's exports were agricultural goods and wood. Since the 1950's, light industry has gained in importance, and its products in the past few years amount to 25 percent of the total export. In 1950, agricultural goods had decreased to 50 percent of the total export, reflecting the rapid rate of industrialization.[3]

Yugoslavia's search for foreign markets has increased also. Exports grew from 125.4 million U.S. dollars in 1937, to 323.4 million U.S. dollars in 1956. Ten years later in 1966, this figure quadrupled to 1,223 million U.S. dollars, a ten-fold increase in thirty years. Imports, however, increased fifteen times in the same period.

In addition to the technological revolution of industrialization, the Yugoslav economic environment has been going through the decentralization process, which is, in itself, a major source of turbulence. Yugoslavia went from a centrally planned economy before 1950 to a comparatively market-socialist economy after the 1965 economic reform.

---

3. I. Drutter, "Sistem Cijena I Tržišnih Odnosa," in D. Gorupić, M. Novak, and I. Drutter, *Poduzeče u Reformi* (Zagreb: Informator, 1968) p. 107.

18

Immediately after the war, all economic resources and means of production were nationalized. Obligatory plans, indicating what and how much production should be carried out, were made on the federal, regional, and county levels. The state determined the rate of corporate savings, totally absorbed them, and then allocated these resources for specified investments to various industries and companies. Company directors were appointed by the government and no one, including the director, could be hired or fired without approval of the government. Prices, which were determined by the government, served, for accounting purposes, as a mechanism of transfer prices among various government enterprises.

The market was primarily a seller's market.[4] Demand was highly inelastic, and producers believed that the way to increase revenue was through increasing prices or production. Profit margins were regulated, and profit was defined as the difference between planned and realized cost and revenue. Since most factors that affect the planned and realized costs and revenues were beyond the control of each company, profit motivation was meaningless. Instead, the motivation of the company was geared toward surpassing the production plan; this was the only factor left to the discretion of the companies. However, maximizing production as an exclusive goal could be functional only as long as a seller's market existed.

In 1950, the Yugoslavs replaced the centrally planned system with the well-known Marxian concept, "the plants to the workers." In favor of the change was the claim that centralization of planning and state ownership of the means of production only increased the centralization of power. Power centralization is in disharmony with the idea of "destatization," the "withering away of the state," which is a cornerstone of socialism as the period of transference to Communism.[5] Moreover, Yugoslavs claimed that central planning had economic inadequacies.[6]

---

4. *Ibid.*
5. Dušan Bilandžić, *Social Self-Government* (Belgrade: Medunarodna Politika, 1965), p. 2.
6. Zeković, Novaković, p. 174.

The "plant to the workers" meant establishing Workers' Councils which, instead of the central government, could manage the companies. (At that stage the Workers' Councils had only advisory powers.) The change, however, was nominal, for the crucial factors in business decision-making still were controlled by the government: (1) Most revenues still were absorbed by the government through taxation; thus, the enterprises did not have economic resources to back independent decisions. (2) Investment decisions still were made by the government, frequently on the basis of political rationale reacting to various nationalistic pressures. (3) Prices were strictly regulated; 70 to 80 percent of the production had government-controlled prices. (4) Exports were encouraged by a multiplicity of exchange rates which were changed at the will of the government; thus, many products were profitable or nonprofitable according to the whim of the government and, therefore, were beyond the control of individual companies. Furthermore, exportation was carried out according to lists of exporters, and companies had to use their influence from all sources to achieve a position on the right list. (5) The Communist Party was extremely influential, and Party directives were channeled into the company to be implemented. Thus, external political intervention was very important, while market economic mechanism as such did not exist.

Accordingly, companies could increase their growth and income more effectively through haggling with governing agencies than through productive, efficient operations.[7] To all these factors should be added the fact that Yugoslavia experienced inflationary pressures as a result of high investment rates and rapid industrialization which were not always well balanced. If the cost of living index in 1956 equaled 100, then it amounted to 102.7 in 1957; in 1960 it was 120.4, and in 1963 it was 151.4.[8]

Because of market instability on the one hand and, on the

---

7. K. Džeba and M. Beslać, *Privredna Reforma* (Zagreb, "Stvarnost," 1965), p. 58.

8. *Ibid.*, p. 117.

Table 3—Distribution of Net Revenue* (in %)**

Allocation	1960	1961	1962	1963	1964	1965***	1966***
To the society (Local and Fed. Gov't)	56.8	54.1	54.4	54.3	49.0	45.2	40.3
Remains in company	43.2	45.9	45.6	46.7	51.0	54.8	59.7
Total	100.0	100.0	100.0	100.0	100.0	100.0	100.0

*I.e., total amount allocated to the various social organs outside the company as compared to how much remained within the company.
**K. Džeba and M. Beslać, *Privredna Reforma* (Zagreb: "Stvarnost," 1965), p. 104.
***M. Novak, "Privredna Organizacija . . ." in D. Gorupič et al., *Poduzeća u Reformi* (Zagreb: Informator, 1968), p. 42.

other hand, management's inability to make independent decisions on subjects crucial to company success, companies tended to develop short-range policies. This tendency was reinforced by the fact that government posed one main goal to the companies: maximum production, high and above the planned level, if possible. In this situation, many dysfunctional phenomena developed, such as the establishment of low planning objectives in order to surpass them, and high cost estimates in order to show a high level of savings. Both practices proved to be highly dysfunctional later on when, as a result of further decentralization, market forces began to operate, and deliberate misinformation taxed heavily the ability of companies to make competitive decisions.

Between 1950 and 1965 the powers of the Workers' Councils for decision-making, as well as the discretionary economic powers of each enterprise, were increased. This change was effected by increasing the share of revenue which remained within each company. Moreover, banks were delegated the function of allocating resources for investment based on economic criteria, a move which also effected a partial "thawing" of the political influence for those decisions.

But the decentralization process was still not carried out on all fronts. Prices were still government-regulated; in 1965, 70 percent of the industrial production still had regulated prices[9] as well as limits on the profit margins a company could realize.

---

9. Drago Gorupič, *Tendencije u Razvoju Radničkog Samoupravljanja u Jugoslaviji* (Zagreb: Informator, 1967), p. 113.

The complexities of running a highly regulated economy were great. As Dzeba put it:

Under the conditions of strong economic instability and inflationary tendencies, wide administrative interventions . . . the results of business activities and the material interests of the individual and the company did not depend sufficiently on the results of work, real productivity and economic efficiency. On the contrary, it depended largely on administrative decisions, the interplay of regulated prices, etc. . . . Under these conditions, working collectives *[companies] tended to devote a large part of their time away from questions of productivity and cost, spending it haggling with the various governmental organs, exercising pressures, and arranging for subsidies and higher prices for their products.* . . . In such deformed conditions we could not conclude how much each production really cost. . . . Lacking objective measurements of value hampered designing a healthy economic policy.[10] [Italics mine]

Yugoslavia's attempts to spur productivity led to the economic reform of 1965, which in fact consisted of further decentralization. This reform contained several facets.

In order to stimulate competition through international trade, and in order to diminish the ponderousness of the system with its distorting effects, the *dinar* was devalued drastically and the number of the various rates of exchange was decreased. In addition, customs tariffs were reduced from an average of 23.3 percent to 10.8 percent, thereby increasing the competition of foreign goods in Yugoslav markets.[11] In 1965, 18 groups of products, and in 1966, another 31 groups, were freed from price regulation.[12] In 1967, the freeing of prices from regulation reached a new height. To encourage competition, companies were allowed to keep and use a larger share of their revenues at their discretion (see Table 3). One interesting aspect of the reform is the fact that, according to the new regulations, international prices in Yugoslav markets were meant to reflect world prices. The changes in customs rates

---

10. Džeba, p. 58. Above passage translated by I. Adižes, 1968.
11. *Ibid.,* p. 123.
12. Mijo Novak, "Privredna Organizacija . . . ," in Gorupič et al., 1968, pp. 37, 38.

and the new pricing regulations were aimed at increasing competition to the Yugoslav producer so that higher productivity would be achieved.

The economic reform was accompanied by political statements. *The Communist Party resolved to fight for higher market competition,* and felt that its members should oppose any pressures to maintain unprofitable companies through price regulations, bonuses, and other subsidies which might hamper adequate operation of a market mechanism.[13]

Further decentralization of the system after 1965 was not an easy goal to achieve, since the central government wanted to decentralize without losing control. Since economic power was being decentralized, the way to maintain control was through legislation of procedures to permit or limit use of the delegated resources. In 1966, the Secretary of the Treasury issued 630 regulating orders. Innumerable federal laws pertaining to the economic environment were issued:

in 1963 753
1964 718
1965 982 (or 3 every working day)
1966 800

The customs laws changed 8 to 9 times per year. These were only federal laws. The number of local and state laws was even larger, and companies often could not identify the most recent law which would regulate certain activities.[14]

The changes described above altered the nature of uncertainty under which companies operated. Uncertainty was more a function of political atmosphere, political connections, and the economic policy of the government before the decentralization than after it. The uncertainty was thus determined by factors which were beyond

13. *Aktuelni Problemi Borbe Saveza Komunista Jugoslavije za Sprovodenje Reforme,* Treći Plenum CK SKJ (Belgrade: Komunist, 1966), p. 323.
14. Novak, "Privredna Organizacija . . . ," in Gorupič et al., 1968, p. 55.

The Chamber of Nationalities at work on the Constitution, disregarding the tailoring injunction to "measure three times, cut once."   *Borba* (Belgrade), February 17, 1966.

the control of individual companies or at least were not related directly to the productivity efforts of each company. In reality, companies enjoyed a sort of security by default, for they could not be hold responsible for decisions they were not allowed to make. The effect of decentralization was that companies making competitive decisions were required to assume a certain amount of risk formerly absorbed by the central government. Furthermore, maximum production, which was a goal in the past, revealed itself to be dysfunctional as a unique goal, since it could lead to the stockpiling of inventory rather than an increase in sales.

Increase in risk absorption requires an increase in rewards in order to maintain the contribution-inducements equilibrium.[15]

15. According to the theory of J. March and H. Simon, *Organizations* (New York: Wiley, 1958), an organization is viable as long as its members get out of it as much as they put into it.

The signs read, from bottom to top: "New Economic Steps, Newer Economic Steps, Newest Economic Steps." *Borba* (Belgrade), June 13, 1965.

25

Increasing the rewards to those who absorb risk in making competitive decisions may mean the nurturing of an entrepreneurial spirit. Entrepreneurial spirit is related to individual freedom; rewards to an entrepreneur are allocated according to exploited opportunities rather than according to genuine laboring on the production line. However, these changes (individual freedom and rewards to an individual for opportunities exploited) may lead toward "capitalistic" social values which have potential political repercussions for the political ideology.

The trend toward greater freedom for business to make decisions, which is necessary for the development of the entrepreneurial spirit, led to pressures to change government legal regulations. In a centralized or highly regulated economy, "everything is forbidden unless specifically permitted. What was necessary in the new conditions was that everything be permitted unless specifically forbidden."[16] Such a change in the legal environment would have had significant political repercussions and would have enlarged the existent scope of freedom of choice. However, this appeared to many conservative politicians, labelled "syndicalists," as too radical a change. In the post-reform era, internal political struggles developed on the desired magnitude of economic political decentralization, and this increased the uncertainty within which companies had to operate.

THE SOCIO-POLITICAL ENVIRONMENT

The economic and technological changes were setting the stage for social, demographic, and political changes. With the emphasis on productivity as a measure for company success, emphasis on education and qualification, as well as on specialization and professional expertise rather than political affiliation, became apparent. The movement to the cities aggravated housing conditions, which were already extremely grave as a result of the wartime destruction. Under these conditions it was a challenge to maintain a high morale

---

16. Novak, "Privredna Organizacija . . . ," in Gorupič et al., 1968, p. 56.

among the workers. On the political scene, even after the reform, it was not clear how far the government was really willing to go with its political decentralization policies. There seemed to be continuous internal struggle between those who favored central control and those who were willing to experiment with decentralization. The political repercussions could be substantive. Economic decentralization enlarged the scope of power centers which could challenge the government's policies. For instance, economic pluralism encourages labor mobility which may encourage freedom of expression. In centrally planned economies, a government employee who opposed government could be deprived of his source of livelihood, since the government was the only employer. In a state where economic decision-making is largely decentralized, the individual does not consider the dependence on adequate relations with the government as the exclusive condition for his survival and progress and is thus enabled to criticize government issues.

Decentralization of economic power was necessary but not sufficient for an increase in political freedom. The political structure itself had to be "thawed." In Yugoslavia, apparently because of nationalistic rivalry, both Rankovic, the Secretary of the Interior, and Stefanovic, who was in charge of the Secret Police, were ousted in 1966. Both were Serbians and apparently there was a struggle for power inside the Party.[17]

Limiting political intervention in economic decisions, freeing individuals from the threat of the Secret Police, and increasing the discretionary economic power of each company, were all factors in the growing freedom for companies to operate in the post-reform market-oriented mechanism. Further freedom was granted when the Secretary of the Trade Union, Todorovic, expressed the view that striking was a worker's right, a freedom of action which formerly had not been fully recognized. However, it would be too simple and misleading to say that the transformation was total. The threats of political intervention were still present

17. For some description of the developments, see Ilija Jukic, "Tito's Last Battle," *East Europe*, 16 (April, 1967), pp. 2-11.

when this study was conducted in 1967. Party resolutions were interpreted carefully and cautiously and time was allowed to test their validity, particularly since the major force behind the decentralization, Tito, was old and there were serious questions being raised as to his successor's identity, nationality, and philosophy.

It appeared that from these environmental changes the companies learned several things: (1) It is hard or impossible to predict the future; thus, it is not worth trying too hard. (2) Take advantage of any opportunities, since they may not appear again. (3) Maximize production or increase prices as much as possible; this will increase revenues and profits. (4) The political environment is hard to predict; therefore, the safest course of action is to follow regulations.

This was the atmosphere which prevailed at the time of this study. Its effect on organizational behavior will be discussed in Part II of this book.

THE IDEOLOGICAL ENVIRONMENT

Not only are the Yugoslavs undergoing simultaneously the industrialization process and the economic decentralization process, but they are also seriously attempting to develop a society with post-industrial values. It is apparent from the self-management ideology that this system emphasizes qualities of self-actualization, self-expression, and interdependence, in addition to encouraging collaborative relations, linked objectives, and social ownership of resources. This is different from the salient values of the industrializing society, which emphasize achievement rather than self-actualization, self-control rather than self-expression, independence rather than interdependence, competitive rather than collaborative relations, separate rather than linked objectives, and a state in which resources are regarded as owned absolutely rather than as belonging to the society as well.[18]

---

18. For a brief introduction to changes in the salient values of the industrial and post-industrial society, see Eric Trist, *Urban North America, The Challenge of*

The basic concepts of self-management are as follows: (1) It is a process, a transition period, in which a "New Man" will be educated and trained to operate in a stateless society and in which he will be guided by his conscience. (2) A member of a given organization should be liberated from the bonds of hierarchy and alienation; these are the by-products of a vertical organization which distinguishes between workers and managers. In self-management, all are workers *and* managers. (3) The sources of influence in self-management are not supposed to be based on vested hierarchical positions but on professional authority and pure authority by acceptance.

The individual in self-management must be socially conscious, skilled, and trained to make decisions which are for the good of society as well as his own good. He should be a "servo-mechanic individual" who does not have to rely on directives and controlling actions by a superior about whose nomination he has had nothing to say. The "New Man" should seek self-actualization and self-expression. He should seek his rewards by collaborating with his immediate peers in a group in whose composition he has played a part. His objectives, his group's objectives and social goals should be harmonized through the reward structure and the individual's conscience, the guiding light of the "New Man" who fully participates in determining the destiny of his company.

Thus, "participation," "decentralization," "involvement," are the slogans of this system. Workers should not be hired. To be "hired" means subordination to an owner; it means enslavement. Workers join organizations as equals, are accepted as equals, and participate in production and distribution of rewards as decided by a democratic vote. In self-management there is no elite group which "manages" others; all the members of the organization manage themselves. There is a group of coordinators and administrators but

the Next Thirty Years; a Social Psychological Viewpoint, Keynote Address to the Annual Meeting and Conference of the Town Planning Institute of Canada, Minaki, Ontario, June 26-28, 1968, p. 20.

not managers. Self-management rights, the right and responsibility to participate and decide, are constitutionally guaranteed and defended by law; violation of them by an autocratic manager leads to prosecution.

One of the cornerstones of the self-management system and of the Yugoslav socio-political system in general is the concept of social ownership. In Russia, social ownership means state ownership; the state hires, fires, and determines rewards. In Yugoslavia, social ownership means that resources are owned by the society at large and not by one individual or agency within the society. Thus, a company's assets belong to the society; the members of the organization can utilize these assets, make a profit, and distribute it among themselves after allocating part of it to the society as interest for the utilization of these resources. An individual can enjoy these assets as long as he works for the company. Once he leaves the company, he cannot ask for a share of the assets; he has no claim on future or past accumulation of wealth, and the company is bound by law not to decrease its own net value. For example, the company cannot sell assets and distribute higher wages.[19] Furthermore, the director is legally bound to represent the society at large and to see that social interests are not being undermined.[20]

Because of the social ownership pattern, the internal formal authority in Yugoslav companies is such that no one group within the company can claim to be representative of the owners, and thus, that it has the exclusive legal right to make decisions.[21] As the ownership is by the society, an abstract legal entity, and as all the members of the organization have rented the means of production, there is legal equality among the members to manage on equal

---

19. *Osnovni Zakor O Preduzečima* (Belgrade: Službeni List, 1965), paragraph 17.

20. Compare this to the Electrical Companies' Price Conspiracy in the United States where some top executives claimed ignorance of the conspiracy.

21. For a discussion of social ownership, see Radomir Lukić, *Društvena Svojina i Samoupravljanje* (Belgrade: Savremena Škola, 1964), pp. 18-52.

terms those resources. A new member has the same rights and responsibilities in management as a senior member of the company. The janitor and the general director have equal rights and obligations to see that the company is well managed.[22] Thus, even the slightest source of exclusive formal authority to be derived from above, hierarchically, is eliminated and full emphasis is put on authority by acceptance.

Social ownership and the process of liberation from hierarchy are supposed to remove the alienating characteristics of the management-labor confrontation. This confrontation allegedly exists in privately owned, vertical organizations. In order that the liberation process be a continuing one, self-management should abolish any bureaucratic tendencies (i.e., hierarchies may establish themselves by perpetuating themselves, acquiring power which is not controlled by the ruled). This is done by introducing the principle of rotation.

No one can be elected several times in succession to any public or political function (except for Tito).[23] Every elected person should go back to his previous job, back to the people who elected him, when he terminates his period of public service. In self-management, everyone should have the opportunity to manage and become involved.

Braut states that self-management in an organization includes the following rights and duties of the members of the organization:

To manage the organization *directly* or *indirectly* through governing bodies which they have elected, to organize production or other activity which is a subject of business activity in the organization:

To decide about *all the business matters* of the organization; to decide about distribution of income, insuring the future development of the com-

---

22. See Bilandzić, p. 33. As defined by law: Decree to Promulgate a Basic Act Representing Employment Relationship, Belgrade, Službeni List, No. 17, April 7, 1965 (translated by the International Labor Office, Geneva), paragraph 2, subparagraph 2.

23. Mirko Perović, *Društveno Uredjenje SFRJ* (Zavod Udbenika SRS, Belgrade: 1964), p. 92.

pany, i.e., making *investment decision,* etc. . . . To decide about accepting new members *[hiring]* or termination of membership *[firing].*[24] [Italics mine]

Self-management theoreticians interpret Western management theory as one which starts from a centralized state of affairs and specifies under what conditions it should or can be decentralized, and then determines how to do so and still maintain control. In contrast, the self-management system starts the other way around. It starts with the state of absolute decentralization where everyone participates and decides. Then it questions when decisions should be delegated upwards, what rights the members are willing to give up, and how they can control the outcome.[25]

Once the reader is familiar with the economic, political, social, and ideological environments, the self-management organizational structure is described. This description is necessary in order for the reader to understand how the ideological concepts were implemented. Furthermore, it will serve as a means to understanding the apparent inconsistencies between the constraints of the organizational structure and the requirements of the changing environment which are described in the next chapters.

The Self-Management Organizational Structure

GOVERNING AND ADMINISTRATIVE BODIES

In order to free the individual from the bonds of hierarchy and give him the right to govern himself, the self-management system distinguishes between administrative and governing functions (*rukovodjenje* and *upravljanje*). Together, these two functions constitute what is commonly known as the management process.

---

24. R. Braut, A. Jaeger, and M. Novak, *Priručnik o Organizaciji Podužeca* (Zagreb: Informator, 1966), p. 70.

25. M. Novak, *Organizacija Podužeca u Socijalizmu* (Zagreb: Informator, 1967), p. 2.

(The term "management" *per se* does not even exist in the Yugoslav language.) Distinction between the two types of power—power to govern and power to administer—constitutes the basis of industrial democracy. The general membership governs, while the nominated or elected administrators administer.

The administrative branch of the self-management system is supposed to *suggest* decisions to the governing branch and to *implement* them, while the principal function of the governing branch is to *make* the decisions. The limits within which decisions are made are spelled out in numerous laws which give the governing bodies the power to handle production as well as financial, personnel, and marketing decisions. The authority and duties of the administrative bodies are to be specified by the governance of each company.

It should be noted that this is a significant deviation from the managerial practice in Western business institutions, where a "top-down" rather than "bottom-up" flow of formal authority exists. An American executive is free to act as he sees fit, within a "zone of indifference" of the interested parties and as long as he does not violate any laws and fulfills the requests of the Board. In Yugoslavia, the executive is *not free to act unless* the right for that action is rendered to him by the company's governing body, which is the general membership or its elected body.

The governing function is composed of several organizational bodies. The largest governing body is the total membership of the company, and it governs through referendums or meetings (*Zbors*) of the various shops or departments. Furthermore, the general membership elects the Workers' Council, which in turn elects its executive body, the Governing Board. The Workers' Council nominates the Director, who stands for reelection every four years, and all the top executives of the company.

Each company is composed of several Economic Units. Each Unit is a separate entity based on its technological, economic, and social independence from other Units. In other words, if a boundary can be delineated technologically and economically (cost

3 3

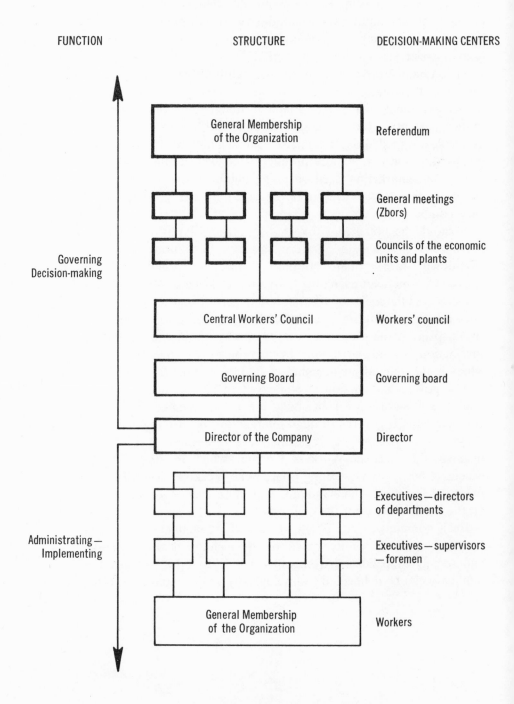

Chart II

FUNCTIONS, STRUCTURE, AND DECISION CENTERS

FUNCTION   STRUCTURE   DECISION-MAKING CENTERS

General Membership
of the Organization — Referendum

— General meetings
(Zbors)

— Councils of the economic
units and plants

Governing
Decision-making

Central Workers' Council — Workers' council

Governing Board — Governing board

Director of the Company — Director

— Executives — directors
of departments

— Executives — supervisors
— foremen

Administrating —
Implementing

General Membership
of the Organization — Workers

can be identified), and if the group's size is not too large, an Economic Unit is designated. The Economic Units competitively buy and sell services to other Units within or outside the company, and in the most decentralized companies, they distribute the created profits among themselves. Depending on its size, each shop, or plant, has a Workers' Council which governs its internal socio-economic environment. The foreman of each Unit is elected, as are the various governing committees, including the disciplinary committees. In addition, each Unit has a recruitment committee which hires and trains new people. The Council of the Unit decides on production norms, budgeting, and on human relations questions within its authority. The foreman is there only to suggest and coordinate activities toward the achievement of the goals determined by the Unit itself.

Each company has a large variety of manuals which are legislated by the governing bodies and which serve as standard operating procedures for the administrators. Each company has a *Statut,* which is the internal constitution of the company, and a statement of goals, means, basic policies, and rights of members and various organizational bodies. The *Statut* and the various standard operating procedures are legislated by the general membership through extensive participation in discussions and a democratic vote. This assures the control of the constituents over their administrators whose discretion is thereby limited.

As can be seen from the above description, each member of the organization is involved, or has the chance to be involved, in the decision-making process. A member may exercise his influence through a referendum, through conventions, or through membership in Economic Unit Councils, the company's Workers' Council, Governing Board, or their various committees. Company XYZ, observed for purposes of this study, may serve as an illustration. XYZ's Workers' Council has 6 permanent committees with a total of 26 members, while its Governing Board has 3 permanent committees with a total membership of 20. In addition, there are 6 ad hoc committees with a total of 54 members. Therefore, the company as a whole contains 15 committees with a total membership of 100, of whom only 15 are on the regular governing bodies such as the Council and the Board. If one adds the 34 members of the Plant Council, the 54 members of the company's Workers' Council, the 73 members of the 11 plant-level committees, and the numerous committees on the Economic Unit level, it becomes apparent that representative decision-making positions are available to about 40 percent of the membership. Since there is rotation in each position, virtually no member of the organization can escape confrontation with the company's problems and participation in the decision-making process.[26] Participation at a level of 100 percent may even be achieved, if one includes events such as elections or nominations, referendums, or a company convention, where members make decisions directly, rather than through a representative.

The system also encourages involvement in socio-political organizations such as the Communist Party, to which a person has to be nominated and elected, the Trade Union, to which all members of the company belong, and the Youth Brigades, to which the younger generation belongs. These three organizations have their own decision-making bodies which discuss company matters and contribute their judgment to the total decision-making process. Theoretically, they may not enforce a decision, but may only take a position and argue convincingly.[27] In this system a janitor could be a member of the Communist Party's Executive Committee, a member of the Workers' Council, and Chairman of his Economic Unit's disciplinary committee. This organizational interlinkage

---

26. As to the various laws which govern the decision-making process in a self-management company, see I. Adizes, "The Effect of Decentralization on Organizational Behavior, An Exploratory Study of the Yugoslav Self-Management System" (Ph.D. dissertation, Columbia University, 1968), chapter 4.

27. In reality, however, the difference between taking and forcing a position is very dubious, since these organizations derive a large amount of their power from their powerful "parent organization" outside the company.

allows a flow of information and reevaluation of goals and means from various organizational, social, and political angles.

The socio-political organizations are supposed to ensure that responsibility to the society will underline major decisions. This social responsibility is discussed and defined by the central organs of these external organizations. Since the top activists in each political organization are members of the local or statewide political committees, various political resolutions are carried swiftly into the various enterprises.

1. The Governance Function

The members of the organization govern themselves through various means such as referendums, *Zbors* (conventions), Councils on various organizational levels and their committees, and the Governing Board and its committees. This subsection describes the legal authority and duties of each of these bodies.

Referendum: According to the company's *Statut*, a referendum must be called whenever the company has to relocate its plant, whenever a merger is being considered, or whenever there is a disagreement between the company's Workers' Council and an Economic Unit. Thus, major decisions with long-range effects require a referendum.

Zbors: The *Zbors* (conventions) elect and recall the governing bodies and vote on changes in the *Statut*. They are consulted on all main decisions such as modernization, manpower policies (e.g., increasing or decreasing the labor force), and budgetary decisions which affect wages.

Economic Unit Councils: Each Economic Unit has an elected Council composed usually of 11 members who serve for two years and are not subject to dismissal during their tenure. The *Zbor* delegates authority and duties to its Economic Unit Council. For instance, in XYZ the *Zbors* are assigned the right to schedule paid and nonpaid vacations, to make decisions concerning firing and

37

hiring, and to determine the allocation of funds. In contrast, in ABC these rights are assigned to the Unit Councils, whereas the *Statut* makes no provisions as to the rights of the *Zbors*. Therefore, in these respects, XYZ was much more decentralized than ABC.

The Central Workers' Council: The Workers' Council is the highest decision-making body in the company except in instances where the *Statut* assigns decision-making function exclusively to the general membership. The Workers' Council legislates (casts the final vote) the *Statut* and the various manuals of the company. It budgets, makes production policy (e.g., products to be produced and their prices, unless regulated by the government), and marketing policy (e.g., marketing channels and advertising strategies to be decided upon), and determines the size of plants and the organization of the company (e.g., the establishment or elimination of Economic Units). The Council decides on the rate of investment by the company and the portion of revenue to be distributed as personal income. Even decisions which do not necessarily concern policy-making—such as decisions to scrap machines, to determine levels of depreciation, to buy a single new machine or a new car—are assigned to the Council. If legislated in the *Statut*, some of these decisions can be delegated to the administrators.

The Council must establish personnel policy: the method of income distribution, the appointment of executives, promotions, and approval of vacations, travel, and scholarships for study. On the basis of a recommendation by the Economic Unit Council or *Zbor,* the Council makes the final decision on firing a member.

The Council also approves the annual plan as it is submitted by the administrative branch of the company, and it approves or rejects the balance sheet at the end of the year. Any changes in prices, internal transfer prices between Economic Units, changes in manuals, basic salaries, job definitions, etc., require the Council's approval.

In order to prevent the administrators from manipulating the Council merely by neglecting to convene it, the law states that the Council has to meet at least once every six weeks and that it is the administrators' duty to report at each meeting on their activities.

The Governing Board: The Board is assigned the responsibility of translating Council decisions into operative tasks for implementation by the administrative body. The Board also makes preliminary findings on material that is to be submitted to the Workers' Council for final decision. As an intermediary body between decision-making and implementation, the Board proposes to the Council changes to be introduced in manuals, suggests annual and long-range plans, approves changes in the annual plan if the basic proportions of the plan are not altered and if the planned income is not changed.[28]

In ABC and XYZ, the Board has the right to veto business trips to foreign countries by Directors or members of the collective. In addition, it is the Board's responsibility to see that the company is managed by the administrators in accordance with all decisions and in the spirit of all relevant laws.

On matters pertaining to changes in salary or job positions, the Board also serves as a grievance-resolving body for the workers. However, if the change requires significant amendments in the manuals, the question has to be decided by the Council. (Grievances against executives are considered in the various elected disciplinary committees.)

2. The Administrative Function

In the Yugoslav self-management system, the Director of the company, directors of plants and departments, and the foremen make up the administrative branch. The organizational structure of the administrative branch is vertical, and it follows the scalar chain principle.

---

28. *Statuts* of Companies ABC and XYZ. (As a rule, whenever the laws are internal, they are derived from the *Statuts* and other manuals of the two companies we studied.)

As mentioned in previous sections of this book, the theoretical difference between the vertical structure (typical of American business organizations) and the self-management horizontal structure is that the power for decision-making in self-management is segmented. The administrative branch has power only to administer, not to govern. Thus, the self-management administrative hierarchy contains neither a correlated increase in discretion in *decision-making* nor more extended control over the sources of reward and punishment. In self-management, a higher executive position coordinates a larger organizational space, and the power that accompanies this coordination is specifically delineated by the governing body.

In order to understand fully the self-management system and the complications that the administration-governance distinction introduces, it is necessary to describe and analyze at length the Director's formal authority, determined by government legislation. Legal constraints on the administrators' decision-making powers are among the crucial factors that affected the behavior of the administrator.

The Director:[29] The Director is primarily a coordinator whose magnitude of authority depends on his leadership capabilities.[30] Together with the professional staff, he advises the general membership of what should or could be done. The membership, or its elected body, discusses the suggestion and then approves it in its original or amended form. The Director is then delegated the task of implementing the decisions with the aid of the professional staff and *with* the organization's membership at large. The word "with" instead of the word "through" has been used in the previous sen-

---

29. For a discussion of the Director's legal rights, see a published doctoral dissertation: Hussein I. Kratina, *Položaj Direktora u Sistemu Samoupravljanja* (Belgrade: Institut Društvenih Nauka, 1965), and Hussein I. Kratina, *Pravna Odgovornost Direktora i Rukovodilaca Sektora* (Zagreb: Informator, 1967), and *Direktor u Samoupravnim Odnosima* (Zagreb: Informator, 1967), which includes a selection of contributions. See the Bibliography at the end of this book.

30. Note that it can be Machiavellian leadership as well.

tence, because, theoretically at least, the collective should be most interested in carrying out activities whose purpose, significance, and character it has previously decided.

From all the relevant material, it would appear that the legal duties and rights of the Director are primarily administrative. With the exception of the right to vote in the Governing Board, virtually no governance rights are assigned to the Director by federal laws or the manuals of the company. Furthermore, there is some ambiguity as to the amount of decision-making authority he can be delegated through the internal legislation.

The federal constitution states very generally that the Director of an organization administers its activities, implements the decisions of the Workers' Council and other governing bodies, and represents the organization,[31] i.e., he is the only person authorized to sign in the name of the company. (The constitution also states when and to whom this right of signature can be delegated.) Identification of the other legal rights of a Director is difficult, particularly since these rights are not listed in as much detail as those of the governing bodies. This situation exists because theoretically the right to make decisions belongs exclusively to the governing bodies, not to the Director.

In order to gain a more complete understanding of the Director's legal rights in implementing decisions, interviews were held with the Directors themselves. However, this method was unsuccessful, because it appeared that even they were not fully cognizant of their rights.[31] In a study made by several members of the law faculty at the University of Belgrade[32] on the legality of the *Statuts* and their functioning in Yugoslav companies, it was noted that the rights of

---

31. Yugoslavia, Federal Constitution, Paragraph 93.

31a. A current Yugoslav joke asks, "What is the difference between a bear and a Director?" Answer: "The bear is protected by law; the Director is not."

32. Draškić, Petrović, Subotić, *Funkcije Statuta u Privrednim Organizacijama Yugoslavije* (Belgrade: University of Belgrade, School of Law, unpublished study, 1965). Page numbers could not be obtained since the document was retyped several times and each version had a different pagination.

the Director in disciplinary matters have been diluted through frequent changes in federal law to such an extent that it is almost impossible to determine what he is entitled or forbidden to undertake. To update and interpret these changes in the federal laws would take a battery of lawyers whom the administrators would have to consult if they wished to avoid the future inconvenience of being accused of illegal decision-making.

Similarly, internal laws, the *Statuts,* do not determine adequately the Director's rights. One reason for this is that most *Statuts* follow very closely federal recommendations or laws on what should be regulated. Thus, if the federal law has not dealt with a subject, it is improbable that the *Statut* will. Accordingly, the *Statut* of the two companies analyzed in this study state Directors' rights as no more than an authorization to sign in the name of the company and to represent it in negotiations.

Although the federal laws and the *Statuts* of Companies ABC and XYZ do not state definitively the extent of the Director's decision-making rights, they do assign to him the *personal* responsibility for adequate implementation of decisions. Within the vaguely delineated tasks that are assigned to him, i.e., implementation of governing decisions, the Director is free to act independently. To "act independently" means that within the boundaries of his defined tasks he can issue solutions, resolutions, and other coordinating directives without having to convene a decision-making group for approval. (In governing bodies, on the other hand, *no one* individual has this independence. The decisions are made by a majority vote.) "Solutions," "resolutions," and "coordinating directives" are specific Yugolsav terms used to define the managerial tools that a Director has at his disposal for guiding a company to the realization of its decisions. Emphasized is the fact that he has no direct power to enforce these decisions—a concept different from that of "ordering," which usually implies the existence of power.

Listed above are the Director's limited rights; an analysis also must be made of his legal responsibilities. The law determines that the Director has the responsibility of insuring adherence to the federal, republic, and internal laws—the *Statuts* and the manuals. If a Director is aware of a legal violation on the part of a subordinate, and has neglected to take measures to prevent it, he can be brought to trial.[33] He has *legal* responsibility to see that the financial and other business activities *within* the scope of his activities are carried out according to legal constraints. Upon proof that a Director has been negligent, i.e.,

He has not followed the right business practices or ethics in his business relationships and connections with other people—he may have neglected the supervisory work of the governing bodies in the company, or other responsible people in the enterprise.[34]

or if he has signed a contract which was harmful to the company and for which he had no permission from the governing bodies, he may be held personally liable[35] (within certain limits)[36] for damages to the company resulting from such negligence.

Violations of some of the Director's responsibilities are considered *criminal* offenses. For instance:

. . . if he has not adhered to the law for labor relations, or if he has consciously neglected to follow the Manual for the Distribution of Income, working time, or regulation of overtime.[37]

If the Director signs a contract which *he knows* will be damaging to the company, or if he signs a contract without first having been delegated the authority to do so by the governing bodies, he is not only liable according to the civil law (see above) but also liable for criminal prosecution.[38]

The Directors and other executives are also responsible to

---

33. Hussein Kratina, *Pravna Odgovornost* . . . , p. 222.

34. *Ibid.,* p. 223.

35. Paragraph 190 of the Basic Law for the Establishment of Enterprises, quoted in *Ibid.,* p. 224.

36. H. Kratina, *Pravna Odgovornost* . . . , p. 222.

37. Paragraph 314 of the Criminal Law, quoted in *Ibid.,* p. 227.

38. Paragraph 217, sub. 1, Criminal Law, quoted in *Ibid.,* p. 226.

socio-political organization,[39] particularly to the Communist Party if they are Party members (as most of them are), for adherence to the resolutions of the various Congresses of the Party—specifically those resolutions that deal with self-management practices and rights. The sanctions for violating these norms are moral, the most stringent being expulsion from the Party. Usually the Director is called to Party headquarters to explain why his company has not followed Party directives, etc. Lack of democratic practices at work, lack of an exhibited drive on the part of the Director to develop the workers' participation in self-management (i.e., leading the company in an authoritarian manner, taking over and dominating meetings, suppressing the workers' opinions), inability to adapt himself to the decentralization process by increasing the share of the workers' discretion in decision-making, or interference resulting in a delay of the delegation process to the Economic Units—all may be considered in violation of socio-political responsibilities.

By virtue of the fact that promotion and reelection are dependent in some cases on the Party's backing, the Party gains the power to obtain compliance with the political norms that it has set. If the Party cannot affect promotion, it can request a member to explain his actions, a nuisance most Directors try to avoid.

The ambiguity surrounding the delineation of a Director's independent authority may result from the difficulty in distinguishing between governance and administration. The distinction seems to be one of magnitude in discretionary decision-making powers. While on the one hand, due to this ambiguity, authority is highly limited, on the other hand the required responsibility is large since the Director, as leader of the company, is expected to prescribe the correct decisions to the governing bodies and to generate adequate results. Thus, a gap is created in which the responsibilities outweigh the Director's authority.

Other Executives: Except for the Director, an executive has personal responsibility only for those duties explicitly assigned to him

---

39. Hussein Kratina, *Pravna Odgovornost* . . . , pp. 228-230.

Chart III
FLOW OF AUTHORITY AND CHARACTER OF RESPONSIBILITY

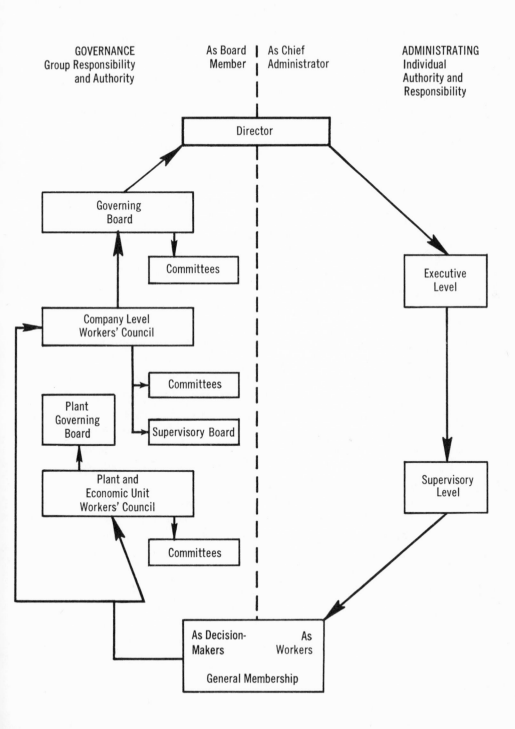

GOVERNANCE
Group Responsibility
and Authority

As Board
Member

As Chief
Administrator

ADMINISTRATING
Individual
Authority and
Responsibility

Director

Governing
Board

Committees

Company Level
Workers' Council

Committees

Plant
Governing
Board

Supervisory Board

Plant and
Economic Unit
Workers' Council

Committees

Executive
Level

Supervisory
Level

As Decision-
Makers

As
Workers

General Membership

by the *Statut*. At XYZ, foremen are elected by the Units which they head. Their authority is limited to suggesting decisions to the governing bodies and to implementing decisions already made. If a worker has to be moved from one machine to another, this change must be within the scope of the decisions made by the Council. For instance, the foreman cannot order a worker to another machine as a punishment; there must be a production need for such a change.

The foreman plans his Economic Unit's activities, but this plan has to be approved by the workers and by the executives above him. Although one of the foreman's main assignments is to train workers, he may not discipline them; i.e., he cannot fire or punish anyone. He can make a complaint, but the verdict will be given by the disciplinary committee of the Economic Unit. He cannot determine production norms, since these are decided by the *Zbor* on the basis of time and motion studies made by a professional group in the company. The foreman reports deviations from the norm to the *Zbor* or the Council of the Unit, but it is up to these bodies to issue the corrective action.

The Collegium: In each company there is an executive group, called the *Collegium,* composed of the top administrators, which aids the Director in making the various decisions necessary to effectuate the company's tasks. Its members include the heads of the various departments, and it is presided over by the Director. (This is the only group in the company which is presided over by the Director.) The *Collegium* does not possess the right to make decisions legally assigned to the governing bodies; thus, it is in essence a staff meeting where various alternatives are discussed and where those to be offered to the Workers' Council for evaluation and final approval are determined.

The Extended Collegium: In addition to the existence of the *Collegium* as an *executive group,* there is a larger group which is foremen, the shift foremen, and most of those individuals in ad-composed of the members of the *Collegium,* the plant and shop ministrative and staff positions, e.g., economists, planners, analysts, R & D engineers. The *Extended Collegium* discusses matters submitted to it by the *Collegium,* and it is convened as the need arises. (Its specific function is described below.)

Politikal Aktive: The *Politikal Aktive* is the only group which includes all "branches" of the self-management system. The top members of the administrative hierarchy, such as the Director and the heads of the departments, are represented. Furthermore, the heads of the governing bodies are invited, e.g., the President of the Workers' Councils on all levels: company-wide, plant-wide, and from the Economic Units, as well as the President of the Governing Board. Represented also is the third "branch" of the system—that is, the Secretaries of the Communist Party Committee, Trade Union, and the Youth Brigade in the company.

The *Politikal Aktive* discusses matters put on its agenda by any group included in its membership. It should be noted that the *Collegium, Extended Collegium,* and the *Politikal Aktive* are non-elected bodies and are not mentioned in the federal laws or company by-laws. These groups are convened by the administrators and invariably exist in every company with almost the same membership composition. (Their existence and operation seem to be dictated by organizational necessities; a central, unifying group is needed as a centripetal force when the organization's authority and power are highly segmented through administration, governance, and socio-political intrusion and when there is extensive decentralization irrespective of technological necessities and time constraints.)

INFORMAL GROUPS

Majstors: This group is composed of the skilled workers, "masters," who repair the machines. They do not appear anywhere in the organizational chart, but may be located between the foreman and the workers. They are mentioned specifically because the researcher found them to be a highly cohesive and influential group. Because all workers are remunerated according to the results of their work, the power of the *majstors* is derived from their ability to affect the income of the workers through slow or rapid repair of the machines.

Potential Drop-outs: The researcher also noted an informal group composed of those workers who were on the verge of being fired by the *Zbor* either because their results at work were unsatisfactory or because their conduct with their colleagues was unacceptable. However, since the members of governing bodies are immune to firing, one way to avoid being fired was to be elected to the Workers' Council or any other elected governing body. This common interest united these workers who would start their own campaigns to insure election. On the other hand, the administrators would make frantic efforts to find a legal loophole to justify the erasure of these workers' names from the list of candidates.

Other Informal Groups: Another type of informal group within the company is the club. The Trade Union and the Youth Organization have many clubs of their own to encourage social life in the company. Chess, mountain climbing, and "book of the month" clubs have their small groups which associate both during leisure time and at work.

Each company has its executive training courses, where, after working hours, workers and executives study operations research methods, new technologies, economics, business policies, etc. These courses also encourage informal groups, which associate during leisure time as well as during work.

ROTATION AND ORGANIZATIONAL PLURALISM[40]

In order to avoid the development of an elite, which would govern the company without having roots in the general membership, rotation and organizational pluralism were introduced. Rotation operates within each governing body. The Workers' Council is elected for two years, and, every year, half of its membership is reelected; no one can be elected twice in a row to the Council. The

---

40. This term was coined by the author in order to describe the phenomenon.

Governing Board is elected for one year, and no one can be a member of the Board two times consecutively.

In addition to rotation, pluralism makes the development of an elite even more difficult. According to this principle, the Director cannot be the President of the Council or of the Board; the President of the Council cannot be a member of the Board. Thus, the three top positions—those of the Director, the Presidents of the Council, and of the Board—are held by three different people. Furthermore, the Secretaries General of the company's Communist Party, the Trade Union, and the Youth Brigade normally are three additional people. Since each has some vested power in his position, this pluralism in power and the rotation process described above make the development of one governing, self-perpetuating group difficult. (However, this also makes the development of a cohesive managerial group difficult, since the administrators have to readapt themselves and company policies to new governors each year.)

THE SYSTEM OF REWARDS

One of the goals of self-management is to facilitate the withering away of the State. The system maintains that, toward that goal, each individual should be trained to make his own decisions. This can be implemented by establishing a system of rewards and punishments which encourages self-guidance. The rewards should be in accord with results achieved, and each individual should be rewarded for cooperating with his immediate producing group and be remunerated according to how well this Unit performs.

Thus, the Yugoslav personal remuneration system is based on several components: individual basic salary, bonuses based on personal achievement, shares in the Economic Units' profits, and shares in the profits of the company. Any sum in addition to the basic salary and personal bonus is termed "variable part," because it changes according to the performance of the membership as a whole.

1. Basic Salary

Basic salary is determined by job evaluation and its relation to the desirable gap between the highest and lowest basic salary in the company. For instance, the general membership, through the legislation of the Manual for Income Distribution, may decide that the Director's salary should not be more than five times that of the janitor. Thus, at ABC, the janitor's basic monthly income is determined as 31,408 dinars and the Director's as 157,506 dinars. Everyone else in the organization fits into this spectrum through an evaluation of his job.

Work hardship, responsibility (i.e., how much one's position affects the total performance of the company), level of education, and years of experience determine one's position in the scale. The Council determines the minimum education and training level which must be attained for each job. (In both companies studied it was decided that, by 1970, those who have not acquired the desired training will be transferred automatically to another job.) Work hardship is an important variable in determining basic salary. There seems to be considerable respect for genuine sweat as a determinant of remuneration; thus, the blue collar worker by the boilers will be given a higher basic salary than another unqualified worker who sweeps the floors.

Basic salary serves as the basis for the proportional distribution of the variable part of income: the higher the basic salary, the greater the worker's variable portion of the profits.

2. Bonus on Individual Achievement—Workers

For those workers for whom a norm can be designed, there is a table indicating the amount of the bonus to be given for various levels of performance above the norm. At first, the bonus was based only on physical output and cost of production. When there were difficulties in marketing products, and inventories started climbing, the companies introduced quality as another determinant of the norm (in ABC).

It was decided that norms could be changed only once a year. The par for a norm usually was set *below* the maximum that people could produce. This practice was apparently a remnant of the central-planning era when overshooting of norms was the desired goal. It still satisfied the workers, because they received their bonuses, and satisfied production managers, because it showed that they had exceeded the plan. However, some informal value was attached to the maximum "fair" variance between par and performance. Fifteen to 20 percent in XYZ and 5 percent in ABC were considered the right disparities which might be attributed to harder work than normal. Thus, everyone performed at a level higher than the norm. The difference lay in how much higher. (The 15 to 20 percent represented the difference between par and the production of the average worker.) The rate buster—the one who produced more—got a higher bonus, but he also contributed to the performance of the Unit. Since the Unit's profit is split among all the workers, everyone enjoys the rate buster's high achievements. Thus, he appeared to be a welcomed rather than a rejected member.

3. Bonus on Individual Achievement—Staff

The principle behind evaluation of staff is to measure those factors a person can affect and to set a par which is considered as normal. For executives, the table of stimulating bonuses lists the variables that are considered to be under their control, including total profit and revenue, and cost of sales. The rate of bonuses is not uniform for each executive; instead the amount of his bonus depends on how much he can affect the variable which is being measured.

Table 4 indicates the emphasis given to various elements in different jobs; for example, the percent of the basic salary which will be given as bonus for each percent of the realized result which deviated from 95 percent of the planned (according to each controlled element of decision-making, Company ABC).

Note that at ABC the Director's bonus is determined according to the increase in profit, sales, and reductions in cost of production,

Table 4*—Administrators' Bonus Rates**

Positions	Profit from Production	Total Sales	Cost of Production (Bonus for Under 95%)	Total
Director	3.60	2.16	1.44	7.20
Director of the Division of Yarn Production	3.84	2.56	—	6.40
Director of Marketing	2.56	3.84	—	6.40
Director of the Unit for Maintenance	1.80	1.20	3.00	6.00
Director of Quality Control	2.60	1.56	1.04	5.20
Director of Finance	3.00	1.80	1.20	6.00
Procurement Manager	2.60	1.56	1.04	5.20

*Company ABC, Manual for the Distribution of Personal Income.
**Percent of basic income to be given as a bonus for each percent of realized income above (or below if desired) 95% of the planned.

but it is assumed that his control on production cost is lower than that of the head of maintenance. On the other hand, it is judged that the Production Manager (Director of the Division of Yarn Production) can affect most the profit from production, which usually means more production than planned and at a lower cost than planned. However, when the total bonus rates are considered, there is a hierarchical order by which the Director receives the highest share. (See Table 4.)

4. Distribution of Profit—Economic Units

The income of each Economic Unit is determined by the amount of its production at planned costs (without basic salaries). If the Unit realizes lower cost, or produces more than planned with the same cost, it receives a bonus which can be distributed to personal income or funds or both. Transfer prices between Units are determined either according to the prevalent market prices or by cost plus formulae of the production unit producing and supplying the production service. The sum of the increments in transfer prices theoretically should not be higher than the market prices for the final product. The word "theoretically" is used to qualify the previous statement, because if prices change in the market, it is difficult to change accordingly the transfer prices within the company. Thus, it may happen that the company's final price at a given time is higher than what the market is willing to pay.

Between the production units and the service units, there is one basic difference in the determination of income. The service units receive their income from contributions of the productive units, and these contributions are determined by the amount of services planned and implemented by the service unit. For these services each productive unit is charged a certain fee. For incentives, the service units receive a bonus based on savings in the planned cost of production. Therefore, they are supposed to offer services which will result in the largest possible decrease in production costs.

The administrative staff, which is a separate Economic Unit, receives bonuses according to the whole company's financial results. Thus, while the maintenance unit is paid a bonus even if the products were not sold, if production costs were lower than planned, the administrative services have to achieve results in the market in order to get their variable share of income.

Transfer prices, bonuses, etc., are regulated in the Manual for Distribution of Income, which is a legal act and requires legal procedures for change.

5. Distribution of Profit—Company Level

The company as a whole generates revenues by selling its products and services to the market. The revenue is distributed to the Economic Units proportionately to their realized income which is determined by the transfer prices and their production lots. Each Economic Unit decides how much of this allocated income is to be distributed for personal income, as variable income, or for funds (reserve funds, recreation funds, funds for homes, etc.).

Assuming that all products will be sold, income is distributed to

5 3

the Economic Units according to production levels of the company. Periodically, sales are reevaluated, and distribution of income is readjusted to fit sales rather than production. It may happen that if a company is producing but not selling, i.e., its inventories are climbing, it would see at the end of the year that it had distributed income which was not realized. In such a case, all employees may be asked to return that part of their salaries which does not reflect the sold products. Because of the fact that what has been distributed cannot be reobtained since it may have been consumed, less is distributed in the months to come until personal income reflects total sales rather than total production.

Since a large part of personal income is related to the whole company's effectiveness as well as that of the Economic Units, a member of a Yugoslav firm cannot predict his exact income for a certain month until he opens his pay envelope. To illustrate the large variations in income, and the lack of downward rigidity in salaries, the following data were collected on the paycheck of the Deputy Director of one of the observed companies. These data reflect the trends in salaries of all the other members of the organization.[41]

The total personal income per month of the Deputy Director was as follows:

1951-1952	5,800 dinars per month—a fixed salary determined during this year by the Federal Department of Industry.
June, 1952- July, 1953	8,700 dinars.
July, 1953	13,000 dinars on the average.
1953-1955	The income varied *every month* during these years; the extremes were 18,500 and 26,000 dinars.

---

41. No comparison can be made of dinars to dollars because Yugoslavia went through several devaluations. In addition, the salaries do not represent a comparable purchasing power because of price index differentials.

1956	*Down* to 18,500 dinars on the average.
1957-1958	*Up* to 22,500 dinars on the average.
1959	January, 31,000 dinars; February, *up* to 51,000 dinars; March, April, May, *down* to 33,000; June, July, August, *up* a bit to 34,000 dinars. In September, October, and November, it *doubled* to 68,000 dinars per month. When December arrived and the final balance sheets were prepared, and readjustment made so that salaries reflected sales rather than production, the Deputy Director's income for that month was less than *half his preceding month's salary:* 33,000 dinars.
1960-1961	These years also had large variations in monthly income; the extremes were 41,000 and 82,000 dinars.
1962	This year the personal income per month was significantly lower, because revenue was lower and production costs higher. The company was going through a merger, and machines had to be transferred, people retrained, etc.
1963-1964	The income remained between 61-62,000 dinars per month on the average.
1965	In January, the income soared. The technological integration started bearing fruit. The Deputy Director grossed 101,000 dinars in January, and by December, his income was 221,000 dinars.
1966	The growth continued and the income varied between 146,000 dinars and 278,000 dinars.
1967	This seemed to be the year when the economic reform started to affect income. In January, it was *down* to 166,000 dinars; by March, it was 130,000 dinars.

There were differences between XYZ and ABC in terms of the distribution of income. Following the latest trend in decentralization, XYZ delegated the "power to form profit" to the Economic Units. This meant that the Economic Units themselves determined the transfer prices, based on planned cost plus, or market prices.

Some "give and take" exists between the central administrative unit and the production units by which the transfer price is determined. They bargain to define the adequate cost to which the planned profit as a percentage is added. Obviously, each unit will try to establish the highest cost possible in order to realize the highest possible savings which in turn will result in high bonuses. ABC did not delegate these powers, but retained them within the authority of the Central Workers' Council and the planning staff (see below under planning). Furthermore, the authority for the distribution of income remained centralized at ABC, while XYZ delegated it to the Economic Units.

The manner in which total revenue is distributed may be illustrated by an examination of ABC.

6. Distribution of Revenue

ABC sells its products and services. The income derived is called *realized income,* as distinguished from *planned income. Planned income* can be defined by the formula, planned production $\times$ planned prices, while the formula for *realized income* is quantity sold $\times$ prices obtained. *Realized income* minus bad debts and accounts receivable leaves a sum designated as *collected income.*

Collected income is distributed as follows:[42] 86 percent for personal income and 14 percent for funds. In case the income was derived from factors not under the control of the company as judged by the Council, the entire income (including the 86 percent designated for personal income) goes into funds. For instance, if prices were elevated by the company and this increased the income, a total of 86 percent of the incremental collected income would go to

---

42. This ratio is determined in the Manual for the Distribution of Income, par. II, Company ABC.

personal income and 14 percent to funds. If, on the other hand, the price of the product was regulated by the Price Control Government Agency, and the price increase was allegedly accomplished without any company intervention, the entire amount of this windfall would go to funds. The same situation would apply to any changes in customs regulations or the rate of exchange for exported dollars. In other words, if the collected income is a result of changes in the environment over which the company has no control, the newly derived income is not allocated to personal income. The underlying principle is that one should enjoy only that portion of income he has actually helped realize. Because of the fact that windfall gains are not controllable and, thus, there is no real labor contribution to its realization, they are not subject to distribution as personal income.

This, incidentally, is an interesting illustration of how the ideology presented above dictates managerial techniques. The self-management ideology claims that it is establishing new social relationships among people, that is developing a "just" relationship where a person will be rewarded, remunerated, etc., only for what he has contributed. Income generated by external forces is allocated to funds which are used for the social needs of the members of the collective and of the society at large, such as modernization of the firm or building homes for the workers, and is not distributed as personal income for consumption.

Conversely, the same holds true for windfall losses. If the government changes transportation rates, thereby increasing company expenses, and there is no way to influence the transportation fees or find a cheaper alternative, the entire amount of the loss is subtracted from the funds.

The existent funds are:

1. Reserve fund—required portion (required by the federal law).
2. Reserve fund—nonrequired portion.
3. Fund for communal expenses—its cash balances.
4. Working capital of the company—its cash balances.

The portion of the income required by federal law to be allocated to the reserve funds amounts to 2 percent of the average current assets of the company during one year. Money is allocated to this fund until it amounts to 10 percent of the average current assets the company has had over the last three years. This reserve fund is deposited in the bank and can be utilized whenever the company realizes operational losses of a magnitude which prevents the payment of the workers' basic personal income. How much of the reserve fund will be used for this purpose is left up to the Workers' Council. The fund can be used as working capital as well, but federal law has severe limitations on when this may occur.

If a company (Workers' Council) desires, it may allocate even greater resources to another reserve fund (which is optional) to assure the workers' incomes in case the company realizes abnormal losses in the future. These deposited reserve funds, which do not yield interest, resemble the primitive "family" type of budgeting, where liquid cash is put aside for a "rainy day." This serves as "income insurance" for the workers. The researcher inquired about the reasoning behind the existence of this "income insurance" fund and was told that because of the frequent and seldom consistent changes in Yugoslav economic policies, companies often find themselves unprepared to cope with the new situations and are often insolvent and unable to pay the members of the organization. Therefore, a fund is established to assure minimal salaries if the company encounters such difficult times.

Economic Units also have reserve funds, which are used when a Unit has not realized sufficient income to distribute to its members. This can happen only through the fault of the Unit rather than through external, uncontrollable forces. In such a case, the Unit is allocated its planned income from the common fund to which all Units contribute. Economic Units should not differ more than 20 percent in income. In other words, if a market price for an item produced by a certain unit soars, it should not lead to more than a 20 percent increase in income over the other units. Increases in

Chart IV
INTERNAL DISTRIBUTION OF INCOME

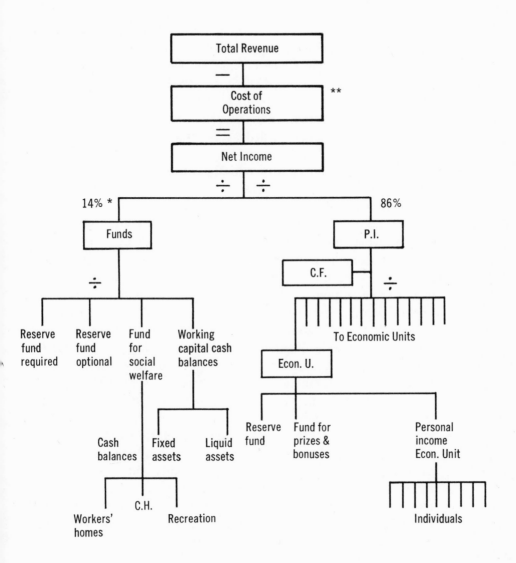

KEY: C.F. = Common Fund; P.I. = Personal Income; Econ. U. = Economic Unit;
C.H. = Children's Homes.

*100% of the income is allocated to funds if this income was generated by uncontrollable factors.

**Including taxation; <u>excluding</u> wages and salaries.

income above 20 percent go to the common fund where they are used as indicated earlier.

This reward system is designed to enhance the achievement of two goals: equality within competition, and income distribution according to measurable results. Equality is achieved through determining the boundaries within which income can vary. Income distribution according to the contributed share toward results, which should be measured, is meant to encourage higher productivity and "justice," since no one is rewarded unless he contributes to the created value. In other words, money earned as a result of being in "the right place at the right time" is considered as windfall effect and is allocated for modernization or housing construction.

Distribution according to contribution requires the measurement of results, which leads the Yugolsav system to quantify almost every process input and output. Each individual's income is tied to other people's work, and, through the establishment of Economic Units, this connection is identifiable and controllable by the individual.

It should be noted that this system creates conflict, since it fosters competition in the distribution of income. Those who operate better than planned, when "planned" is allegedly the "normal" state of affairs, receive bonuses. However, since what is a "normal" state of affairs is determined through a consensus of the membership, and since there is never perfect information on which to establish purely objective norms, the subjective inputs in this process of the development of a consensus can lead to widespread organizational friction. In other words, rewards are determined by appraisal of an individual's contribution, and, since appraisal is always made through group decision-making, the participants in the group are evaluating each other and competing for a share of the "pie" of rewards. The obvious result is friction among individuals, especially if the competition for rewards is tense and the objective standards for measuring contributions to results are questionable.

3.

The Organizations Studied and
Their Output Measurements

Using as background material the previous discussions of the environment, ideology, and organizational structure which prevailed in Yugoslavia at the time of the study, this chapter, by describing in detail the environment of Company ABC and Company XYZ, serves as a bridge between the general environment described earlier and the specific behavior observed in the organizations studied which will be presented in Part II of the book.

The "Black Boxes"

HISTORICAL BACKGROUND

Company ABC and Company XYZ both were located on the outskirts of Belgrade, and both companies had a plant a few miles from their main divisions. (The two plants of XYZ are designated as TC and RN in this book.) The headquarters of the two companies were located half a mile apart, and ABC's plant about a mile from XYZ's plant. Both in the textile industry, ABC produced cotton fabrics and XYZ produced wool fabrics. Their technology was basically the same, as were their markets in terms of channels of distribution and government regulations. However, they were not in direct competition with each other. The two companies were also the same size; XYZ had an average of 2,600 workers, and ABC, an average of 2,900 workers. Except for their modernization efforts, the history of these two companies is similar. ABC was established in 1903, while XYZ was founded in the 1890's.

A summary of ABC's history will familiarize the reader with the organizations, will offer him a worm's eye view of the environment, and will give him an idea of the "organization's memory" which may have affected organizational behavior at the time of the study. XYZ's history is not significantly different from what is described below.

ABC was established in 1903 by an absentee owner, who was in France and Italy "spending the money," as one worker said. The company operated with eight spinning frames until 1914. In 1917, the owner sold half the ownership in the company to the Director, top executives, and top *majstors* who came from Czechoslovakia and settled in Belgrade. ABC's production at that time was about 2 million meters of fabric per year.

The Czechs brought with them old equipment that Czechoslovakia, already a developed nation, no longer needed. In 1934, because of the Depression, the company went bankrupt and was purchased by an English firm. In 1941, six bombs, direct hits, destroyed most of the factory; an unexploded 400-pound bomb from this raid had not been removed from one of the plants by 1967. During the Second World War, all the foreign employees escaped; the Germans managed the company and destroyed the machines through lack of proper maintenance. The workers and the *majstors* who survived the war returned to the company in 1967, and the company still employs a few workers with thirty-five years seniority.

When the war was over, little but a trademark remained. Virtually no operating factories existed, the management was abroad, the machines were old (some dating from the nineteenth century), and most of the buildings had been destroyed.

In 1945, immediately after the war, the company was nationalized and taken from its shareholders by the government. A military management was appointed, and the company began to produce cotton piece goods for the Army. In 1946, the military management was replaced by Directors appointed by the Ministry of Labor. The division of the Ministry for Leather, Textiles, and Rubber determined the production lot and allocated raw materials, working capital, and labor force. No one had the right to hire or fire employees without a license from the Ministry; in this way, it was claimed, the qualified manpower, which was in enormously short supply after the war, could be "nationalized" and allocated where needed throughout the country.

It took the workers until 1951 to rebuild by voluntary work what had been destroyed. For eight hours a day, six days a week, they produced cotton goods, while after working hours, and on weekends, they rebuilt the factory and repaired the plant. It was not until 1951 that production achieved its 1917 level of 2,600,000 meters of fabric (by 1967, the production had reached 20 million meters).

At this time, there existed a great deal of *esprit de corps;* people rejoiced when the siren announced that a production plan had been achieved. They competed to see who could triple or quadruple the production goal. The people with the highest status were those who could make their machines work the fastest and, thus, produce the most, and there was a direct and close correlation between production quantities and monetary rewards. The people felt little uncertainty as long as they did not question the political situation. Many who were interviewed recalled this time with longing and nostalgia, even though food was not in abundance. Bean soup was distributed daily to Director and janitor alike from a common barrel in the middle of the plant. A feeling of togetherness and equality prevailed. One executive spoke with pride of this period:

I remember that we did not have gloves. It was the middle of the winter. Freezing. Transferring machines from one place to another was a terrible job. Hands would stick to the frozen iron and you could not take them off. But it was a period we will never forget. We worked together. Now [1967] everything has changed.

On June 26, 1950, a law was passed which transferred the plants to the workers. This was the birthday of self-management. The workers elected their first Council with 56 members, and its first President was a blue-collar worker. However, the Council's function was only advisory, since it had no decision-making powers as yet.

Most of the workers lived in villages around Belgrade and travelled to work by rail or bus. As the first shift started at 6:00 A.M., and train connections were far from perfect, some workers had to leave home at 4:00 A.M. in order to get to work on time. (These conditions still prevailed in 1967 when this research was done.) Those who moved to the city lived in small apartments built primarily by the company. Those who were not allocated an apartment lived in half-ruined homes or in small dwelling units under congested conditions. Illiterate, without industrial working traditions, without trained professional management, and confronted with a ruined plant, they had to pool their common sense in order to manage and rebuild the company.

According to the new self-management law of 1950, the company had the right to decide what to produce, but investments were allocated by the government and prices were regulated. The one factor left under the control of the company was production lots. In the post-war period, demand was high, production increased enormously, and, as a result, the company moved to three shifts. By 1956, production had reached 3 million meters; anything produced was sold.

In 1958, the company began making its own plans and budgeting its revenue, most of which went toward building homes for the workers and administrators. With time, more power was given to the company to make decisions, and larger parts of the revenue were left to its disposal. These changes led to modernization.

The modernization of the firm was of minor magnitude, including adding machines and dyeing equipment, furnishing, etc., until 1960, when a major change occurred—a new spinning plant was built. The time needed for its installation was a record in itself, since workers built it after working hours, and it was producing at full speed by 1962. The next step in modernizing took place in the weaving department, where all the old machines were removed and the latest automated equipment installed. In 1963, the company underwent a merger, and ABC was established. The integration was vertical, thus freeing ABC from dependency on suppliers for its cotton yarn. The merger helped achieve the greater efficiency demanded to meet competition which had begun to be noticed.

It took a year and a half to integrate fully the merged companies (in 1967, XYZ still was struggling to integrate TC and RN). All the workers had to be consulted; the company Trade Union, the Party and community of Belgrade representatives discussed the matter and had to give their approval. Economic feasibility and personnel policy, i.e., what should be done with the surplus labor, were among problems tackled. However, it is claimed that not a single worker was fired as a result of the modernization process and the merger. The company simply did not hire new people, but maintained and retrained its existing labor force and shifted it wherever necessary. There was an outflow of workers to West Germany and to other companies in Yugoslavia, but voluntary exit was the only way in which the company dealt with its surplus labor.

Since 1963, ABC had been able to export to Italy as a result of a very favorable rate of exchange for dollars obtained from exports. During that time, the company was working on three shifts, and production was still its main goal and key result area. In 1965, the economic reform was instituted. For some time, the market kept absorbing all the production, but, in 1967, the market was saturated and foreign goods flooded the country. ABC's inventory started piling up, because the company was experiencing internal difficulties in cutting planned production (see Chapter 5 on planning). By March of that year, three months of sales had accumulated in inventory, but three shifts were still in operation. Quality started falling, and personal income fell as well. A wildcat work stoppage took place, and the feeling of togetherness was not as strong as before. The company faced tough competition, had no resources to pay salaries, and was saddled with surplus labor which could not be fired.

Described and analyzed below are the organizational charts of ABC and XYZ as they existed at the time of this study: the formal administrative chart and the governing chart, neither of which include the socio-political groups.

THE ADMINISTRATIVE ORGANIZATIONAL CHARTS
(ANALYZING THE DIFFERENCES)

Company XYZ was strongly production-oriented. The Technical Director's position was most emphasized; he was second to the company's Director. Compared to ABC, marketing was almost neglected. (The company did not have a Marketing Director for several years; instead, the Director of the company filled that job.) XYZ's marketing department had less than a dozen people, while ABC's had 39.

ABC was obviously more market-oriented. The company employed Market Research people, was departmentalized according to products, contained a strong economic planning department, and even had electronic data processing equipment. It also had a strong personnel department with 12 people to XYZ's 5. With strong headquarters staff, it was more centralized than XYZ, and it had developed an economic staff with referees to analyze the results of each Economic Unit and planners to plan the activities of the Units within the company. XYZ had only 5 people in the planning department, while ABC had 30. The same pattern held true for the financial sector: ABC employed 54 people while XYZ had less than 20. Furthermore, discretion for making decisions (like planning) was more centralized in ABC than in XYZ (see below). XYZ had several double chains of command, emphasizing the characteristic of joint responsibilities, which ABC did not have.

By and large, XYZ had more governing bodies on more levels than ABC. Since the delegation to these bodies of the right to make decisions was more extensive than in ABC, XYZ was far more decentralized. Additional evidence of decentralization may be found in the number of committees, which was significantly greater in XYZ than in ABC. With respect to political bodies, XYZ was also more decentralized because each of its two plants had a Governing Board, which ABC did not have. Furthermore, its political bodies on the plant level seemed to be more active and more aggressive than those at ABC. Thus, it may be concluded that in nearly every aspect ABC was more centralized than XYZ.[1]

The major difference between the two companies, however, was rooted in the personalities and power of their General Directors. Based on evidence obtained from numerous interviews, it would appear that the above differences in organizational structure were an outcome of the differences in leadership.

ABC's Director was a young man in his thirties, aggressive, strong in the Party, and owning a most phenomenal ability to convince people. When he addressed workers, he gave a highly structured, well presented talk. He was a university graduate with an engineering degree, which ranks between the master's and doctoral degrees as given in the United States. While studying at night, he had worked as a technician in ABC, where he became the Production Manager and finally was elected Director. He had extensive connections with external political and economic organi-

---

1. We realize that we are not using the common definition of centralization, which does not necessarily include departmentalization as a variable. The common definition considers only the distribution of discretion for decision-making. However, having more people in administrative jobs in the center, and fewer decision-making bodies at the Unit level because there are fewer Units, may affect the location of decision-making, as we will see in later chapters.

Chart V

EXECUTIVE CHART—XYZ

SOURCE: Company's files.

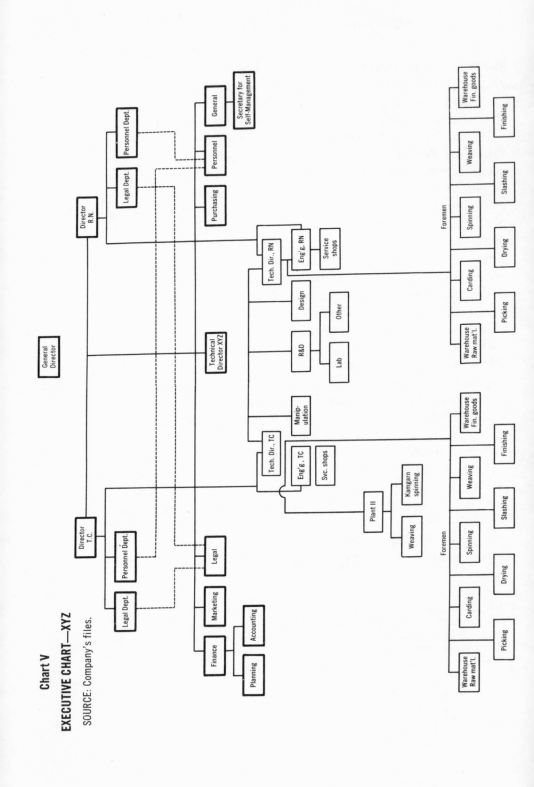

Chart VI

EXECUTIVE CHART—ABC

SOURCE: The Manual for the Distribution of Income states the various units.
An organizational chart did not exist as such.

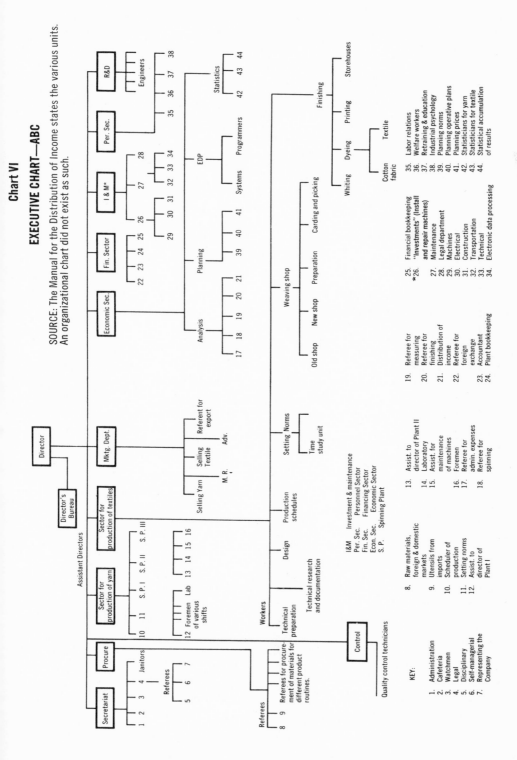

KEY:

1. Administration
2. Cafeteria
3. Watchmen
4. Legal
5. Disciplinary
6. Self-managerial
7. Representing the Company

8. Raw materials, foreign & domestic markets
9. Utensils from imports
10. Scheduler of production
11. Setting norms
12. Assist. to director of Plant I
13. Assist. to director of Plant II
14. Laboratory
15. Assist. for maintenance of machines
16. Foremen
17. Referee for admin. expenses
18. Referee for spinning

19. Referee for measuring
20. Referee for finishing
21. Distribution of income
22. Referee for foreign exchange
23. Accountant
24. Plant bookkeeping
25. Financial bookkeeping
*26. "Investments" (Install and repair machines)
27. Maintenance
28. Legal department
29. Machines
30. Electrical
31. Construction
32. Transportation
33. Technical
34. Electronic data processing

35. Labor relations
36. Welfare workers
37. Retraining & education
38. Industrial psychology
39. Planning norms
40. Planning operative plans
41. Planning prices
42. Statisticians for yarn
43. Statisticians for textile
44. Statistical accumulation of results

I&M   Investment & maintenance
Per. Sec.   Personnel Sector
Fin. Sec.   Financing Sector
Econ. Sec.   Economic Sector
S. P.   Spinning Plant

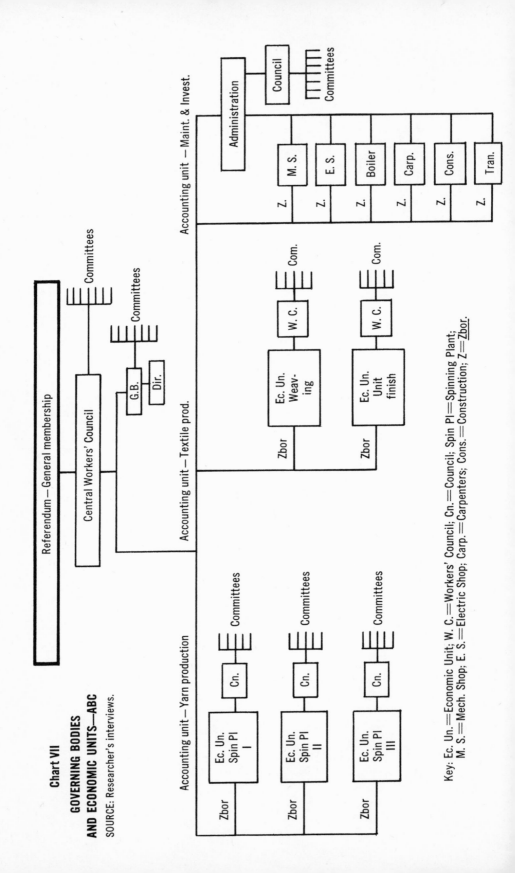

Chart VII

GOVERNING BODIES
AND ECONOMIC UNITS—ABC

SOURCE: Researcher's interviews.

Key: Ec. Un.=Economic Unit; W. C.=Workers' Council; Cn.=Council; Spin Pl=Spinning Plant; M. S.=Mech. Shop; E. S.=Electric Shop; Carp.=Carpenters; Cons.=Construction; Z=Zbor.

Referendum—General membership

Central Workers' Council

Committees

G.B.

Dir.

Committees

Accounting unit—Textile prod.

Zbor
Ec. Un. Weaving
W. C.
Com.

Zbor
Ec. Un. Unit finish
W. C.
Com.

Accounting unit—Yarn production

Zbor
Ec. Un. Spin Pl I
Cn.
Committees

Zbor
Ec. Un. Spin Pl II
Cn.
Committees

Zbor
Ec. Un. Spin Pl III
Cn.
Committees

Accounting unit—Maint. & Invest.

Administration

Council

Committees

Z. M. S.
Z. E. S.
Z. Boiler
Z. Carp.
Z. Cons.
Z. Tran.

Chart VIII

GOVERNING BODIES AND ECONOMIC UNITS—XYZ

SOURCE: Researcher's interviews.

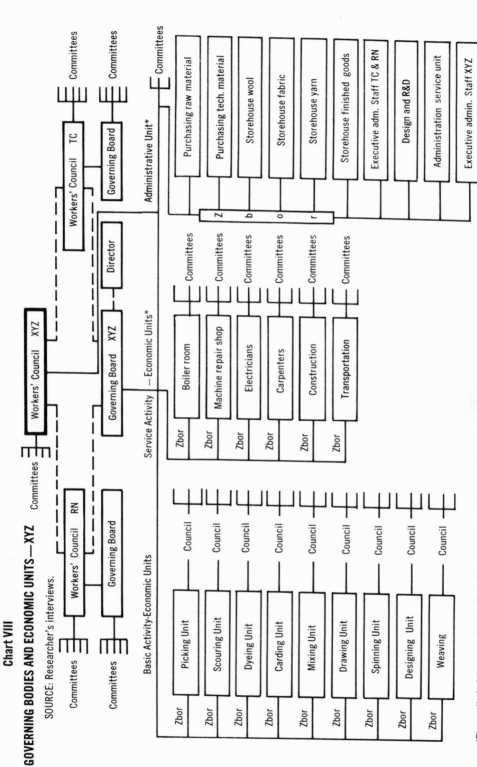

*These units don't have councils since their size is too small. The Zbor serves the function of the Council.

zations. He was the elected vice president of the local bank and a member of the Party's decision-making bodies and of the Serbian Republic Cabinet. He was feared and respected by many; there were also some who strongly disliked him. His grip over the company was noticeable—almost no one wanted to talk to the researcher without the Director's permission. However, in terms of the American view of authoritative management, the Director of ABC would be considered rather permissive. He attended all workers' meetings, visited Units, chatted with workers (most of whom he knew by name), and maintained an open door policy. It was a common phenomenon for workers who wanted to complain against some resolution of the Governing Board, their elected body, to come to the Director. At a time when the company was in a difficult financial situation, he voluntarily lowered his salary to set an example. His strong leadership brought many fine people to the company, because they believed ABC could succeed under him. At ABC, there was respect for administrators, but this was not the general case in Yugoslavia at the time of this research. Although attempts were made by other companies to lure executives from ABC by offering them higher salaries, they preferred to remain, trusting that ABC would continue to grow under the leadership of its Director.

ABC's Director derived his power mainly from his ties with the local bank and the Party, his technical experience, and his personality. The bank was important for loans. The Party ties were important, because only a strong Director could oppose the pressures of the syndicalist stream of thought toward maximum decentralization within the company, pressures that frequently oversimplified the managerial complications involved.

The Director had a specific leadership style. He made it clear where he stood on issues, suggested atlernatives (always two), and used his powers of persuasion to obtain acceptance of one of them. He made it clear that he bore the responsibility for the quality of the alternatives and for the outcome if either of the alternatives was accepted. He spoke on radio and television and was elected to prominent political positions. However, it should be noted that no noticeable leadership existed one or more levels below the Director.

XYZ's Director was an older man in his sixties, awaiting retirement. He had only high school training, but he was an excellent salesman, a significant factor in his rise to the top. He was a Party member but was not very active. His external sources of power seemed to be minimal. Unlike ABC's Director, who clearly was politically ambitious, he had no apparent political aspirations. His behavior pattern was to seek the consensus, identify the law of the situation, and yield to it, rather than to take an aggressive lead. He placed the responsibility on the total membership and seemed to see his role as a balancing power or as one of crystallizing the existent ideas. His participation in discussions was less than any other executive (ABC's Director took the lead 90 percent of the time).[2] XYZ's Director was well liked and well respected and was feared by almost no one. Not a single complaint or unfavorable remark was made about him during this study. Under him there was a layer of noticeable leaders who were capable of taking his position at any time and, in effect, led more discussions to the delineation of alternatives and the making of a choice than he did.

The Economic Output

The economic results[3] of the two companies were different. Table 5 shows a computation of economic results in both companies as well as a comparison of both of them to the industry in general (after being multiplied by a constant in order to protect the companies). The method is called *jedinstveni pokazatelji* (uniform indicators).[4]

---

2. See my doctoral dissertation: *The Effect of Decentralization* . . . , chap. 7.
3. Human capital outputs will be presented separately, Chapter 6.
4. As to the method, see *Metodologija koriscenja jedinstvenih pokazatelja i uporedivanja poslovnih rezultata privrednih organizacija* (Belgrade, Jugoslovenski Zavod za Produktivnost Rada, 1963).

Table 5—Uniform Indicators*

Year and Company	Uniform Indicators	Business Success**				Operational Conditions**							Distribution**					
													In 10,000 Dinars			In 10,000 Dinars		
		1	2	3	4	5	6	7	8	9	10	11	12	13	14	15	16	17
Industry '66		135	1999	58	199	5871	2915	68	87	111	52	92	793	969	13	447	82	117
ABC '64		164	1435	42	203	4008	3210	96	87·	72	42	127	525	776	NA	NA		
ABC '65		194	2162	29	220	5030	3011	80	92	100	44	83	718	1184	13	486		
ABC '66		103	1620	39	190	5169	3488	86	92	100	64	125	788	969	NA	NA	39	109
XYZ '64		NA	1949	83	216	4910	1713	21	81	103	36	86	568	1002	12	263	NA	NA
XYZ '65		264	2547	100	260	5091	2033	38	84	113	52	68	724	844	34	862	NA	NA
XYZ '66		65	2097	55	221	6656	2657	47	78	109	37	95	846	1086	12	445	NA	NA

Key: NA: Not Available.

*All figures were multiplied by a constant in order to protect the companies.

**As to the various indicators used, see page 75.

Source: Computed by the researcher for XYZ from their balance sheets. ABC had its own computations. Industry figures taken by interview from the Agency for Social Accounts, Belgrade, Yugoslavia.

LEGEND: The following numbered explanations refer to the identically numbered column headings in Table 5.

Please note that the translation of the terms is done rather literally. There is no identity between what the Yugoslav considers cost of production and what it may be considered in the U.S.A. Exact translation is impossible because we are not aware of English terms which can be used to express Yugoslav accounting terms; however, the goal of comparing ABC to XYZ and of deriving some insight as to their economic performance can be achieved.

This translation was obtained from the Institute for Productivity in Belgrade through personal correspondence. Because of the above-mentioned disparities in accounting methods, it may not be precise.

1. Trend of the "net product" (i.e., value of total sales minus material costs and provision for capital consumption); base year=100 percent.
2. "Net product" per employee of the enterprise; the respective values in 10,000 dinars.
3. Efficiency of working capital (i.e., the ratio between "net product" and working capital).
4. The ratio between value of total sales and "costs of production" (i.e., material costs plus provision for capital consumption, excluding wages).
5. Value of total sales per employee of the enterprise; the respective values in 10,000 dinars.
6. Total initial value of machinery and equipment per employee of the enterprise; the respective values in 10,000 dinars. (Indicates capital intensity.)
7. The ratio between the initial value of machinery and equipment, and the present value of total fixed assets, in percentage.
8. The ratio between the present and initial value of machinery and equipment, only, in percentage.
9. The ratio between the "income for distribution" (i.e., the value of salaries and wages plus net profit of the enterprise) and "net product," in percentage.
10. The ratio between salaries and wages only, and "net product," in percentage.
11. The ratio between salaries and wages including contributions for pensions and medical purposes, and "income for distribution," in percentage.
12. The average value of the paid annual salaries and wages within the total sales value, per employee of the enterprise, in 10,000 dinars.
13. The average paid salaries and wages within the total output of the enterprise per employee, in percentage.
14. The ratio between net profit and capital of the enterprise, in percentage.
15. The net profit per employee of the enterprise, in 10,000 dinars.
16. The part of net profit assigned for social purposes per empoyee, in 10,000 dinars.
17. The ratio between effective productive hours corresponding to the paid hours within total sales, and total effective productive hours within output, in percentage.

The tables should be interpreted with great care, since more significant differences between managerial efficiency and organizational efficiency can occur in a regulated economy such as Yugoslavia's, than in a less regulated economy. The difference between the two is that organizational efficiency includes managerial efficiency, while managerial efficiency includes in the input and output measurements only those parts that could be regulated by management's efforts.[5] Thus, in highly but not totally regulated environments, organizations can show satisfactory results, not because of favorable decisions on the part of management, but because of favorable economic environment or government regulations.

The growth rate of the average income per worker (which is called "productivity" in Yugoslavia) was higher at ABC than XYZ. This may result from ABC's early investments. Columns 5 and 12 indicate that, although XYZ and ABC have almost the same average income per worker, XYZ distributed more as personal income than ABC. Part of the explanation for this may be that ABC spent more on modernization, thereby cutting personal income. This coincides with indications in labor relations[6] to the effect that ABC was able to make more "painful" decisions than XYZ.

Indicated in column 6 is the beginning of XYZ's modernization, which occurred slightly later than ABC's.[7] Columns 9 and 10 further substantiate this fact and indicate that the process took place at XYZ on a moderate scale. The company still had its funds as sources for personal income, while ABC, having exhausted most of its sources in modernizing, found itself in 1966-1967 with no

---

5. For a relevant discussion on comparing organizations, see Barry M. Richman, "Empirical Testing of Comparative and International Management Research Model," *Proceedings* of the 27th Annual Meeting of the Academy of Management, December 27-29, 1967.

6. See Chapter 6, below.

7. Columns 3 and 4 of Table 5 indicate the conclusions given above: that XYZ did not modernize as much or as fast as ABC.

resources for salaries, especially since its liquid assets were absorbed by inventories. Upon examining the data presented in this chapter, it would appear that ABC is a faster-growing company, which has modernized at a more rapid rate despite the turbulence of governmental policy changes. This may mean that ABC is willing to take more chances and is more market-oriented, while XYZ proceeds more cautiously and seems to consider workers' short-term interests first and the company's interests only when necessary as dictated by general trends in the economy.

The policy implications, particularly in the area of growth strategy, appear to be that ABC should curtail its growth and begin a "strategy of entrenchment," whereas XYZ has moved too slowly and needs to accelerate its modernization if its wants to survive. ABC needs to decelerate its growth rate, because its short-term financing is extremely heavy. The company innovated at such a rate that difficulties in utilizing the modernization have arisen. If its modernization does not yield results, ABC may find itself in a very uncomfortable position. Conversely, XYZ invested during the years when the profits were good, but, when the situation in the market deteriorated, the company curtailed its investments rather than workers' salaries. This trend can be seen in the changes in personal income. In 1965, XYZ cut personal income in favor of funds; in 1966, personal income was increased in order to balance the effect. ABC, however, continued investing, whether the market was good or bad, and it seemed to be able to persuade the collective to modernize despite cuts in personal income.

Thus, from the table of economic results, it appears that ABC modernized faster, i.e., was able to adapt faster, and perhaps even over-reacted to environmental conditions. ABC took more risks and was able to make more "painful" decisions, such as cutting workers' income. On the other hand, XYZ had good results in the short run, because it produced with old equipment whose value and cost were low, and thus XYZ had to pay very low interest on it to the government. XYZ would be in a dangerous position, however, if the laws were changed, and the company had to rely fully on its equipment and productivity to survive.

Both in terms of organizational structure (specialized and with a clearer authority assignment) and in terms of equipment, ABC was more modern than XYZ. However, XYZ had better labor relations, as will be shown in Chapter 6.

PART II

The Decision-Making Process

How does a Yugoslav enterprise operate in reality? How does an organization operate when decisions have to be made by consensus of the general membership, which has the exclusive right to make decisions? How does an organization operate when executives serve in a staff function with highly controlled power since they are appointed by their (otherwise) subordinates for a limited term and are subject to possible recall?

What are the external pressures to which this system is reacting? How does it cope with the extremely turbulent environment in which it has to generate economic results for purposes of survival, and continue to operate "democratically" as well? Can consensus-seeking and competitive decision-making be carried on simultaneously?

The next three chapters describe the process of decision-making under these conditions—a process which may be familiar in nonprofit, nonmarket-competing organizations, but which is unique for a business, economic results-oriented institution.

4.

Modernizing the Firm

At the time of this study, both Company ABC and Company XYZ had undergone extensive modernization and organizational changes. This chapter describes the managerial process by which a decision to modernize is achieved and implemented. The first part of the chapter discusses decision-making on major organizational changes. In the second part of the chapter, three case studies are presented to illustrate the decision-making process, and conclusions based on this material are offered.

The Process

Although many similarities and differences exist in the processes that developed in XYZ and ABC for making major decisions, one phenomenon, common to both companies, should be noted. In order for a decision of great magnitude to occur, two conditions have to be fulfilled. One is that a general feeling of, "it is time to do something about the present situation," must permeate the collective. The second condition is that an individual with strong support has to be interested enough to take the time and the effort to try to secure a decision and its implementation.

A general sentiment toward favoring changes diffuses throughout

the organization with time and through events that stimulate thinking on the subject. It may start with one individual or with several
because of external pressures, stimuli, or because of internal interests, or both. If there is enough reward anticipated from the proposed change, the desire for change spreads relatively fast. Usually,
in order for action to be taken, the desire must root itself deeply
and widely enough to achieve some level of saturation. Such conditions normally develop when the situation deteriorates at such a
pace that most of the members of the organization take notice.
When the saturation level is reached, various individual suggestions
to improve the situation are considered. These alternative courses
of action may have been formulated previously and may have
existed in the "organizational subsconscious,"[1] but apparently they
do not "float" to the surface for consideration until the saturation
level has been achieved.

An originator of a suggestion must be strongly motivated to
propel his suggestion through the various phases of decision-
making, because his suggestion will have to pass through several
"filters" where different groups discuss its validity. His motivation
may be based on the satisfaction that is derived from assuming the
role of leader. If personal interest is his only motivation, this fact
usually will be detected early in the process and his suggestions will
be defeated. The originator may be from any group—executive,
governing, or socio-political. If he comes from other than the
executive group, his ideas will be screened by his own group before
they are brought to the *Collegium* for discussion.

In order for the initial idea to gain some degree of formulation,
a support base from a nucleus of people is necessary. If the need
for change exists, and the realization of this fact is at a high level
of saturation within the company, the nucleus forms fairly quickly.
The factors involved in determining who becomes a part of this

---

1. "Organizational subconscious" is a term we are coining in order to describe a
situation where various bits of data and suggestions for action exist in the organization, but lie outside of the usual channels which deal with choice making or design
of alternatives.

group include: an individual's previous training, his perception of reality, his position in the organization in terms of information networks, and the potential gain or loss he may derive from joining the group.

The nucleus is neither elected nor appointed but is comprised of volunteers. The group has to formulate a proposal and gain an even wider support base, if it ever hopes to see the proposal accepted and implemented. Gaining this support base is not an easy task. First, an exchange of opinions concerning the proposal is conducted at the top levels of the executive hierarchy or group to which the originator belongs. Several alternatives are then discussed, new alternatives are formulated, and new nuclei are formed. Because an extremely strong core is needed in order to propel a major decision, the proposal does not leave this group until the various nuclei are integrated, thereby creating a joint front. If this joint front does not develop, two alternative courses of action are available to the initiator of a proposal. One is to let the proposal lie until conditions develop to an extent that the law of the situation will dictate the solution. The other alternative is to bypass the executive hierarchy and to start building pressure at the bottom levels until it becomes evident to the executives that a base of support exists and that the wisest course for them to follow is immediate action.

A wide support base for a certain alternative is gained by the possession of more powerful data than that of the opposing groups. Such data must be difficult to refute; a propelling group may resort to the use of international sources, statistical proofs, etc., for its arguments. "Playing politics," in terms of exchanging favors, does not seem to exist here, because the decision-making body, i.e., the general membership, finally votes for one alternative or another and will defeat a proposal which lacks obvious value for all members. Unless the group propelling a suggestion can convince the general membership of the value of its proposal, its suggestion will be defeated. "Playing politics" might take place if a compromise were needed for a decision, i.e., if several groups found an intermediate alternative and secured a majority vote. Yet this is not the case because decisions should be made by all—a unanimous vote must be sought.

An ever-widening support base is acquired in the following manner: the group supporting a certain issue presents it to a meeting of the key executives from the administrative function, the *Collegium*. This group then debates the proposal. Each individual has an equal right to vote and an opportunity to express his opinon, but, in these discussions, one's position in the hierarchy has no vested advantage. Top administrators are challenged by their colleagues or by the workers and, thus, have to resort to strong arguments based on data if they want to convince. These arguments

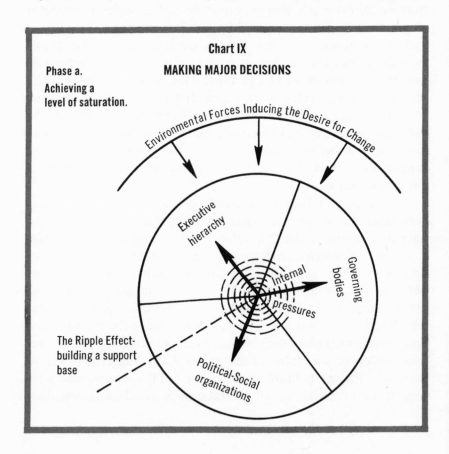

Chart IX

Phase a.
Achieving a
level of saturation.

MAKING MAJOR DECISIONS

Environmental Forces Inducing the Desire for Change

Executive hierarchy

Governing bodies

Internal pressures

The Ripple Effect-building a support base

Political-Social organizations

are not always understood because of educational differences among the members of decision-making groups. However, a unanimous decision is sought. The pressure for unanimity decreases as a ripple effect spreads to larger and larger units of organization.

As a result of the meeting, the administrators have clarified their position on the issue, and a new proposal with new constraints is prepared. There is nothing secret about this meeting. Secrecy could provoke intimations that the administrators were deciding "behind the curtains" and then confronting the legal decision-makers with fully formulated alternatives with the Council or general membership serving only as a rubber stamp. Administrators can be prosecuted for this, because they have no legal right to make decisions independently. Most members of the organization know that various alternatives are being debated. In the self-management system where organizational interlocking is fostered, any secrecy is difficult to maintain. If "kitchen cabinets" exist, their usual purpose is to formulate new proposals before another phase in decision-making takes place.

As the process matures, the informal group propelling the proposal increases in membership to include more and more key men from all levels of the organizational structure and from the various "branches," socio-political groups, offices of the governance function, etc. Simultaneously or subsequently, the company's Communist Party Central Committee and the Trade Union Secretariat discuss the problem and the proposals considered by the administrators. These discussions are accomplished easily because the chief administrators typically are members of the Party; even if they are not Party members, they are still asked to participate in the meeting and explain their positions. The Trade Union does not usually enjoy a level of status which would enable it to summon the Director, but its top officers attend Party meetings and thus can easily convey information.

The Party and the Union take stands on the issue, although, formally, they can neither make a decision nor attempt to manipulate forces in the company to obtain acceptance of the Party or

Union suggestion. Their position should serve only as an additional input to the decision-making process. Theoretically, the distinction between "taking a stand" and "forcing a stand" is that the Party should not use its power to distribute rewards to its followers, i.e., propel its own people, etc. Instead, it should deliberate the issue and then make its conclusions and supportive reasoning available to the collective.

In the next step in the process, the three "branches" of the Yugoslavian managerial system convene in the *Politikal Aktive:* (1) the administrators who have the information, (2) the political and social leaders who are allegedly the guardians of conscientious value judgments, and (3) the Presidents of the governing bodies who are

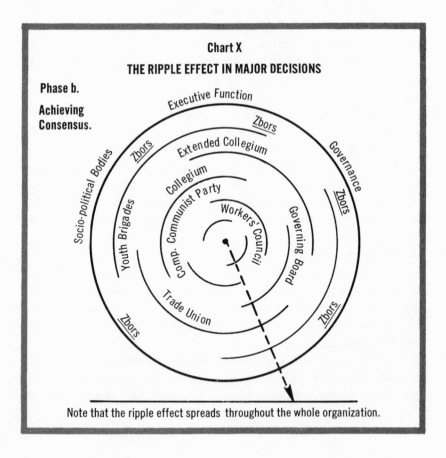

Chart X

THE RIPPLE EFFECT IN MAJOR DECISIONS

Phase b.

Achieving Consensus.

Note that the ripple effect spreads throughout the whole organization.

the formal leaders of the legal decision-making bodies. All have been acquainted with the topic early in the process through the formal and informal discussions in their organizations. During the ensuing discussion, the administrators and the top political leaders usually "bore from within" until a consensus is developed about what should be done. A feeling of urgency usually assists the process of achieving consensus, as does the cohesiveness exhibited by the group supporting the proposal.

This phase of the decision-making process usually involves discussions of the various constraints and may also serve as a "clearing house" for numerous questions from the floor. Because of the composition of the *Politikal Aktive,* questions may be posed by members from the various ranks in the organizational hierarchy. Janitors, who happen to be political leaders, question the effect the proposal may have on their work. The same question may be asked by a foreman who is President of the Governing Board, etc. Administrators achieve an awareness of the proposal's potential implications, which they never would have achieved otherwise, because of their organizational distance from the various jobs. This is a free-for-all discussion which presumably ends in a consensus.

The next to the last step is to "go to the collective." At this stage, all the formal leaders have deliberated the proposal and accepted it. Informal leaders were not identified at XYZ, primarily because there were so many formal leadership positions in the existent system that anyone who wanted to be a part of it could have done so easily. In other words, the system was so participative that no leadership external to that already in existence had to be forced. Also, if someone who had leadership status and whose opinion was respected had not been included in formal discussions, he still could be heard in the *Zbors.*

In the *Zbors,* the discussions are either held separately for each Unit and shift or a general convention of the shift is called. Which strategy is used depends on how much discussion is being sought and what the potential danger is that the proposal may be grounded by red tape or conflicts of interest. Usually, conflicts have been ironed out at previous meetings of the various groups; otherwise, the proposal has little chance to pass the *Zbors* intact. This forum is used also to air anxiety, answer questions, reassure the doubtful, etc.

If this phase passes without noticeable opposition, the proposal in its semifinal form is put on the agenda of the Governing Board. Once it is approved by the Board, it is submitted to the Workers' Council. Most of the Council members are completely familiar at this stage with the modernization proposal. They receive the final proposed alternatives as well as a list of suggestions which were not accepted, together with the reasons for rejection. (XYZ's Governing Board performs this function.) If all the previous phases of decision-making went swiftly, and little opposition developed to hinder the formation of a consensus, the discussion in the Council then turns to a matter of formalities, that is: the voting procedure. Such is usually the case, since the proposal would not have arrived at the Council table had there been strong opposition in previous stages. The Council apparently votes for what it feels the general discussions have indicated.

The implementation of the decision follows the same pattern as above. Each significant problem which occurs and was unforeseen in previous discussions is treated by developing a support base for its solution. Data is collected and arguments are presented until a consensus is established on how to implement the decision.

The process is not as swift and painless as it may appear from the above description. Since a consensus for action has to be developed, and there may be a conflict of interests involved as well as time pressure introduced by prevailing conditions, arguments become more emotional, and the end result may be that close associates within the company, who must communicate by virtue of their jobs, do not talk to each other for weeks in a row.

The process may be represented in schemes as shown above. Chart XI describes alternative No. 2, where the suggestion is deadlocked at the administrative branch, and the individual propelling the suggestion for change will turn to the collective if he insists on putting his idea to use. In this case, as well as in the first, he has to develop a support base. He will start with one Economic Unit within which he can capitalize on personal friendship. The support base in the Unit may yield itself naturally, because of random circumstances, or be developed through persuasion and nurturing of individual needs. The link between the support base and the general membership of an Economic Unit usually is provided by the *majstors,* those who are neither executives nor workers but are "in between," and highly respected. They are a crucial link and their support has to be secured. If their support is obtained, and if the Unit has the necessary resources for implementation, the idea spreads to other Units where it is applicable and advantageous to those groups. The pressure, then, is from below; the administrators have to follow, because their authority and position depend on their being accepted by the collective. (To the best of our knowledge, this second alternative was never used at ABC.)

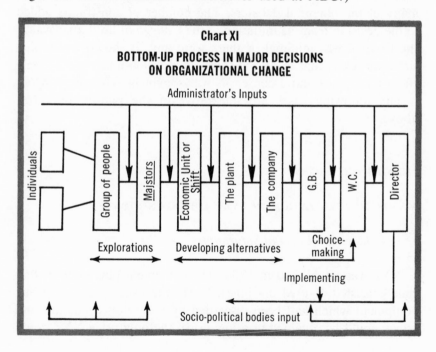

Chart XI

BOTTOM-UP PROCESS IN MAJOR DECISIONS
ON ORGANIZATIONAL CHANGE

Administrator's Inputs

Individuals — Group of people — Majstors — Economic Unit or Shift — The plant — The company — G.B. — W.C. — Director

Explorations   Developing alternatives   Choice-making

Implementing

Socio-political bodies input

THE DIFFERENCE BETWEEN ABC AND XYZ

There was no major difference in companies ABC and XYZ in the sequence of the pattern described above, but there was a difference in its content and character.

In ABC, the idea was initiated by either the Director or other executives; no evidence was found of the "bottom-up" strategy for achieving a major decision. In addition, it would appear that, because of the atmosphere in the company in which the general membership relied on the administrators to take the lead and the administrators relied on the Director, such a strategy could not have been put to use. In the stages of decision-making, the time dimension between initiation and choice was significantly shorter at ABC. The various groups were consulted, but the orderly manner in which meetings were conducted and the overwhelming personality and professional knowledge of the Director seemed to quiet many of the potential debaters. The number of constraints added to the decision from its initiation at the *Collegium* until approval at the Council was minimal, if there were any. It should be emphasized, however, that in *all* the stages of decision-making the ripple effect took place and a consensus was sought in ABC as in XYZ.

The following cases are illustrative of the pattern described above.

Illustrative Cases

MAJOR MODERNIZATION IN XYZ (TOP-DOWN STRATEGY)

1. Achieving a Level of Saturation

XYZ was established in 1898. The equipment purchased at that time consisted of used machines. It was the usual practice to buy equipment which had been discarded by a developed country and which could be obtained at a low price, the only price XYZ could afford. (In 1967, XYZ still had machines which had been purchased *used* in 1905 and 1910.)

The accounting unit in the company had noted a constant rise in the cost of repairs and indicated frequently that there was need for change. The workers themselves—who were losing income because their machines required frequent repairs—were voicing a cry for modernization. Whenever the administrators complained to the workers that the company's production quality was low and asked for more personal involvement and commitment to improve the situation, the workers would retort: "Let us see you work with these archaic machines. Give us something to work with." Thus, there had been for a long time a feeling that change was needed.

The Director of the R & D Department, Rajko, was instrumental in the modernization that followed. It is the opinion of the researcher that his activities and personal characteristics represent the kind of leadership and motivation which was necessary in order to effect a decision in XYZ.

Rajko had joined the company as a production-line worker. He was very active in XYZ's governing bodies and was elected President of the Workers' Council. Upon completion of his term, the Council supported him for two years of study with pay—a common occurrence, since a portion of company revenue normally was devoted to educating members of the organization. Rajko subsequently graduated as a textile engineer and was appointed the Director of R & D. In addition, he served as the President of the Supervisory Committee.

He spent at least 12, and sometimes 14, hours a day in the company, of which 8 were spent at his job and the rest at meetings in the plant or with various Units that had to be persuaded about one thing or another. Twice a week, he attended afternoon classes in the company, where management theory, quantitative methods, and at least one foreign language were taught. He was also married and had two children. It should be noted that he received no additional basic salary for his extra hours spent in the company.

Rajko's ability to convince people was notable. During the four months he was observed, it was noted that his opinions were always listened to with interest and his arguments debated with respect. Rajko had convinced the company to subscribe to numerous foreign publications. From these publications, he noted that the productivity of XYZ (the ratio of output to labor) was lower than in other countries.

According to interviews held by the researcher, the following developments took place. In the past, productivity was not of crucial importance for the company's successful operation. Until 1963, raw materials were imported and the license to import them was granted comparatively easily on the basis of the company's *production capacity*. The prices of the products were regulated, as were the prices of raw materials. There were few internal funds for investments, because most of the revenue was absorbed by the government. Productivity was not encouraged to exceed 5 percent above standard; if it was higher, the Government Price Regulating Agency changed the prices to retain the 5 percent ceiling. The government allocated investments as well and, until about 1963, was interested in investing in basic industries where the payoff period was the shortest. Thus, there was neither the stimulus nor the financial means to modernize, even if the company felt that it was necessary.

In the 1960's, several changes took place. In terms of supply, the government began allocating more funds for consumer industries, while in terms of demand, as a result of the rapid urbanization of Yugoslavia and increases in personal income, there was a booming demand for textile goods. In addition, competition became tougher, because industries were freed from government regulations and started making competitive decisions. About this time, a new law regulating the foreign currency exchange was enacted. It tied importing to exporting—if the company wanted to import raw materials at the value of $1.326, it had to export at least a dollar's worth of its goods. Furthermore, exportation was encouraged through bonuses for dollar exports to Western markets.

As a result of the changes in supply, XYZ was pushed into

9 2

competition with more sophisticated and competitive markets. The company tried hard to export, but noted that its goods could not be placed in Western Europe because of their high cost and low quality. With respect to supply of capital, it was noted that if a good case could be made, the company would be able to obtain funds for modernization.

In Rajko's words, "Now was the time for action. What we felt had to be done all the time had to be done with the new conditions. It was either compete well or bankruptcy. No more subsidies; no more help from the government."

2. Conceiving Alternatives

In 1962, several XYZ weavers from the line were sent to visit other textile firms in Yugoslavia. They saw that XYZ's competitors produced *kamgarn*,[2] which is easier to weave, and, as a result of these observations, began posing questions to the Workers' Council regarding the desirability of *kamgarn* modernization. In addition, Rajko, from his reading of international literature, noted that international production was using more and more synthetic fibers mixed with wool (*kamgarn*) rather than 100 percent wool (*štrajgan*). For XYZ, this meant not just new machines but new technology as well.

In 1963, Rajko submitted a suggestion to the *Collegium* to modernize the company through *kamgarn* technology. In the ensuing discussion, the Director of the company suggested a second alternative: to modernize and expand along the existing technology of wool production—*štrajgan* technology.

Because of budget constraints, there was a question of allocation and its purpose. Among those who opposed Rajko's suggestion in the *Collegium* were the executives of the spinning departments. For them, the change to *kamgarn* would be major and would not facilitate work as it would for the weavers. The General Director of the

---

2. Synthetic—fiber made partially of wool and partially of synthetic fibers.

company, who had been in the wool industry for forty years, supported *štrajgan* as well. Conservative in his thinking, he declared that wool fabric was far more versatile and longer-lasting than synthetic material, which he claimed was merely a current fad. The Production Manager of RN Plant who had worked for twenty-five years in *štrajgan* would not even listen to Rajko's suggestions. The main reason for his attitude seemed to be the fact that RN was largely on *štrajgan* operations, while the TC Plant had been established more recently; if new technology could be introduced, it would go to TC rather than to RN.

The Production Manager of XYZ supported *kamgarn*. He had worked for the ex-owner of the company before the Second World War and before it was nationalized. The owner had been an entrepreneur who had several textile plants, spoke several languages, and traveled extensively—in the words of an executive, "he was exposed to the modern world." After the nationalization, the government made the ex-owner a paid consultant to his former company. He had been trying for a long time to convince the workers to move toward *kamgarn* production, but he had been ignored. The present Production Manager of XYZ who had worked for this person for many years had apparently inherited the desire to modernize by adopting the synthetic process.

The Finance Manager supported the least expensive alternative, since he wanted to have maximum liquidity in the bank. The Marketing Manager supported *kamgarn* because the market was asking for synthetic material. The Procurement Manager was also in favor of the change, because synthetic components could be obtained more easily than wool. Rajko had worked on *kamgarn* machines as an apprentice; he was familiar with this alternative and supported it for reasons already stated.

During his four months in the company, the researcher became familiar with the way the meetings of the *Collegium* were conducted and, from his observations, was able to derive an impression of the manner in which the specific meetings on modernization may have proceeded. The participants included all the top executives of the company: the General Director, XYZ's Director of Production, Director of Production at RN and TC, the Marketing Manager, Rajko (the Director of R & D), the Procurement Manager, and the Finance and Accounting Managers. The Director of Self-Management, i.e., the Secretary of the company, who was responsible for the self-managerial practices and the guidance of the governing bodies (the Governing Board, etc.) through the decision-making process, participated in *Collegium* meetings, but he was ignored and made almost no comments. (However, in the meetings of the governing bodies he was the epicenter of many of the discussions.)

The most important members of the *Collegium* after the Director were Rajko and the Production Manager of XYZ. Both were dealing with production, which had been the activity most crucial to the company's success until the economic reforms. With the new market orientation, the function of the Marketing Manager started gaining importance. Since the previous Marketing Manager had left the company for a higher salary elsewhere, the Director took it upon himself to perform this job. During the research period, the company tried to recruit a Marketing Manager, but failed to find one who had some professional experience. Because of its importance, the function was not delegated to anyone else, but was concentrated upon by the Director.

3. Obtaining Consensus—the Ripple Effect

Collegium Meeting. The meetings of the *Collegium* were comparatively calmer than those of the Council or Governing Board. The participants sat around a long table in the Director's office; there were no designated seats and whoever happened to be nearest sat in the Director's chair. Furthermore, the Director, himself, seldom sat at the head of the table, and it was hard to identify the chairman of the meeting. Everyone talked in turn, holding on to his argument, i.e., outvoicing the others, and gaining the floor by speaking first. Black Turkish coffee was served and the cups were the ordinary, inexpensive ones used in the workers' cafeteria. On the wall was the picture of Tito. By the Director's table on the floor, leaning against the wall, was a framed organizational chart of the company. It was never used or referred to during all the meetings attended by the researcher, and it was not available anywhere else in the company (ABC did not have any at all). By the wall were book stands which held very few books: one by Marx— *Das Kapital;* the others were on marketing (in English) and on other managerial subjects.[3]

The words most frequently mentioned at each meeting were "sincerely," and "do we agree that . . . ." The word "sincerely" was repeated by almost every participant and appeared to be used to support an argument which did not contain personal interest, but which tried to forward the interests of the collective at large. The phrase "do we all agree that . . . ," which was used by different participants at different times, seemed to serve as a means of identifying the pockets of resistance to certain arguments. The discussion would continue in this way until no one questioned the "do we all agree that . . ."; this was usually the sign that a conclusion had been achieved through a consensus. No voting took place and the minutes were recorded as "conclusions" of the meetings. According to general procedure, the minutes were distributed only to the members of the *Collegium.*

During one of these meetings, Rajko presented an argument in favor of *kamgarn* modernization. His foreign subscriptions came in handy, since his readings enabled him to compare the number of spindleframes in Greece with that in Yugoslavia. He claimed that even though Greece was smaller, it had twice as many spindle-

---

3. The researcher was told in another company that the books by Lenin, Marx, etc., were being replaced by managerial books, and that the best sellers were the translations of P. Drucker's books. In one company, the researcher noted M. Starr's *Production Management* on the Director's desk. This same trend was noted in the display windows of bookstores. During the summer of 1966, the researcher noted several Russian books, but, by the spring of 1967, he rarely saw any. The windows displayed mainly English books on economics and business.

frames. He used these data to support the argument that there existed a place for the textile industry in international markets and that Yugoslavia and, therefore, XYZ were behind the times. Next, he provided U.N. statistics showing that the growth of the natural production of wool was limited, while there was a growing demand for textile goods as a result of the population explosion. "It is inevitable," he said, "that synthetics will be needed to fill the gap."

After several discussions, a consensus to change to *kamgarn* and to suggest the change to the Workers' Council was obtained. When some of the executives were asked to comment on how the Director of XYZ and the Director of RN were convinced to favor *kamgarn*, they answered, "We discussed the matter until they were convinced." It seems to the researcher, from his observations of numerous similar processes of mutual convincing, that their response represented reality. Deliberations always took place as long as the arguments of each side were strong. Each side employed more and more convincing data—U.N. statistics, Russian statistics, etc.—until one side ceased to resist. Also, the time factor served as a variable; if the decision had to be made in a hurry, and the expected value was high, an individual was likely to yield more rapidly to another's arguments. Consensus was arrived at through increasing pressure on the individual to conform to the group.

During the four months in which Company XYZ was observed, discussion always continued in each group until a unanimous vote developed. This process may stem from the fact that, historically, collectivism rather than individualism was encouraged; involved also may be the need to develop a strong, cohesive support base with a high degree of locomotion in order for a decision to evolve through the diffusion process. The ripple effect apparently consumed large amounts of this locomotive energy.

When the consensus developed at the *Collegium,* Rajko and the three other members of the group who supported the idea took it upon themselves to develop a proposal for the Council. Such groups are voluntary; in the words of one executive, "if there are no 'fanatics' for the subject who will foster and push the idea through all the decision-making phases until it is fully implemented, nothing really happens."

The proposal, which was prepared by this group, was 150 pages long. It contained all the international arguments discussed above, the production plans, sources of funds, and expected income. The assumption was made that what was produced would be sold, and no serious attempt was made to research the market. The researcher was told that the reason for the lack of such research lay in the fact that no manpower was available, although at that time the company was looking desperately for someone with training to fill this capacity.[4]

Another section of the proposal included information on the potential distribution of the incremental revenue to be created by modernization. For instance, information was given on anticipated raises in personal income, construction of new homes, modernization of the cafeteria, new showers for the workers in various units, etc.

"If we don't show them what they get from the modernization, we will not get them to vote for it," commented Rajko.

Extended Collegium Meeting. The next step in the decision-making process was to convene the *Extended Collegium,* a larger group consisting of foremen, department heads, and some high Party and Trade Union officers, in addition to the *Collegium* members. This meeting usually was presided over by the Production Manager of XYZ, who, although neither appointed nor elected to this job, was looked to for guidance because of his seniority and status. He was an extremely permissive chairman and, as usual in the meetings of XYZ executive bodies, the discussion flowed in a free-for-all manner.

Development of a consensus on the course of action in this group differed little from the way consensus developed in the *Collegium.*

---

4. There are no business schools in Yugoslavia, and only recently, because of the tremendous pressure from the market, has an attempt been made to establish some.

The only difference noted was that each foreman contributed his bits of data on the possible implications, difficulties, and advantages that the modernization might bring. In this discussion, information relevant to various levels of the organizational structure and with different levels of importance (the latter evaluation is a value judgment of the researcher) was offered. This was a phase where, in a sense, the administration, with the assistance of the political functionaries, attempted to consolidate its opinions on what course of action should be taken before conclusions were submitted to the next discussion group. "Consolidation of opinions" should not be understood as the establishment of a pressure group to forward its own interests; this particular group could not benefit from the modernization except as a part of the whole because of the system of income distribution. "Consolidation of opinions" was necessary in order to maintain group cohesiveness, without which the locomotion necessary to propel an idea would have been limited. The output of this "consolidation of opinions" often was the imposition of various constraints on the initial proposal.

Politikal Aktive Meeting. Once the *Extended Collegium* terminated its discussion and agreed to submit the proposal to the Workers' Council, the *Politikal Aktive* was convened. (The Council was confronted with the proposal only at the last stage, when it was already clear that a consensus existed in the company at large and in its various discussion or decision-making bodies. Although this process was not formally required, it was followed almost invariably.)

The *Politikal Aktive* was composed of the members of the *Extended Collegium*, the Presidents of the Central Workers' Council, Plant Council, and Economic Units, the Governing Board Chairman and Secretaries of the political and social groups in the company, and some *majstors*—in other words, all those who had power or influence in the company.

The meetings of the *Politikal Aktive* were held in the large conference room of the RN plant. Tables were set in a "U" shape, and the Director of the Company, the Production Manager, and the

Finance Manager sat at the head of the room. Rajko always sat among the workers. Members of the various groups that comprised the *Politikal Aktive* sat randomly as they arrived or according to personal friendship, but never as a body. The meeting usually was opened by the Production Manager. No one dominated the floor, and even the Director rarely tried to dictate the course of the discussion. From time to time he would ask for permission to speak, and frequently he would have to wait until permission was granted. He rarely took the floor as other exectuives did by "fighting his way through." The President of the Governing Board, who clearly dominated the meetings of the Governing Board, seldom tried to do so at other meetings. Usually, the meetings were immediately after working hours. Virtually no one the researcher talked to had had lunch, and no food was served during the meetings. At one meeting, several people feel asleep out of sheer exhaustion.

The meetings of the *Politikal Aktive,* which seemed to be the most important group to be convinced of the validity of an action, were the most vocal of all those attended by the researcher. Blaming each other for various company problems, side-tracking the major issues, and becoming involved in hot discussions on the most painful problems facing the company at that moment were common occurrences among the participants. The meetings were highly unstructured, which noticeably frustrated the Finance Manager. He would try from time to time to lead the discussion back to its original track, but would clash with the Production Manager who had his own axe to grind.

It may be assumed that the pattern of discussion on the modernization and the process by which a consensus was developed on this topic were identical with those observed in this study. As a practice rather than a formal requirement, once a consensus developed in the *Collegium* and was accepted by the *Extended Collegium,* those groups comprised the core which tried to convince the others to agree. This group had no formal power to distribute; it had to use convincing arguments in order to evolve a decision. Although the *Statut* forbids calling to account a dissenting member of the *Col-*

legium, as a practice the *Collegium* and the members of the *Extended Collegium* still appeared as one group. Apparently, unless the *Collegium* was united, it was almost inconceivable that the ideas would pass swiftly through the *Politikal Aktive,* and the *Politikal Aktive,* in turn, had to be united in order to affect the next support base.

In the particular meeting here described, Rajko, in the name of the R & D Department, suggested *kamgarn* modernization, specifying both needs and advantages. He did not submit any alternative suggestion for *štrajgan;* nevertheless, at the meeting of the *Aktive* a discussion developed on the extension of the existing *štrajgan* technology. However, because Rajko had a detailed project for *kamgarn* which had been fully discussed and supported in previous meetings of the *Collegium* and *Extended Collegium,* and because no one had such support for *štrajgan,* it was comparatively easy for him to persuade the *Aktive* to decide in favor of *kamgarn.*

The opposition could have suggested a postponement of the decision or the establishment of a committee, or could have made its own detailed proposal. Any of these courses of action would have defeated Rajko's project immediately. He would then have had to return the matter to the *Collegium* and establish a new support base as well as a new proposal with new and more attractive features for the legal decision-makers. In this case, however, the *Politikal Aktive* decided to recommend *kamgarn* to the Workers' Council, although one constraint was added: that the modernization must increase personal income. In other words, the funds for modernization could not be obtained even partially by slashing the personal income of the members of the organization; instead, personal income had to increase. This condition had widespread repercussions as will be evident from the results XYZ achieved (see below).

If too many constraints or modifications are imposed on a proposal during any phase of the discussion, either in the *Collegium, Extended Collegium, Politikal Aktive,* or even in the *Zbor,* the group propelling the proposal withdraws it, claiming that its initial goals cannot be achieved under such conditions. Usually, a bargaining process then develops, where the opposing groups relax constraints and the proposing groups relax the goals. This result is achieved by again utilizing maximum *external* independent data and by appealing to personal *consciences*. Trust plays a crucial role; if trust is lacking, one outcome of these discussions may be that some executives may be involved in a conflict (among themselves or with other workers) resulting in their not communicating with each other for long periods of time. Whether the decision passes this stage in the development of a consensus seems to depend on the amount of interest on the part of the support base in pushing the proposal through, the strength of its arguments, the importance of the decision to the company's achievements, and the strength of vested interests of other groups (i.e., the contents of the proponents' arguments and their ability to deliver them, and the potential effect of these arguments on other groups).

In the case examined here, the opposition was not strong enough. On the other hand, Rajko's formal proposal was the only one which was well organized and which promised benefits in terms of personal income, housing, etc.[5]

"Spreading the Message." In the next step in the process, each representative in the *Politikal Aktive* took the subject to his group for discussion; this was an informal practice but was usually followed. Simultaneously, Rajko and his group began to design a new, more thorough proposal. The Party officers convened the members of the company's Central Committee of the Party to discuss the various implications of modernization. They considered the value judgments made and whether the project had any social implications for the collective, e.g., what the effect of the modernization on the size of the labor force might be. Generally speaking, the Trade Union dealt with the same topics, including their par-

---

5. Those top executives who had originally supported *štrajgan* and could have provided leadership for the opposition, had joined the *kamgarn* camp during the intermediate stages of the discussion and could not defect back to *štrajgan* at this point in the discussion.

ticular set of constraints such as communicating to Rajko that no one should be fired because of modernization. However, such communications were neither official nor compulsory. The "clearing houses" for many of these messages were the Central Committee of the Communist Party in the company (of which Rajko and most of the central figures of the *Politikal Aktive* were members), the cafeteria, and the afternoon management courses which served as informal meeting places for purposes of discussion. The Governing Board may have discussed the modernization but, if so, only briefly. Usually, such discussion at the Board was held only if workers began to complain or if there were organizational implications in the issue.

Of particular interest are some of the researcher's experiences relating to the development of a general consensus. Riding in the company's bus to their homes after work, the workers continued the discussions from the meetings concerning the managerial aspects of the company and its financial and marketing policies. The weaver, who had only elementary school training, sat with the accountant, who had a university degree in economics, and the two argued about the present policies. Many workers lived their company's affairs and, during parties attended by the researcher, the discussion would revolve around the latest subject raised in the meetings. Many of these topics were controversial and led to some hot arguments. From knowledge of the kind of conflicts arising from modernization, it may be assumed that the arguments in these places probably involved the distribution of income. Once a Unit modernized, its productivity increased and with it the "total pie" to be distributed among the members of that Unit. *Uravnilovka*, i.e., trying to equate conditions, would be attempted by those in other Units and this might have been a topic for these informal discussions. Thus, while the subject was carried to the Party, the Union, and the *Politikal Aktive*, a grapevine began to operate, which was utilized by the group that prepared the proposal. After all the groups had discussed the modernization, a new proposal with the newly suggested constraints was prepared by Rajko's group, which,

Wage leveling—a form of an *uravnilovka*.
Ekonomicka Revue (Prague), No. 6, 1966.

in the meantime, had grown in membership to include several more *majstors* and foremen. This new proposal was now taken to the collective at large, i.e., the *Zbors* (the recommendation had been to take it to the Council).

Zbor Meetings. In order to avoid the undesirable effects mentioned at the beginning of this chapter, where a suggestion becomes deadlocked, a general convention was called. In a general meeting, a meaningful discussion is difficult to achieve. Such a result was desirable since the executives apparently were aware of possible intentions for *Uravnilovka* because of the differences raised among the units.

Observation of several such meetings, indicated various ways in which such a situation can develop, e.g., executives can take so much time explaining the issues that discussion finally occurs at a time when the workers have been in the factory for ten or twelve hours. Under these conditions, it is easy to develop consensus, especially if time pressure is introduced. Also, consensus may be achieved because most of the members of the organization have already discussed the matter either in the *Politikal Aktive* or in the *Collegium, Extended Collegium,* Party, Trade Union, or Governing Board. These groups may include about 20 to 40 percent of the total membership and, thus, a large number of the formal and informal leaders of the company, who create social pressure on others to conform.

If opposition occurs in the *Zbor*, it may be because the proposal developed too much opposition along the way, i.e., the *Collegium* was not totally convinced and, hence, not totally involved in support of the issue, thus affecting the possible support and involvement of the *Politikal Aktive*. When the proposal arrives at the *Zbor*, the opposition may ally to defeat it.

However, such opposition does not have to be organized. The dissenters sense during the meeting that their group consists of more than what appeared to be a meaningless minority, and they will support each other's arguments until the proposal is returned for further elaboration, i.e., delegated to a committee established for this purpose. During the research period, no evidence was noted at XYZ of any organized activities of opposition behind the formal organization "curtains" (this was more apparent in ABC).

Generally speaking (it is assumed that the meetings were the same on this specific subject), the meeting of the *Zbor* has a different character from those described up to this point. At the *Zbor*, the group which presents the proposal explains why modernization is needed. They proceed with a lengthy discussion of the situation in the international markets, the state of competition, the state of the economy, the anticipated effects of modernization, and the rewards to be gained by the members of the organization. They present all data which have been accumulated in the previous discussions. The workers ask questions, which are answered or explained by the Director and the top executives. Part of the explanations and answers is provided by the members of the *Politikal Aktive* who by now are committed to the idea of modernization. This meeting, unlike previous ones, is not for the formulation of alternatives but for exchange of information, the sensing of opposition, and the securing of commitment to an already formulated alternative. If there are no further questions or personal conflicts, the meeting is then adjourned.

The researcher was told that at the end of the meeting on modernization, a consensus developed to recommend *kamgarn* to the Council. Rajko and his group reworked the proposal once again. It should be noted that sometimes there may be hundreds of suggestions, questions for clarification, comments, etc., from the floor that have to be considered. They must be submitted to the Governing Board for consideration.

Workers' Council Meetings. What is submitted to the Council is the final proposal, which incorporates any suggestions accepted by the support base as well as a list of rejected suggestions and their sources. The rejected items are accompanied by an explanation for their exclusion from the body of the proposal. This material is submitted weeks before the Council meeting and at both ABC and XYZ, it was noted that the members read and commented on the document.

At the Council meeting, there was usually less discussion than in other groups. Those members from the *Politikal Aktive* had already strongly supported the proposal. The collective at large had discussed it and was willing to accept it; in addition, most of the Council members sat at the meetings of the *Zbor*. At the Council, there was an informal practice of joining the majority, and from direct observation, it was noted that this was the way consensus developed. If someone was very vocal in his opposition but was in the minority, the group would pressure him to conform. Executives were called to explain certain parts of the proposals and to submit more data if needed.

In the case described here and in all others, the Council formally announced that it had *decided* to ask the bank for a loan for the modernization and to initiate the necessary steps to purchase the machines. The previous deliberations were not formal decisions, but were merely recommendations.

4. Implementing the Decision

The modernization project then moved into the implementation stage. The bank checked the feasibility of XYZ's proposal, particularly the company's ability to sell their product and repay the loan. If the bank had considered the project too risky, i.e., the market for the product was not of the expected magnitude, or if it considered the company's financial situation shaky, the loan would have been refused. In this case, the loan was granted and Rajko was sent to East and West Germany and to Czechoslovakia to purchase the equipment. Workers from the line were sent abroad to learn to install and operate the machines.

A question XYZ faced later was how to transfer the necessary manpower from the existing Units to a new *Kamgarn* Unit. There was no geographical problem, since the new department was going to be established in the existing plant. The problem was to prove to the workers that the new Economic Unit would be at least as profitable as the old Units, and that no variable personal income would be lost. Members of the *Collegium* began visiting Economic Units to convince workers of the expediency of moving to a better Unit. Their argument was based on the claim that the existing Units would have to decrease existent production because of the introduction of a new product, and that lower production would necessarily mean less income to the existing Unit. The only way the workers could keep their current level of income would be to transfer some of their group to the new Unit, so that fewer people would be sharing in the "smaller pie." Usually, the members of the *Collegium* did not try to identify individuals to be transferred. These decisions were left to the *Zbors* of the Units. However, the executives tried to convince the *Zbors* to accept the fundamental principle of transferring certain numbers of people.

What the executives had to beware of was the possibility that the units might transfer their worst workers, i.e., the least disciplined, laziest, or hardest to get along with, to the new Unit, which would then begin at a disadvantage. Much of the opposition to the transfer of workers was caused by this very factor, e.g., workers feared that the transfer would mean the group did not recognize them as valuable members. These fears would create a whole series of dysfunctional reactions such as weeping, arguing loudly against the transfer, cursing, slamming the tables, or simply displaying apathy to the whole issue. The members of the *Collegium* had to deal with these situations, despite the fact that they were not very well-versed in sensitivity training or human relations theories. If no solution could be found, the problem was taken to the Council, which decided on a list of those to be transferred. (It should be made clear that once the Unit was established, the in-transfer of workers would require approval of its *Zbor* as well.)

The law forbids transfer to a job with a lower basic salary. Therefore, the transfer could have changed only the variable part of the individual's income; in this case this portion could have been higher because of the modern equipment. If a person refused to change jobs even though the Council required it, and even though he would receive the same basic salary, the Council could fire him. (See Chapter 6, on Labor Relations.)

When the new Unit began operating, no norms were established. A time and motion study specialist recorded and analyzed the work, and later a temporary norm was established. According to the company's Manual for Labor Relations, a norm cannot be changed more than once a year. However, there was an informal, unspoken judgment as to what was a "right" norm. Usually, a total of 20 percent was considered as a fair variance between the realized production and the par. Thus, if most of the workers produced to 135 percent, the norm for the following year probably would be raised by the Council to 120 percent with 15 to 20 percent leeway permitted for incentive purposes. If a discussion developed with respect to raising the norms, the process of convincing the workers was resumed, using again international statistics, the state of the nation, competition, etc. Consensus had to be developed as described above.

If there was serious discussion about what constituted a "just" norm, the Party entered the picture. Its recommendations were based on what was supposedly regarded as "justice," or "independent judgment." The Party's recommendation did not have to be accepted, but it was another part of the support base the executives had to develop if they wanted to evolve certain decisions.

In 1967, a new suggestion was being considered: the closing of 40 percent of the *štrajgan* machines and the opening of more *kamgarn* production. It was noted that, because no market existed for them, *štrajgan* goods were piling up in the storeroom, while the *kamgarn* production could not satisfy the demand. This suggestion initiated a whole new series of discussions which resulted in the Council's decision to undertake some long-range planning. The job was delegated to Rajko, who, with his department, had to prepare a proposal describing what XYZ should look like in 1970.

The program of action that Rajko prepared was based on the assumption that full integration between RN and TC was not going to take place, i.e., that half the modernization would go to TC and half to RN. This proposal was submitted to the *Collegium*, but it succeeded only in reaching the *Politikal Aktive*. There it was grounded. There were so many comments on it that it was never presented to the general membership or to the Council. These comments were basically critical of the compromise achieved in the proposal between RN and TC, since many toes were stepped on. At a further meeting of the *Collegium*, a decision was made to design a new, more aggressive strategy. According to this strategy, no compromise would be sought; TC would produce all *kamgarn*, while RN would absorb all the *štrajgan* production. For this purpose, an exchange of machines and manpower would be made between TC and RN.

This new proposal, which seemed to step on *all* toes rather than on some, together with the old proposal and all the comments, was to be submitted to the Council for a final decision. When the researcher left the company, no decision had yet been made. The Council was consumed by current problems created by the 1965 reform and could not allocate the necessary time for long-range planning. (See Chapter 5, on planning.) Apparently, the Council did not intend to approve any changes unless there was a consensus of opinion among the total membership as to what should be done. As the economic results were deteriorating after the reform, there seemed to be reluctance on the part of the collective to make long-range commitments which would tie up income.

THE BOTTOM-UP STRATEGY FOR ORGANIZATIONAL CHANGE (AT XYZ)

1. Achieving Saturation Level and Conceiving Alternatives

In 1962, after the integration of TC and RN to form XYZ, the question was again raised as to the best manner of increasing productivity. A comparison was made between the average labor/ output ratio in the United States and the TC plant. The Director of TC, who had started with the company as an apprentice, made the study and found that TC's productivity was incomparably lower than that of the U.S.A. At the same time, there were difficulties in marketing TC's products because of their high prices, which were dictated by high production cost. He concluded, therefore, that some changes would have to be made. Two alternatives were considered: either to fire 250 workers, determined by the Director as the extent of surplus labor (about 10 percent of the labor force), or to establish what he called an "extended front." The idea of "extended front" was to increase the number of machines on which each worker labored, and to transfer the surplus labor to a third shift. Presumably, increased productivity would result from these moves.

TC's Director developed the idea of "extended front" when he noticed that, although 5 workers were assigned to every two spinning frames according to the organizational scheme, a yearly average of only 3.5 workers actually operated the frames because of sick leave, labor turnover, and vacation time. Also to be considered was the fact that the initial assignment of 5 workers had been made before the workers had known how to operate the machines; once they had learned, the workers were continually underutilized. TC's Director concluded that if 3.5 could do the work of 5, then comprehensive extension of assignments was feasible. The "extended front" provided that the 3.5 workers would get the salary of 5 (assuming they could achieve the same results as the 5), and that the surplus 1.5 workers would be transferred to another shift.

2. Obtaining Consensus

The idea was brought to the *Collegium* for a discussion. No decision was made primarily because workers' opposition was expected. However, Ivan, the Director of TC, wanted to see his idea implemented and decided to work independently. In the department where he had been an apprentice, *majstor,* and foreman, and where he felt most confident, he called for a meeting (*Zbor*) of the two shifts comprising 180 people. At home, he worked with the time and motion staff man to prepare a detailed program for the meeting as well as a scheme including workers' names, the number of machines, and their assignments. Indicated also was the amount of increased income which might be gained by each person if the "extended front" were implemented.

"At the meeting," Ivan said, "I knew I had to present the proposal very carefully. First, I gave a long description of the situation in the company: the level of inventory, the higher sales of competitors because their prices were lower, the high cost of our production, and our low level of productivity compared to our competitors and to the United States."

The next topic he discussed was XYZ's low personal income relative to the potential he believed was possible. He then suggested two alternatives:

1. To let some workers go so that lower costs could be achieved, or

2. To increase the number of machines on which each person worked and to transfer the surplus labor to a third shift.

111

Then he distributed papers containing the new production line scheme—3 workers on 2 machines, rather than 5 on 2 machines—with the figures indicating the anticipated increase in personal income.

They almost "lynched" him. "You want to exploit us!" they shouted. "We will write to SIV.[6] We thought that by having you [as a Director] you would know our needs." The norm setter, Bora, was pulling his sleeve. "He wanted to leave immediately," a worker told the researcher. Ivan suggested that they think about the idea; he also pointed out that they were not obligated to accept it, since they would make the final decision anyway.

The next day, Ivan called in the foreman and the old *majstors* and spent the whole day going over calculations. "They argued until my head spun. We checked every fact and my assumptions. The *majstors* are the most conservative force in the company, and I knew if I convinced them I would be on my way to convincing the others. They were not convinced."[7]

At that same time, two girls on the line became sick. Ivan asked the other three to experiment with his suggestion and promised them that, whatever happened, they would not lose any salary. Legally, he had no right to make such a promise, but he felt certain that no income could be lost. The girls agreed to the experiment, and every day, in order to encourage them, Ivan informed them of their earnings.

"Weren't you afraid you might create so much opposition that the workers would recall you?" he was asked.

"I believe in what I proposed, and I was willing to take the consequences," he replied.

---

6. The Federal Cabinet.

7. J. Woodward, *Industrial Organization, Theory and Practice* (London: Oxford University Press, 1965), p. 194, noted in her studies in England a similar phenomenon. The greatest opposition to change comes from the most self-assured and successful individuals and groups. These groups were composed of people whose word was relatively important to the firm in the eyes of both management and fellow workers. They tried to get something out of the change. The resistance was rational rather than emotional.

After one month, he submitted the results of his experiment to the *majstors*. Again, they rejected his proposal; apparently they could not see how they were going to benefit from it. The researcher was told that they feared the "extended front" would increase their work by creating more repairs caused by careless operation resulting from increased time spent on production. The anticipated increase in their own income as a result of higher company profit was too indirect and remote to influence them.

"I saw that my last resort was to go directly to the workers. I submitted all the figures from the experiment to the *Zbor* of the working Unit," said Ivan. This time, the discussion took a different course. Eighty percent voted for the proposal, but approved it only as an experiment. The 20 percent who objected were not compelled to join, but continued to work as before. However, at the end of one month, when it became evident that the other workers were receiving increased income and were not necessarily working much harder, the dissenting 20 percent asked to "join the front."

The Workers' Council of TC knew about the experiment, but had not officially discussed it. Once the experiment succeeded, however, the proposal was put on their agenda, and it was decided to apply the method wherever possible.

3. Implementing the Decision

"Was the 'front' made mandatory wherever the executives thought it could work?" several executives were asked. They answered that it was mandatory; however, if the workers objected, the new method would fail, the executives would be held responsible, and it might even be insinuated that a Workers' Council decision had been misapplied. Thus, they asked only for volunteers. The *Zbor* decided whom to transfer; the executives only suggested who should go to the third shift from the newly created labor surplus.

When the Director of TC first presented the plan to the *Col-*

1 1 3

legium, the Director of RN plant opposed it. However, when the method had operated successfully in TC for a year, the workers at RN, through their Council, started to pressure their Director to adopt the plan. He refused for a while, but finally had to follow their decision.

Once the method was applied to the workers, the administrative members of the organization asked that the principle of the "extended front" be applied to them, too. Therefore, whenever someone left the company, no one was hired to replace him; instead, company workers were asked whether they would like to assume the job with an increase in salary, in addition to the one they already had. For instance, when a new spinning unit was opened in 1965, only 60 of the 260 workers needed were hired from outside the company. The remaining 200 came from this "extended front."

"My limitation in extending the front in an Economic Unit was within the clearly identifiable labor fluctuation resulting from turnover, sick leave, etc. If, let us say, I see that I have a surplus of 30 people but the average turnover is 15, I can take out only 15 through the front. To take out 30 requires new decisions and agreement of the *Zbor,* which may put the method itself into question. I don't push that far," said one of the executives.

4. Altering a Decision

In 1967, there were many discussions about the abuse of the extended front. For example, if an executive went on vacation and someone else took his job temporarily, even if the replacement did nothing whatsoever that person received an increase in salary. Furthermore, there were machine operators who, through the "extended front," received twice as much as the legal counsel of the firm. Those who were unable to assume an "extended" job were becoming jealous and trying to change the system. In addition, automation led to the phenomenon of people obtaining through the "front" jobs which no longer existed. Also, there were people who took additional jobs they could not possibly perform. To avoid this last situation, the executives generally made an agreement with the person, defining his job exactly before approving his participation in the "extended front." When the case arose of someone over-extending himself, the Council had the right to revoke that particular extension.

When the researcher visited the company in 1967, he attended meetings where ways of eliminating abuse of the method were being discussed. Such abuse was attributed primarily to the fact that modernization of the firm was outpacing the ability to change job definitions and the Personal Income Distribution Manual that regulated the allocation of income according to the "extended front." For instance, when new equipment was installed in the energy power unit (boilers), several workers were transferred because their jobs were eliminated; those who remained did less manual work, but continued to share the total income of the unit among themselves according to the "extended front." This was legal under paragraph 96 of the Manual, and changing the Manual was a tedious job. As a result, various meetings were held to readapt the paragraph to eliminate the abuse of the system.

During the discussions attended by the researcher, no final decision was reached. Fists were slammed on desks, people exploded in anger, the President of the Governing Board left the room for a while to cool off, but no one succeeded in obtaining a consensus on a solution. One of the alternatives was to eliminate paragraph 96, which regulated the "front," but abolition of this paragraph would have meant abolition of the "front." Those individuals who benefited from the method or considered it a fair solution to the company's surplus labor problem opposed this suggestion.

The following pages offer a description of one of the meetings which characterized the general atmosphere prevailing when a confrontation of vested interests existed. The purpose of this description is to present a sample of such a meeting and to show the place on the agenda of a discussion of the "front." Included in this material are the researcher's comments on the events taking place. It should be noted that these comments are a subjective evaluation by an outsider, but the conclusions derived, when presented to other Yugoslav researchers, were supported as observations of general value rather than observations of a single case.

5. Resolving Conflicts

The meeting[8] is opened by the President. The Secretary of the Council takes attendance. Everyone is present—a situation which does not always occur, but this meeting seems to be of importance; no one is even late. The time is 2:15 P.M. and, since those present finished working at 2 o'clock, no one has eaten lunch. At the head table are the President and the Secretary of the Council, the Production Manager of XYZ, and the Finance Manager. The Director is somewhere among the Accountant and several heads of shifts at one of the corners of the "U"-shaped tables. I am sitting by the Director of TC, who remarks:

"You can see how many meetings we have—the Trade Union, Party, *Collegium,* Collective, and now this." He really looks exhausted.

"You don't have to come," I comment.

"If they send you an invitation, *you come,*" he says. "They have questions; we have to answer."

The Production Manager of XYZ is stating the problem. Because of the need to produce different products than those planned, people have to be transferred from one Unit to another. Weaving Unit No. 1 will have to give up thirty people. The Unit is refusing to do so because, with thirty fewer people, they will not be able to fulfill their group norm and, thus, will lose their potential bonus for surpassing the plan. The Production Manager is asking permission to transfer workers and to pay the bonus to the

---

8. Workers' Council meeting, Company XYZ, April 7, 1967. About seventy people attended.

weaving department even though the unit's plan will not be fulfilled. Another alternative is to alter the plan, but he thinks such a move would be unwise because the change he is requesting is periodic and no one really knows how long it will be in effect. Alteration of the plan is more permanent; thus, if conditions change again, another change of plan will be necessary, a costly procedure for the company. The Production Manager further argues that his request for the right to transfer workers and to decide on an adequate bonus to the dispatching unit is a less time-consuming alternative and involves less commitment on the part of the whole enterprise.

The Finance Manager disagrees. He thinks the present planning process is ridiculous. Instead, the company should start from the financial conditions and proceed into the production plans rather than vice versa. On this specific issue, he suggests transferring the people without altering the plan and without giving bonuses to the dispatching unit.

General disagreement occurs in the Council. I cannot hear the words, but I can detect the tone. The Finance Manager has to speak more strongly in order to overcome the voices of disagreement: "But we hardly have money to pay the basic salaries. The inventories are piling up and you want to distribute bonuses. The spinning department has been losing bonuses for years because it did not surpass the plan and it did not surpass the plan because of uncontrollable factors like the one we are discussing."

He is quieted by voices of disagreement. Apparently, the dissenters feel that simply because an anomaly has existed in the past does not mean that it should continue in the future.

The Production Manager of RN tries to explain the issue, and he supports XYZ's Production Manager. Voices are heard: "Yes, that is right." The Finance Manager withdraws and does not participate further in the discussion.

What seems to be the pattern in this specific case is that some individuals discuss the alternatives, while others provide the background noises. It is the workers, though, who will make the final decision by voting. Those who do not fully understand the issues are looking for clues which will guide them in their voting. The voices of agreement or disagreement in the crowd serve as one such clue. Furthermore, the background voices serve as a clue to the executive as to whether his idea is acceptable or not, and his voice accordingly becomes stronger or softer. Thus, even though the participation of many workers may not be structured, words and phrases like "Yes," or "That is right," or "What do you mean?", or "But this is not so," etc., have an effect on the course of the discussion and eventually on the voting.

Workers are taking the floor. They criticize the executives for day-to-day planning: "fire extinguishing," rather than "fire prevention." The executives defend themselves by saying that they cannot offer plans which will not change, since the market is changing so rapidly. It is apparent that some members want the same certainty in plans which they had previously in the stable environment—a situation which cannot be achieved under the conditions of uncertainty now prevalent.

One of the executives, noting my interest in the discussions, whispers in my ear: "The problem is a common one. As long as we operate at full production capacity and sales are high and income distribution on the rise, everything is okay. But now, when there is full production but sales and income distribution are low, everyone is complaining and looking for scapegoats."

It should be noted here that XYZ cannot fire workers because of the internal process of decision-making which would be extremely ponderous; similarly, it cannot hire because of the decision to use internal labor resources which were in abundance and which were underutilized. In order to meet the plan, the company has to move workers from one production unit to another. Transfer of workers means changing the norms and this means new computations, new balancing of interests, etc. All these moves could have been accomplished easily when the "pie" was still growing or was at least stable, but when it began to decrease, achieving consensus

"This is our excess stock!"

Hospodarske Noviny (Prague), April 28, 1967.

began to be a problem. Thus, while the changes in the environment went from decision-making under certainty to decision-making under uncertainty, the internal changes in the company went from operation under cooperation to operation under conflict. Both these changes seemed to put the democratic self-management system to the test.

At the meeting, it is already 5:30. People seem exhausted. Voices can be heard asking the President to conclude. A suggestion is accepted to transfer the problem for study to the Governing Board, which would then make recommendations to the Council. Thus, the Production Manager's request for power to transfer workers and allocate bonuses to the dispatching Economic Unit is defeated, either because of lack of trust in the executives which results in reluctance to hand them a "blank check," or because the Council has not felt that a consensus has been achieved.

Thus, the problem is transferred to a smaller group, which presumably will discuss it in greater depth and possibly reach a consensus, after which the proposal can be offered to the Council for a vote. However, what might happen, and has happened in other cases where a deeper conflict exists, is that the smaller group also fails to achieve a consensus. Its recommendation to the Council is based on the group's points of agreement without specifying points of disagreement, and it is hoped that this omission will be detected and clarified in the larger group. "There are more people in the Council; they know more than we do," is a common reaction. In the meantime, no one group really debates the crucial points which are in dispute because to do so might be too explosive.

However, since time pressure exists to force a decision, the big group apparently prefers to trust that the small group's recommendations are the most prudent, and the small group, in turn, believes it is the responsibility of the larger one to test these recommendations. The end result is that the proposal, even though not fully debated, is accepted in a general, abstract, and thus accepted-by-all, form. The points of disagreement remain unresolved and will reappear repeatedly until the situation itself dictates the solution, i.e., "the law of the situation" resolves the conflict rather than do the participants in it.

An alternative way to make a decision would have been by a majority vote achieved through a compromise.[9] Since decisions are always made unanimously (unless they are decisions with personal flavor, as in specific labor relations issues such as hiring or firing a certain individual), a compromise through voting is not a viable alternative, and a process of delegation back and forth takes place until a consensus develops despite, or because of, the fact that no one can identify the group responsible for the decision.[10] Only then do people seem to be confident enough to accept a suggestion which will not identify them with the consequences.

Another alternative would have been for a top executive to make the decision, resolve the conflict, and absorb the aggression of those whose interests were damaged by the resolution. However, this solution is not viable, because under self-management an executive may not make a decision independently. It must be a unanimous group decision.

Inability to identify those responsible for a decision which involves conflicting interests appears to serve a functional role within the given constraints of the system. If such identification were possible, the various conflicting interest groups would direct their pressure toward those who made the decision, making a consensus impossible. However, the aggressions appear to be against the "system" in general and are, therefore, in the short run rather impotent. As a result the company at least is able in the short run to continue making decisions necessary for its survival.

To continue the description of a specific case, while I am trying frantically to write my impressions of the meeting, the Director of TC becomes involved in a hot argument with the secretary of the

---

9. *Compromise:* an agreement, not necessarily unanimous, to settle differences by mutual concessions. *Consensus:* an amiable (without perceived concessions) and unanimous agreement.

10. Legally, the Council made it, but when the decision proves to be an inadequate one, they blame those that recommended the decision to them.

"Who's responsible?"   *Szpilki* (Warsaw), February 26, 1967.

Workers' Council. She is a typist-stenographer in one of the departments, but she has been involved for so long with self-management
bodies that she feels equal to the executives and argues with them
quite frequently. I missed the argument, but I saw Ivan's pale face
and heard his final statement directed to me: "That b----! She has
no power, but she can definitely start a fire."

Gresham's law of economics operates in many of the discussions.
Unless the matter is complicated, and/or the "good coins" have
strong arguments, they withdraw and leave the floor to the "bad
coins." "Whenever the nuts start shouting the smart ones pull out,"
said one of the executives. That certain people at a meeting may
pull the discussion to their level seems to be a recurring phenom-

enon. For instance, the Finance Director gave up trying to convince anyone while the typist-secretary gained more courage to raise suggestions and fully communicate with other workers.

It is 6 P.M. People are hungry. We go down to the company's cafeteria, which is just closing. The Director of XYZ is pleading with one of the waitresses to reopen, but she does not seem at all impressed by his demands. The cafeteria manager is called, and, after several moments of deliberation, food is finally produced. We then return to the meeting, where a discussion develops on the "extended front" because it is directly related to the questions of transferring workers from one Unit to another and requesting the remaining ones to work on more machines.

The discussion is vociferous. The conflict seems to be on two levels:

1. Conflict between TC and RN: TC has succeeded in fully integrating the method, while RN has not. RN considers the front an unjustified distribution of income.

2. Conflict between the workers and the managers: as one of the workers put it, "The workers work like Negroes on the 'extended front,' while the executives read the newspapers and play. Why should they get the extension?"

This was not the first time the matter has been discussed. Prior discussions have taken place in the *Extended Collegium* and the *Politikal Aktive*. The Party has discussed the matter as well, especially since several of the Communists clearly are receiving extended salaries for nonexistent jobs. Arguments and mutual accusations are heard. The President of the Governing Board is emotional when referring to the unjustified distribution of income: "What kind of Communists are we when we steal from each other?" he asks.

Finally, it is decided to establish a committee to examine the problem. A discussion ensues about its members and names of candidates are suggested. It is apparent that every group is suggesting its own candidates. One of the workers suggests that half be members from TC and the other half from RN, but this brings a wave of vocal disagreement. "This is a shame," says the manager of the weaving department. "We are quarreling for hours over who should be on the committee and only today we hardly had cash to pay salaries. These are hard times for us. We have no money and we don't even know whether we will have any next month. We don't speak about that, do we?"

One of the candidates, a worker in charge of fire prevention in the company, and a member of the Party, asks to have his name withdrawn from the list of candidates, saying, "If we are going to continue fighting for our own personal interests, I don't want to be on the committee."

The mood of the meeting is beginning to reverse itself. People are attacking the idea of interest groups and finally, at 8 P.M., a committee is established. It is composed of the company's senior accountant, several workers, and one of the plant's legal counselors, who are to meet after their regular working hours without additional remuneration for their efforts. They will study job definitions as well as specific cases where an abuse of the system appears to exist.

When the researcher left Yugoslavia six weeks later, the committee was still laboring over the figures and job definitions.

MODERNIZATION OF ABC

1. Achieving Level of Saturation, Conceiving Alternatives, and Obtaining Consensus

Until the mid-sixties, ABC claimed the market would absorb anything the company could produce. Around that time, however, competition became more and more fierce. Customers paid more attention to quality and style and Italian competitive products began to flood the Yugoslav market. The status of the Director of Economic Affairs and the Director of Marketing increased noticeably, and both were questioned by the company's Director as to the best method of solving the problem.

Within the company, each plant was making requests to modernize. However, the Director (not the present one) did not want to make a commitment until a feasibility study was done. This feasibility study, based on payoff period and on the identification of the crucial production bottlenecks for the improvement of product quality, indicated that the spinning department should be the first to be modernized. The next to undergo the process was the weaving and the last, the finishing unit, a sequence which, in a sense, followed the technological process. A timetable was prepared and financial resources reviewed. Very few extensive debates on modernization occurred at ABC. When the spinning department was modernized and new machines had to be installed, the *majstors* worked after working hours and on Sundays, without additional remuneration, in order to install them. If the modernization succeeded and the company obtained higher revenue, everyone, including the *majstors,* would benefit. Thus, all those involved would be instrumental in the success of the company.

When the researcher expressed his amazement at such reasoning, he was told that, with respect to this concept, there is no difference between the U.S.A. and Yugoslavia. In the United States, managers work at home after working hours without receiving direct remuneration. If their work yields results, they are promoted and their salaries increased. The Yugoslavs implement the same idea, but it encompasses the entire company, not just the executives.

There were some discussions on the executive level as to whether to maintain the existent cotton technology or, like the Italians, to modernize to synthetics. The Production Director supported the maintenance of cotton and, as a result, held up the modernization for almost a year, always finding some technological reason for postponing modernization. In 1962, the Technical Director of the company, Peric, was elected the General Director, and the preceding Director became vice president of the local bank, which turned out to be a very fortunate connection for ABC. The new Director, a young and dynamic person, assumed aggressive leadership to modernize the company. One of his first moves was to rid the company of the Production Manager who opposed the modernization.

However, the Director could not fire the Production Manager without legal cause, nor could he discipline the man. If the Director had any complaint against an executive, he had to submit the grievance in written form to the Workers' Council. His technique for obtaining executives' loyalty and adherence was to try to persuade to his point of view those who disagreed with him; if this did not work, he would stop all communication with them. For instance, in the case of the stubborn Production Manager, Peric (the Director) seldom addressed the executive or sent him any information. In time, the executive was so isolated and found his work so disagreeable that he left the company of his own accord. The Director would call the executives to his office almost every day "for a talk," which served as a method of obtaining and harmonizing various perceptions about a given situation.

In ABC, the decision on modernization was conceived by the Director and the Economic and Marketing Managers. Then the proposal was discussed in the *Collegium, Extended Collegium, Politikal Aktive, Zbors,* Governing Board, and the Council. In comparison to those of XYZ, ABC's meetings were calm, short, and efficient. Proposals were sent to the Economic Units, to the various *Zbors,* etc., but unless something directly affected the workers, atttendance and suggestions from the floor were significantly lower than in XYZ.

2. Workers' Council Meeting

From the following short description of the meetings of the Council at ABC, it can be noted that they differ significantly from those of XYZ. The Director and the President of the Council decide on the items to appear on the agenda. ("I don't let them talk about whatever comes to their minds. I argue and try to indicate to them what I believe is crucial.") The meeting is held after working hours, and lunch is served. Tables set in a "U"-shape are covered with white cloths; flowers are everywhere, and there is a feeling of festivity. At the head table sit the President of the Council, the Director, and all the top executives; at the rest of the tables sit the general membership. The President, Director, and those around him are served coffee out of special, gold-rimmed cups. A tape recorder is provided to record what is said. Invariably, the President opens the meeting and then recognizes the Director, who speaks for thirty minutes to an hour about the main topic on the agenda. If a discussion develops, it occurs in a very orderly manner. If people disagree, they murmur softly or repress their feelings; unlike the discussions at XYZ, there are no vocal, disorganized interruptions.

For the Council's meeting on modernization, the Director, a prolific writer, has written a pamphlet about fifty pages long. It deals with the business policy of the company: what is needed, why it is needed, and how it can be achieved. It is distributed to all the members of the Council and the Governing Board. There is no opposition to or comments on his exposé, and it is accepted (decided) unanimously.

3. Side Effects

After the modernization of the spinning and weaving units, ABC moved to the finishing unit. The latest modernization (1967) was the addition of textile printing equipment. The accelerated rate of modernization cost the workers about 15 percent of their income in a period of about three years. Furthermore, for this modernization, the company secured from the Italian partners (buyers) a loan, which committed most of the company's earnings in the near future. However, the Director was not satisfied with the rate of change; rather, he advocated the fastest and largest modernization that the firm could afford. New offices were built with luxurious interiors resembling the latest Park Avenue executive suites; these were allocated to the Marketing and Production Managers, while the Director remained in his old office. During the period of this

127

research, preparations were being made to purchase and use IBM computers.

There was little noticeable opposition to the fast tempo of this modernization, although (see below) personal income was falling steadily. If there was any grievance, it was not manifested through official channels. The Governing Board was especially silent; the President of the Board rarely spoke. If the members of the Board participated in discussions, it was usually to agree with what was being said. However, subdued opposition could be heard in the hallways. People avoided public arguments, particularly because of the feeling that those who dissented from the majority could leave the company. Unemployment was high and people were afraid to lose their incomes. The grapevine provided the researcher with rumors that "workers' eyes were pinched" with the office luxury, while their personal income was barely at subsistence level. The dissatisfaction seemed to manifest itself in different ways: in a wild work stoppage, numerous fist fights in the cafeteria, neglect of machines, and the like (see Chapter 6 on Labor Relations).

At the meetings of the governing bodies, the data presented to convince the workers to modernize usually consisted of a comparison of two alternatives, indicating which would yield more income to the company and, thus, eventually to the workers. Among the constraints specified in these proposals, the primary concern was to avoid firing anyone.[11] Any surplus labor went into services or

---

11. This constraint, avoiding firing because of modernization or periodical slack in demand, was common throughout Yugoslav industry. In other companies, surplus labor was used in a third shift, thus increasing production despite the resulting increase in inventory. In another company we visited, surplus labor was sent home and paid 50 percent of its salary for simply waiting to be recalled. Companies that *had to* decrease their labor force did so in the following way: peasants were first to go, since it was claimed that they could always go to their pieces of land in the village; the rest did not have this security and could not afford to be fired. Next to go were those without families to support. Heads of households without alternative employment were seldom fired. Productivity or seniority were not significant screening variables in this process. XYZ and ABC, for instance, were considering reducing the working week to four working days rather than firing surplus labor.

replaced those who left the company voluntarily. In order to decrease surplus labor, the company closed its doors to new labor from 1962 on, except for those who were highly qualified. However, at any point in time, there existed disguised unemployment which caused little concern. There were strategies taken to squeeze labor out by increasing disciplinary pressure (see below), but this was not sufficient.

In 1967, ABC encountered its greatest difficulty: the quality of its products began to fall. Goods that were shipped to Italy as "A" quality were returned as "not acceptable." Inventory climbed *partially* because of bad quality. It appeared to the researcher, although he could not verify the hypothesis, that *one* of the reasons for this difficulty was the inability of the company to absorb the rapid technological change. Norms were not kept abreast of the modernization; those adequate for old machines were not paced for the new ones. The fiber was not of the same number, a factor which affected the weaving. The coloring was not homogeneous, etc. In addition, the planning of manpower needs seemed to be in a state of confusion. All manpower from the laboratory was transferred to the new synthetics department. There was not sufficient quality control for the old line of products. Thus, ABC appeared to be modernizing faster than it could afford.

In summary, while XYZ was still operating with machines of a nineteenth-century vintage and still deliberating on a method for technically integrating its long-merged plants, ABC was rushing ahead at an accelerated pace, acquiring computers and copying the Italian equipment and methods of production. XYZ's too cautious progress showed in the company's economic results, whereas ABC's too rapid modernization was manifested in its labor relations (see Chapter 6) and product quality results.

SUMMARY AND CONCLUSIONS

The Yugoslav executive walks a tightrope between maneuverability and attainment of a high level of commitment through consensus. While legal constraints and ideology 'require maximum commitment, the competitive economy requires maximum flexibility.

The above descriptions indicate that administrators have to proceed through all the phases of developing consensus in order to secure maximum commitment. At this point, they are faced with a decision which cannot be changed easily even when it is obviously being abused (the "extended front"). A solution to the dilemma would be to delegate power to the executives, with enough discretion to allow some flexibility. However, since administrators were not trusted completely at the time of this research in Yugoslavia, and since their dominance was regarded as a potential threat to the "democratic process," they were not delegated this power and, therefore, this solution was not feasible.

Some degree of flexibility was achieved by reaching a "pseudo" consensus, i.e., external signs such as lack of dissension indicated a consensus even if few workers really understood the issues on which they were voting. This was done by bureaucratic means such as placing the subject high on the agenda, manipulating the order of speakers, etc. People apparently voted unanimously on decisions, because they were exhausted at the end of the day and the matter was presented as if it were imperative that it be acted upon. Flexibility achieved this way had a short life-span, but at least some was obtained.

Is large maneuverability, or commitment more important?[12] Answering this question is equivalent to choosing between a vertical organizational structure with probably higher predictability and short-term maneuverability, or a horizontal structure with greater commitment to processes. Neither extreme is adequate.[13]

In an extremely turbulent environment, when it is hard to predict the future and a company is unable to affect its environ-

---

12. We are concerned here with those cases where commitment and flexibility are incompatible. Achievement of a commitment *for* flexibility results in recentralization, a practice described and analyzed in Chapter 8.

13. See Chapter 8 for further discussion.

ment to any great degree, maneuverability achieved through strong leadership may be dangerous. A short-run follow-up of immediate trends may prove to be disastrous, because a company commitment made under one set of conditions may prove to be inadequate under a new set of conditions which evolved before the primary commitment was exhausted. It is true that maneuverability may make possible a new commitment, but always at cost. For instance, XYZ worked more slowly and was more ponderous, but its decisions seemed to reflect general trends rather than immediate opportunities. Its modernization occurred without the creation of dysfunctional reactions like those at ABC.

In terms of management theory, one may conclude from the above descriptions that the procedures developed for the well-known vertical organizational structure do not necessarily follow for the horizontal democratic structure. In a horizontal structure, emphasis is placed on securing commitment, while in the vertical structure, the primary concern is securing control over results. The whole idea of the ripple effect—of securing a united front from the conception of an idea, a strong core which can bore from within—is one illustration of a democratic principle of management. A further illustration may be found in the assignment to a small committee of the task of discussing a topic, and "kicking it around" until hardly anyone knows who is responsible for it. Thus, everyone becomes involved in the process.

A large commitment achieved for major decisions also has managerial repercussions. From one point of view which states that management serves a bargaining-balancing function between various pressure-interest groups, the Yugoslav system of securing wide commitment enables such a balancing mechanism to evolve even beyond the immediate interests of the company: The Party allegedly maintains the interests of the society at large and promotes the egalitarian political principles; the Trade Union is supposed to support these Party intentions. The community interests, those of the society in the immediate vicinity of the company, are represented through the Party and by representation of members of the company in community decision-making bodies. Capital is represented as well because banks have some control over the loans they give out. Thus when a decision is made, Labor Capital, and Society at large are represented and this representation is instituted through membership on the decision-making bodies. This may be advantageous for a major decision, because many otherwise too-late-to-be-resolved polarizations of interests may be avoided by early and constant confrontation of all interested parties and through a distribution of income which encourages joint efforts to maximize results.

How long this system will continue, with the consensus-seeking process of decision-making, will depend on the pressures for maneuverability. As the macro-environment becomes more predictable and the internal organizational sphere more variable at management's discretion and terms, and as the immediate competition becomes tougher and operates on smaller profit margins, the advantages of maneuverability and promptness of response will increase. These conditions, it is expected, will generate pressure to increase the legal authority of the executives to make independent decisions and thus be partially freed from seeking consensus on every issue. In other words, it is expected that a structure more hierarchical, vertical, than the existent one will ultimately evolve

5.

The Process of Dealing With Short-Term Uncertainty— Preparing the Annual Plan

While the previous chapter dealt with the major organizational changes (commitments), this chapter deals with the process of preparing the annual plan. It describes and analyzes the organizational difficulties encountered by the companies in their attempts to deal with the increasing uncertainty of a competitive economy.

The first part of the chapter describes the technical process of preparing the annual plan at XYZ and ABC, and is followed by a discussion of this process in action and the alterations introduced into it. Actual situations are described and conversations are quoted in order to give the reader the flavor of the interpersonal interaction observed by the researcher. Finally, the chapter presents conclusions derived from an analysis of the case studies.

The Process

COMPANY XYZ: THE PHASES OF PREPARING THE ANNUAL PLAN

Described below are the various steps through which a consensus is formed and an annual plan designed in Company XYZ.

1. In July, the marketing department submits to the planning

department a list of products, quantities, and prices believed to be what the market will be willing to bear. This is called the "Production Plan."

2. The Planner of the company meets with the Production Manager to analyze production capacity (a decision already should have been made on continuing to work with three shifts or less; to change the number of shifts would constitute a separate decision requiring separate treatment similar to long-run commitment decisions like the modernization process).

3. The Marketing Manager and the Production Manager meet in order to clarify what can be produced vs. what the market needs. The usual conflict has to be resolved in this meeting: the Marketing Manager wants maximum flexibility in the plan and thus tries to keep several alternatives open, while the Production Manager is interested in minimum flexibility and tries to establish a rigid production plan.

4. After this meeting, the Planner sends a memo to the foreman of each Economic Unit regarding the production line and quantities which are being considered for the next year. The foremen then call in the *Zbors*.

5. The foremen indicate to the *Zbors* the standards for material and labor necessary for the suggested production (these are planned by the foremen together with the planning staff). The standards are discussed in the *Zbors* because many workers may have their own ideas about the necessary labor or suggestions on how to reduce it. The Economic Units are supposed to send their suggested standards for each expense and each product back to the planning office.

6. The plan for maintenance, repairs, and technical improvements of machinery also is submitted by the foremen to the Economic Units' *Zbors* for approval. Then the plan is sent to the Finance Manager, who computes the costs of the proposal.

7. The Economic Unit reconsiders, alters, and approves the plan and then sends it to the Planner for preparation of standards.

8. The depreciation rates, another input to the decisions on standards, are determined by the State.

9. The procurement unit prepares a suggested list of planned prices for raw and other materials for the coming year.

10. This list is submitted to the Governing Board for approval. The list of materials and their prices may constitute as many as five to six thousand items. The Governing Board cannot discuss each one, but, instead, concentrates on the major items, making decisions regarding alternative materials such as the substitution of imported for domestic dyes. Once the list is approved, it is sent to the planning office, which uses it to set the standards.

11. The planning office prepares a suggestion on the utilization of manpower. Included in the plan is the number of working days for each individual, based on data of sick leave, vacation, *meetings during working hours,* etc. The output is called the "Manpower Plan."

12. From the decision on the number of shifts to be employed and the suggestions for norms for material, overhead, and labor submitted by the foremen and approved by the *Zbors,* the planning office prepares cost norms for each Economic Unit. Theoretically, there should be no difference between what the Units suggest and what the planning office prepares; in reality, however, this is a very sensitive point. The Units try to suggest higher cost norms, while the planner tries to reduce them. There are no special difficulties in determining the standards for raw material or the production capacity of machines. Pertinent data, based on historical performance, are available. The discussion concerns the overhead, which can vary significantly. Included in the overhead are maintenance, repairs, parts, waste of raw materials, dyes, etc., where the savings from better operations lie. The following considerations are involved in the preparation of cost norms:

a. Raw materials needed for the production phase of the basic production unit for which the standards are being prepared.

b. Unavoidable waste computed from production of past years.

c. Other materials needed for production.

d. Norms of labor, with allowances for normal stoppages in the technical process.

e. Depreciation, maintenance, electricity, steam, etc.

f. Administrative overhead based on direct salary paid to each Unit.

13. The standards and the production plan of goods to be sold yield the Production Plan. This plan is developed not for XYZ as a whole, but for each Economic Unit; indicated are the items each Unit will produce and their planned cost, the planned labor force, planned utilization of equipment, planned repairs, etc.

14. The foremen bring the Production Plan to the *Zbors* of the Economic Units, who must either approve or reject it. Usually, approval is given, since the plan is so complicated, with its numerous interdependent numbers and computations, that changing even a single computation is very difficult. Any disparity in these figures should have been resolved in discussions on the standards.

15. The *Zbors* append comments or suggestions to the plan. These comments may deal with requests for new machines or for an *increase* in the total production task of the Unit (not the cost standards), if the plan does not fully utilize all available capacity (production at less than full capacity means less revenue to the Unit).

16. The appended plan is sent back to the planning office, where the comments are read. If there are any significant disagreements with the content of the plan, it remains on the planner's desk until the disagreements are resolved, usually through discussion in the *Zbors.* The planner goes to the meetings and either convinces the workers that the plan should remain as it is, or they convince him to change it. For instance, the discussion might concern production standards in the weaving unit, whose production is measured by meters of fabric produced. They may weave a fabric loosely and produce more, but this may affect the next unit, which has to dye and press the cloth. Shrinkage of the fabric may lower the dyer's productivity through no fault of his own.

17. Once disagreements in the Production Plan are resolved, the Financial Plan is added. The Financial Plan takes into account taxes, interest to be paid on loans, and any of the company's other financial dealings with external institutions. The Production Plan and the Financial Plan constitute the "Plan" which is sent to the Workers' Councils of plants TC and RN.

18. The plant's Workers' Council then discuss and approve the Plan.

19. The Plan is sent to the company's Workers' Council for approval.

20. The last step is distribution of the Plan to each foreman and executive for implementation.

Normally, seven months are needed to complete the process described above. The Planner in XYZ, when asked how long it would have taken him to plan if he had not had to go through all twenty steps, replied that only one to two months would have been necessary. It should be understood that there are five to ten thousand computations to be made before achievement of a complete plan—stating which products will be produced on which machines, with what amount of resources, and at what internal transfer prices—is possible.

The Plan is reviewed monthly, and quarterly reports are submitted to the Council and the *Zbors*.

COMPANY ABC: THE PHASES OF PREPARING THE ANNUAL PLAN

At ABC, the Marketing Manager and his salesmen determine a sales plan which, in their opinion, is the most adequate under existing market conditions. Basically, they assume that, as in previous years, there will be growing demand in the market. They are not supposed to consider production limitations; rather, their sales plan should reflect the specific market opportunities for ABC and provide an input to evaluate the adequacy of the production facilities. This plan, which includes the product mix and the prices under which it can be sold, is submitted to the planning service. To

Chart XII

THE PLANNING PROCESS

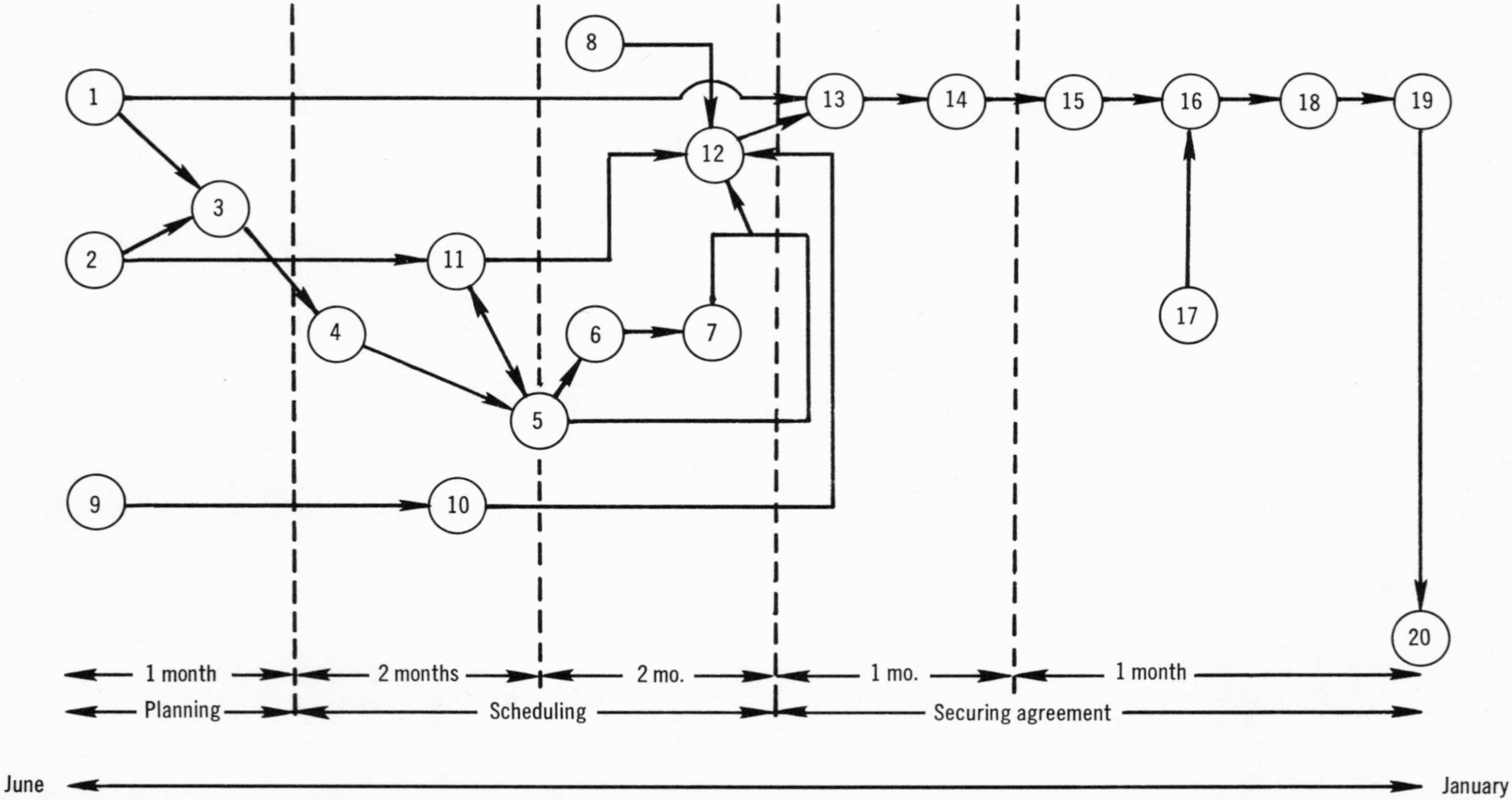

prepare the plan, the Marketing Director, the salesmen, and a marketing researcher make inquiries of the prospective buyers. No attempt is made to predict the state of the economy, but special effort is made to research the foreign market; in fact, the Director himself traveled to either Italy, Germany, Austria, or Czechoslovakia to do so.

The sales plan is compared by the planning unit to the company's production capabilities, which are estimated by the Production Managers and their professional staff of time and motion study specialists, industrial engineers, etc. (This analysis was possible, since the company employed eighty people with academic degrees, including seventeen economists in the planning department—almost triple the number of academic degree-holders in XYZ.) From the sales and capacities plan, another plan is developed by the planning unit, indicating the product mix and quantities to be produced by each Economic Unit; this plan is sent to the foreman of each Unit for comments. Once this process is accomplished, the plan is considered to be a "natural" one, i.e., to indicate the product line and its quantities. The natural plan now serves as the backbone for preparation of the financial plan, which covers the planned cost of production and sales and serves as a par for the distribution of income, bonuses, etc.

The prices of raw materials are determined, wherever possible, according to the prevailing prices for these products in the market. The Government Price Regulating Agency issues a list of prevailing market prices for various products, even those it does not regulate. These prices are used in determining the planned production cost for each Unit. The Procurement Department, which is stimulated to buy at the cheapest price, checks the relevancy of the government list for the future by questioning suppliers as to whether they anticipate a price increase. Once these prices are determined in ABC, any market price change is compensated for by a fund for uncontrollable forces. It is claimed that these changes cannot be predicted and, therefore, should not affect the planned transfer prices, which, in turn, affect the revenue determination of each Unit and, thus, personal incomes.

Overhead cost is added to the direct cost of production and is determined through bargaining between the planning service and the various Economic Units. For each Economic Unit, there is a "referee" from the planning service, a trained economist, and a statistician, who submit to each foreman a suggested overhead based on statistical data from previous years. If difficulty develops in the bargaining process, the Director of the Economic Planning Service Unit in the company intervenes. If he cannot resolve the differences, the Director of the company arbitrates. Theoretically, if the Director cannot help, the Workers' Council makes the final decision. In reality, the process does not proceed beyond the Chief Planner.

Labor cost is added to the cost of direct materials and overhead and is based on manpower standards derived from time and motion studies. These standards are multiplied by the basic salary for each job, and the total computed cost for each Unit plus the planned profit results in the input cost for the next Economic Unit in the technological process.

The final output is a production and sales plan for the company as a whole, and for each Economic Unit, which is sent to the Units for discussion and comments. When this step has been completed, the plan is returned to the professional staff for implementation.

The professional staff designs monthly operative plans from this general plan. On the basis of the monthly plan, need for changing the general plan can be determined. As long as the annual plan does not require alteration in its basic components, i.e., revenue and personal income can remain as anticipated, internal changes in monthly plans can be made by the executives, with regular approval by the Governing Board. The Central Workers' Council must approve an overall change in the annual plan, because it is considered a legal act which only its legislating body can modify.

In terms of time, the planning process at ABC was significantly shorter than at XYZ, primarily because the *Zbors* did not have

1 4 0

the right to make their own plans but could only comment on plans prepared for them by the administrators. The company's Workers' Council voted on a plan; therefore, it was assumed that if there were opposition to a plan it would have been voted down by that body. Furthermore, the *Zbors* did not have the power to determine transfer prices as was true at XYZ. ABC, having larger groups and more qualified executives, was able to exercise stronger control over the Units through professional authority. That this control made the process of planning faster and smoother will be illustrated in the following section through case studies.

The Process in Action

PLANNING MEETINGS AT XYZ

For several years, XYZ has followed the planning process described above. In 1966, because of decentralization pressures within the company, the authority for decision-making on the planning process was transferred to the *Zbors*. Once the *Zbors* made their decisions, the plan was sent to the Workers' Council for its attention only. Even though market pressures called for more prompt decisions, this change required more central coordination and, thus, more time for the *Zbors* to reach a consensus. As a result of this elaborate effort, the plan for 1966, which was to become effective on January 1, was brought before the Council on August 5, 1966. The following discussion about this delay took place in the Council[1]. It is presented in some detail in an attempt to illustrate a meeting where new conditions affecting planning were discussed, and to portray the pressures these conditions put on the managerial processes.

---

1. From the minutes of the meeting of the Workers' Council of August 5, 1966, Company XYZ. Translated by the author.

141

The President of the Council (a technologist in the laboratory): We are approving the plan for 1966 on August 5 instead of in January. It is true that Pera [the Chief Planner] had difficulties in designing the plan, but I don't consider that a justification for this delay. I condemn this delay and I think we should all condemn it.

Member of the Council (head of one of the shifts): This delay is an abnormal shame for us. Only today we are accepting this plan because we must, since it has already been in operation for six months. In the future, we should open our eyes so that we will have a realistic plan on time.

Another Member of the Council (head of a department and member of the Governing Board): It is true that Economic Units planned their overhead expenses and worked according to them. But, due to the fact that no one compared or checked them until now, there are large differences between Units, as a result of which there will be people who wil receive additional income without laboring for it.

President of the Council: I believe that the governing bodies should clarify their relationship with those who do not fulfill their tasks within the given time. The Directors of the plants should request the heads of the departments to explain why they did not show up today.

Pera (the Chief Planner): You have all received the plan, but I would like to draw your attention to several elements which affected the design of the plan. First, the Economic Units accepted the plan a long time ago (in April), and they are operating according to it. The production (quantity) plan was supposed to be lower than in the previous year because we wanted to work in two shifts. But we started to operate the *kamgarn* spinning department and we are already producing more than our last year's plan. In order to operate in three shifts according to a larger plan than we have, we need raw materials. In order to obtain raw materials we need to obtain foreign currency and this can be done only by exporting. But we all have difficulties in exporting. . . . It was difficult to design this plan because many prices of materials could not be obtained. The Procurement Plan was not available in time, and prices were changing rapidly in the market. Also, in February, you changed the basic income of many jobs and the rates of various bonuses given. Besides that, "Desa" [one of the products] was discontinued because it did not sell, which closed production unit number two for the month of April. Thus we had to start recalculating the entire plan. . . .

Member of the Council (the fireman of plant TC): We conclude that something is wrong somewhere, but we should be specific as to whether this person or that person is responsible and request that he be called to account for it, as is done with workers.

Another Worker (a weaver): In the future when we work on a plan, we should coordinate things by meeting with all the executives of the Economic Units so that there will not be large anomalies between Units. The production costs are 58 percent and this means that if we do not decrease the material costs, this year will be a very difficult one. . . .

Member of the Council (worker, dyer in the dyeing department): That's right! In the dyeing unit of plant TC there are fourteen workers more than in RN, but our production plans are the same. Their cost of production in the dyeing department is double those in RN.

Pera (Chief Planner): Overhead expenses are higher in TC because in RN and TC we dye different products, and according to the production line, we determine the dyeing and other materials to be used. It is true that there are anomalies, however. The spinning unit of TC submitted its standards only in April.

Ivan (Director of TC): The Council of plant TC formally accepted the plan and requested that next year the plan be accepted in December. As to the plan's delay, the fault lies with many of us, starting with the government, and ending with some of us around this table.

Finance Director: The plan is not as late as it seems because *the plan is now decided by the Zbors,* and they have accepted it in April and are already working according to it. The Workers' Council should only approve it. Thus, it has already been accepted by those who have the legal right to do so. As for the delay, there are objective and subjective reasons for it. The production service unit discussed the natural [quantity] production plan too long and delayed input. We should keep in mind that this was the first year the plans were made by the Economic Units. They had no experience with them. The realization of the plan for the six months is good and indicates that the plan is realistic. Maybe there were instances of bad coordination between the Units, and this was our fault. We should allocate manpower according to the organization scheme. The plan is made by the *Zbors* and the Workers' Council only accepts it; but it should not be done at any cost; there must be some differences between plans because reality is an operating factor as well.

I believe that the procurement service should start now [August] to design its plan [planned price list of materials to be obtained], so we will not have to wait for their inputs as we did before.

President of the Workers' Council: We are not accusing the whole planning service, but the five or six people whose fault it is. It is not all of our faults. For instance, the executives of the Economic Units whom *it took a month to convince that some of their planned elements were unrealistic,* were they punished? According to our discussion, it sounds like it is the fault of all of us, but no one person is responsible for what is happening. *We should move from group responsibility to individual responsibility,* and people should personally account for what is being done. . . . [Italics mine]

A similar discussion to determine the causes for the delay took place on July 29, 1966, in the Governing Board.

Finance Manager: When we designed the plan for this first year, we changed the process technology. In the *statut* we determined for the first time that Economic Units would make and accept their own plans. Now the Workers' Council simply announces its approval, but it is first made by the *Zbors*. The delay resulted from the new planning process, the exchange in manpower in the planning unit, and difficulties in determining standards.

Pera (Chief Planner): The plan was ready in March, but we had to change it because we closed unit number two and changed the bonuses and basic income for certain jobs. This meant recalculation of five thousand accounts.

President of Workers' Council: It is a shame that we discuss the plan in July or even September because many Council members are on their vacations then.

Member of the Governing Board (head of the weaving department): I had already prepared the data in December. The blame for the delay lies with the productive services. Their job was to determine the planning conferences, *but they constantly postponed them.*

Chief Planner: The procurement services submitted the procurement planned prices only in February, so that *added to the delay too.*

Finance Manager: There were objective and subjective reasons for the delay this year, but next year, we hope it will not happen again, because we have already begun working on it. [Italics mine]

In March, 1967, when the researcher next visited XYZ, the plan still had not been accepted. The following excerpts from a meeting attended at that time by the researcher will illustrate how XYZ attempted to manage the situation. [2] The reader should note (the researcher attended several meetings before reaching this conclusion) that constant postponement of a decision on the plan occurs without any outright action. This could be derogatorily referred to in Yugoslavia as a "bureaucracy." However, as noted earlier, the red tape appears to be a result of an individual lack of willingness (which seems to be a realistic approach) to take the responsibility in a highly dynamic environment for a decision with its long-range commitment and its rigidity. So discussions move in circles for hours at a time. No one suggests *not making* a plan, or making a very *flexible* plan, because either idea appears to be against all the sacred values and practices of the past. Apparently, the practical answer is to change the consensus-seeking process of planning, but this means changing the self-management process of decision-making, which would be revolutionary. The meeting excerpted below was held after working hours, and was attended by forty people.

Director of XYZ (opening the meeting): You have the plan for this year in front of you. You all know it very well by now. The question is, should we accept the plan as it is. I think we should look first at the market. We don't need more labor force because we couldn't sell the extra they would produce.

Production Manager of XYZ: We have here all the components of a production plan. You all participated in making it; you have quantities and qualities suggested by the marketing department. The question is whether the forecasting done is adequate. Can we pursue with the plan by taking into consideration the economic conditions, or must the plan be reworked?

(People are leafing through hundreds of pages of the data contained in the plan. I note that they have made many comments

---

2. Meeting, *Politikal Aktive,* Company XYZ, March 7, 1967.

on the margins and that they seem to be very familiar with the topic.)

Production Manager: Do you believe our plan is realistic? Should we change it?

Financial Manager: I believe we should examine our premises first.

Head of a Shift (a young girl): That's right. In my Unit we cannot produce the planned output because a machine was thrown out.

Director: How come? We get six hundred dinars for the output.

Head of the Shift: But it cost us one thousand dinars.

Director: So, get rid of the machine!

Head of the Shift: Why did you plan its use then?

Director: That's what I'm asking you!

Referee for Marketing: This is really crucial. We don't know the cost of our products. I want to ask the Council a policy question: Can we sell under cost?[3] When I look at the plan, I see we have profit. When I look at each product sold, I realize we have only losses. If we accept this plan and the quality remains as low as last year's, I warn you, we will go bankrupt. I request a special meeting of all executives to discuss this matter. Even if we sell at thirty to forty percent lower prices than our current prices, we still cannot market our products. Our planned prices are inadequate now. I cannot sell with the planned prices and I don't know whether I can sell under the planned prices. In the meantime, our warehouse is so crowded that we have no place for new output. The Production Manager says: "I am for more production at lower prices." I ask, how much lower? I am for production too, but for heaven's sake, only if we can market it! I warn you, tougher times are coming!

---

3. The reason the real cost is unknown seems to be the fact that each Unit attempts to boost its planned transfer prices (based on cost plus) in order to obtain higher income. When the total is computed, the cost is much higher than the prevailing market price.

(I try to identify the person to whom he is addressing his invective. At ABC the addressee was easily identified because he was usually at the executives' table if a worker was speaking, or among the workers if an executive was speaking. Here the speaker is talking to the entire group. No one looks at the Director; he, too, is one of the complainers.)

Director: East Germany flooded us with competitive goods, and we have to cut costs. . . . The low quality is a disgrace. I really don't know what to do any more. I am at a loss. We have six hundred products accumulating in inventory since 1963. No one cares; no one feels responsible.

Director of TC: I suggest it is time we clarify this company's policy. All of us should speak. I don't want to hear threats of striking from anyone anymore. I want those who promise the workers' class higher income to show us how they can realize it. We made a plan based on desires and needs rather than on reality. Now, what should we do? If we let ten percent of our membership go [fire them], we can save three hundred million dinars, but we will lose 950 million dinars in production. We are working without a system. How can we confront the workers like this? Half a million meters of synthetic was produced, none of which can be sold.

(The Director of the company and many other individuals are nodding their heads in agreement, yet I cannot pinpoint just who is supposed to act.)

Director of TC: I suggest we ask ourselves what we can sell this year, at what prices, and then proceed to personal income, rather than vice versa. [That is, deciding what the maximum is that can be sold, which would lead to maximum income, rather than deciding what can be produced maximally and planning income accordingly.]

Rajko (Director of R & D): I can't see that workers will not work up to capacity. We are here to provide work.

President of the Workers' Council: Who can walk up to someone and tell him: you are surplus; you go to the street? The other can answer: why me? Why not you?

Rajko: This plan tells us the maximum we could produce. Until now, we

147

have said: maximize production. We can't go to the workers now and tell them to cut production.

Director: That's right. We cannot.

Financial Director: I said before, a plan should be based on financial premises first, and not on technical production capabilities.

Rajko: The working class wants to live. It wants to work, also. Let them work and live. It is our task to sell. What we should do is solve our internal problems. People don't talk to each other for days. We should look at what is wrong with this plan. We worked on it for two months. Now, let's get going. . . .

"To date, the biggest savings have come from suspending production."
Odborar, No. 14, 1966.

Everyone pitches in, but in a disorganized manner; each talks about the topic with which he is most familiar. The head of the synthetics department explains why his Unit overshot the production norms, while the Trade Union Secretary complains that vacations are allocated inadequately. The Director is silent. I notice that people talk passionately about what bothers them in the system; when they finish, they seem composed and relaxed. The

148

accusations raised are not directed to anyone in particular, but to the "atmosphere": "What should *we* do?" is the question that occurs again and again.

Chief Planner: I can't make a long-term plan because I don't know my market. There is no information, and no one to do research. But will the Workers' Council increase the number of people working in my Unit? No! Because you are against increasing the overhead, against increasing the "administrators."

Head of the Weaving Unit: I am against firing workers or administrators. I am against increasing the overhead, too. I don't know what we can do with our surplus labor. . . .

A Woman Weaver (interrupting): For goodness sake! It is already 6 P.M. [she started at 6 A.M.]. Why don't you let us go?

Head of a Department: That's enough! It's not enough to criticize. It is necessary to suggest a way out of the problems. Cost is rising because of planned transfer prices, but people are paid according to what is sold, and we hardly sell anything. Look, people have hardly any salaries. Tomorrow, we may not have any money to pay them. . . . It is easy for you to speak here, but take your fight to the people down there [in the units] and see how easy it is.

Worker: We have losses, but the balance sheet [pro forma] is showing profit. In this murky water, someone is catching bigger fish than others [sic]. Some units constantly get twenty percent bonuses while we sell to other Economic Units practically free, meters of yarn. . . . Let us get together and find out who really is working and who is just manipulating transfer prices. . . . Let's not accuse the overhead alone.

The Finance Manager: Now, look, we met for something. Let's see what condition we are in. We can start with financial requirements. This is a good plan; we should only take the marketing into account.

Head of Weaving: Okay. Let's talk about the conditions . . . how can we operate in this condition? Last year I paid 30,000 dinars for some material. Now I have to pay 50,000 for the same stuff. Many heads of shifts are ordering tremendous amounts of inventory in order to minimize *their* cost, anticipating price increases, but how much is it costing the company?

Procurement Manager (seems to consider the above remarks an attack on his department): People, understand! In Yugoslavia today, it is difficult to know prices, or to predict anything. Our turnover of raw materials is one month. We are buying at the best price we can.

(It is 7:00 P.M. The researcher has such a headache he can hardly see. The President of the Governing Board is pale, and obviously sick from exhaustion. Now seems the time to move toward a conclusion. . . .)

Director of XYZ: There are many crises in the world. We are not the only ones. Look at Britain, Germany. . . . Other industries are suffering as well. We should not panic. . . . We need preventive action. . . . I suggest we return this plan to the planning unit and suggest to the Council that it give free hand to the marketing department. Also, we alone should approve any expense for any material . . . [centralization of decision-making, I.A.].

Worker: I have been in this company twenty years. There is always a conflict between marketing and production. . . . Now it is too much.

Production Manager: Okay, I agree that not everything is the best in production. But I think we ought to "clean our own houses" before we tell others to do so. This is a difficult time for us. Let's get together and help ourselves. . . .

The meeting is adjourned. The researcher at first has no idea what conclusion has been reached, but finally, he realizes that *the decision is not to decide!* Yet, it *seems* that an informal value judgment prevails which leaves marketing freer to act. A decision to reduce Council power, i.e., to transfer power to the Marketing Manager (implicit in the above-described meeting), would be difficult to achieve. Therefore, no overt decision is made. Instead, a more permissive atmosphere is created *if* (and this is crucial) the marketing unit will be willing to undertake the risk.

Several comments from various executives serve as an additional illustration of the difficulties in planning a company's activities in post-reform Yugoslavia. When an executive of XYZ was interviewed on planning processes in the company, the following reaction was obtained:

There are only so many calculations we can make. Last year, we finished the plan on February 18. On the 26th the Workers' Council changed the basic income, so all our expenses changed and the transfer prices among units had to be readjusted. This amounted to about 5,000 calculations. This should have affected the decisions on the product line we are going to put out, because the price of each product changed, and accordingly, its profitability. But we could not make a change in the product line; changing the product line would have required another three to four months. We had enough trouble finishing our calculations in August.

* * *

We start from production capacity when we make our plan. We do this because if we plan less than what we can produce, we get endless comments and criticisms from the floor. They lose income if they don't produce maximum. In case there is a gap between what we can produce and what we can sell, we bid to other companies to subcontract from them.

The Economic Units plan their overhead. That is the source of their savings on which they get the incentive bonuses. We have to fight here to keep the planned overhead a realistic one. With what they figure for overhead, we can't sell in the market.

The problem is that whenever anything is okay, there is no need for central power. Once we encounter difficulties and conflict, however, there is a need for authority who can absorb the conflict, who can cut it one way or another. I can't do it. I have to convince, analyze, and it takes time, and we have no time anymore. [Italics mine]

. . . We are asked to provide the community and the city with a long-range plan for the next seven years, including what we will produce, how many people we will employ, etc. We submit it even though we all know that it is not worth the paper it is written on. Look, the taxation is constantly changing. We have no idea how much revenue will be left to us. The credit conditions are always changing. The value of fixed assets changes too.[4] Labor laws are constantly changing too.[5] Also, the role of taxation for social security

---

4. Government reevaluated all assets because of inflation. Assets evaluated previously were underpriced. Since government charges interest, which is a tax, on fixed assets, only through reevaluation of assets could interest be raised to meet inflationary conditions. Interest on fixed assets is a way of expressing social ownership over the means of production. Society rents the means to the companies who pay interest on them to the government.

5. The research noted innumerable government supplements to the laws. A full-time lawyer was employed to update the laws in the company. Making a decision in labor law was a major undertaking.

changed, the prices of power, water, coal, etc., change constantly. In 1966, the government raised prices of raw materials. Yet the price of textiles remained fixed by the government. I don't know how long they will remain fixed. We don't know which prices will change again or which regulations will be introduced. The government started pulling money out of the market as a deflationary policy. Other buyers are confronted with the same problem. They don't want to give a long-term order because by then something may change again. So they come in the fall and order for the fall. Only the Army gives long-term orders. In the U.S.A., I heard you get orders two years in advance. [Lamenting.] If only I could get orders two years ahead of time. . . . I can't specialize in the long run either. Now, synthetics are very profitable. If they change the rate of exchange again, they may not be profitable. Thus, people are afraid to vote for modernization because it may commit money for something that no one knows if the market will be willing to buy.

The difficulty in obtaining reliable data for planning purposes is internal as well as external. Because of the incentive method, each Unit apparently tries to inflate its overhead to create a place for savings and bonuses. As a result, the Planner does not know the real cost of products, and cannot optimize the product line to be produced. In several meetings, including the one mentioned above, the Director and one of the Marketing Managers begged the various Economic Units to tighten up their standards for overhead so that products could be priced competitively. Furthermore, because of the fact that production norms are set below the expected production load, there is no clear knowledge of the real cost of production. As an executive stated:

When I suggest the quantity to be produced to the production line, I assume certain quantities and allocate the fixed costs accordingly. The plan is usually surpassed and the fixed costs are the same, while per unit they are less. If I knew that before, I could have changed the product mix, because when the new average fixed cost is considered, other products are more profitable than the produced ones.

To the question of whether a determination of the anticipated expenses, rather than the norms, can be used as a basis for computation, the answer was:

I can't do it because I have to show my computations for acceptance. Suggesting anticipated expenses will set the workers against me because I would be cutting part of the income they get from the incentives for surpassing the plan.

Then how does XYZ operate? How does it plan within these external and internal constraints? The answer seems to be that the company assumes some fixed rate of growth in production and then plans accordingly—that is, according to past experience for growth rather than for a decline in sales. Such a premise fits workers' requests for maximum production and still keeps the historical arrangement of bonuses, incentives, etc., in force. These conditions continue until the situation deteriorates, inventories accumulate, and it is clear that a corrective action is needed by means of a major change in the plan. An atmosphere of crisis prevails which helps obtain a fast corrective action. Then the process of obtaining organizational change, as described in the previous chapter, takes place. This process consumes a large amount of psychological energy, too, but apparently crisis management is the most effective tool under these conditions.

How much deterioration must occur before action is taken? Evidence indicates that the situation has to deteriorate *until it affects the individual in the group*, e.g., until the workers' salaries are affected. Since a balance sheet is prepared periodically and personal income recomputed to reflect sales rather than production, the feedback loop closes and even those least involved in decisions become concerned about the situation.

This process of planning raises a question as to the amount of work spent in preparing the plan—namely, is the XYZ case described above unique or is it representative of general practice? It was noted by the researcher that XYZ had to print every proposal for each Unit, and then had to send several copies of each proposal to the planning service. This material was reprinted with comments from the planning service and sent back to the Economic Units, etc. It is not surprising, then, that the following estimate was made by a leading Yugoslav theoretician:

According to my research, in Serbia, every third member of the organization is working on providing information, and 12 percent of all the employees work in accounting (Cost Accounting-Finance) while the industrial norm for it should be 5 percent. The final reports (balance sheets and profit and loss statements) arrive on the average of four to six months late, at which time they are too late . . . [to be useful].[6]

The cost of exchanging information for planning purposes is large. According to a study by the Federal Institute of Statistics in 1965, a total of 150 billion dinars (about 120 million dollars) were expended for irregular, ad hoc reporting.[7] Divided by the total Yugoslav population of 15 million, the result would be 8 dollars per person per year, or 32 dollars per year for a family of four, which was comparable to 5 percent of the *annual income* of a worker's family of four in Belgrade in 1964.[8] These figures illustrate the partial cost of participation in management in Yugoslavia.

PLANNING MEETINGS AT ABC

The planning process at ABC was more centralized and less time-consuming than XYZ's, with more structured discussions and no apparent frustrations or aggressive behavior. As mentioned earlier the Director of ABC behaved in a manner which indicated his position as leader and the individual responsible for collective decisions.

In the opinion of the researcher, the following description of the Workers' Council meeting,[9] taken from the minutes of April

---

6. Miloš M. Sindjić, *Sistem informacija i privredno upravljanje,* Referat sa I Savetovanja o Složenim Sistemima u Privredi. Belgrade, 1966, pp. 21, 22, quoted in a study on planning to be published by Informator in Zagreb and the author of which is Mrkša Slobodan et al.

7. *Ibid.*

8. *Statistički Godisnjak Beograda,* 1965, p. 106, indicates that the average monthly income of a worker's family of four with one supporter in Belgrade is 58,509 dinars.

9. The process of planning, i.e., information flow, is the same as described in Chart XII.

20, 1966, represents the general character and content of ABC's planning meetings. The Marketing Manager was given the floor first. He informed the Council of the market situation in foreign and domestic markets, the sales opportunities, and the chances of realizing the plan, as well as the volume of sales for the first fifteen days in April to indicate the market trend.

The Chief Planner informed the Council of the financial conditions, results, and cost. According to him, cost of sales was 62.40 percent, and profit was 31.42 percent (presumably before taxes). Next the Product Manager told the Council of the realization of the production plan for the first three months, and indicated the specific production difficulties which had occurred. The Procurement Manager indicated the problems the company had encountered in acquiring raw materials. The Director then interpreted what had been said before, specifying pricing, merchandising problems, financial strategies, and organizing the planning process.

After the Director, a blue-collar worker, who was also a Council member, asked what the new printing equipment was to be used for. Next, another worker questioned the fact that, based on evidence in the plan, ABC was giving higher profit margin to its merchandising outlets. The Marketing Manager answered by saying that the printing equipment was to be used for exported products, and that higher margins were needed because of higher competition. Another worker asked: "Are you anticipating surplus labor?" The Personnel Manager's answer:

We anticipate a labor force of 2,919 workers. We have one group which has not been allocated yet because the new equipment for cleaning parts freed them [made them obsolete]. However, they are qualified as weavers. The Personnel Office will retrain them. If they don't want to work as weavers, they will be sent to the Institute for Re-Employment [they will be fired].

Worker: Why is there such a large quantity of products in process in certain phases of the finishing department?

General Director: Lack of proportion in production capacity of the finishing and weaving units causes the imbalance between the various production phases in the finishing department. The finishing department has free capacity, and depends on the textile that the market demands.

Worker: Why did you plan a loss in export?

The Marketing Referee for Exporting explained the various market penetration strategies involved in exporting. The General Director then explained that during 1965, before the economic reform, a boom in buying occurred. Now, however, there existed increased competition which the company intended to meet by:

1. Offering new products wanted by the market, and
2. Prolonged credit.

The Workers' Council concluded its meeting and decided to:

1. Accept the production plan.
2. Accept the planned cost of sales for the following overhead: for travel abroad, advertising expenses, expenses for representation and expositions.

It may be concluded that the interchanges were primarily for the purpose of an exchange of information on existing alternatives or decisions and not for the design of these alternatives.[10] The workers were informed but were confronted with an almost finished act.

However, under the prevailing conditions, the effectiveness of swift decision-making had its cost. Once a plan was made—and the earlier it was made, the worse the situation became—changes were difficult to obtain. Even ABC, with its strong leadership, had a hard time convincing the decision-makers (the workers) that the original plan, accepted only after the executives had used all their persuasive power, was no longer adequate.[11] Suggesting new

---

10. For a more exact measurement of the decision-making process, see my doctoral dissertation: "The Effect of Decentralization on Organizational Behavior, An Exploratory Study of the Yugoslav Self-Management System" (Ph.D. dissertation, Columbia University, 1968), chapter 7.

11. Descriptions of these difficulties are not presented here (even though they were noted by the researcher) because they are not essentially different from the case of XYZ presented above.

alternatives meant new confrontations with the workers and the assumption of responsibility for the proposed changes. These confrontations, the need to explain why the old plan was no longer adequate, and the risk of being accused of bad planning were all embarrassing to management. Bureaucracy, or delaying major decisions as XYZ did, was more effective in the short term in the sense that less pressure was put on the executives, and more flexibility resulted, which could not have been achieved under the normative setup of decision-making.

CHANGES IN THE PROCESS OF PLANNING

This chapter has described the planning process in its technical form and in action, utilizing the participants' own words to indicate the difficulties encountered in dealing with uncertainty. Furthermore, a discussion has been presented of the various ways in which the two leadership patterns dealt with uncertainty and affected decision-making and behavior at meetings. It is of special interest to note the changes that took place in the planning process in *both* companies. These changes may indicate that, independent of the leadership pattern and organizational structure, the authority distribution on planning was altered.

Changes made in the planning process in ABC from 1966 to 1967 reinforce the researcher's observations at XYZ. Specifically, at the meeting of ABC's Governing Board on January 12, 1967, it was clear that several changes had been decided upon. Decisions were made to emphasize marketability of products rather than just their production feasibility (market orientation) in decision-making, to increase emphasis on managerial training, and to enlarge the managerial discretionary powers necessary for securing flexibility.

According to the new 1967 Plan, income would be distributed not according to quantities *produced,* but according to quantities *sold*. Until 1967, whatever was produced was sold, so there was no pressure to reconsider the technique of distributing income. This was not the case after the reform, which emphasized *profitability* rather than production rate. The difference in desired results was most evident in the accumulation of inventories, which resulted in distribution of income even though products were not being sold. It was even claimed that some companies made fictitious production contracts in order to increase production and, therefore, income distribution. (Note that the previous description of the process took this factor into account and gave an updated report of the situation.)

However, even though inventories were piling up and income was being distributed according to sales and not according to collected revenue, no inventory control methods existed, and no discount of planned revenues for bad debts was taken into account. These techniques were beyond the business training of both companies at the time of this study in 1967 and apparently were unnecessary before. The first technique needed some Operations Research training, and the second required some historical data on operations in a market economy under risk. These data were not available because of the slight experience of the staff. In both companies, however, several production engineers were at work training for O.R., and the financial department was keeping a record of accounts receivable.

Another change lay in the fact that the executives began asking for more discretionary powers to make independent decisions or shorter channels of communication which would enable swifter decision-making. On the 13th of December, 1965, six months after the reform, the Marketing Manager of ABC informed the Council that when the timing of prices was of crucial importance, the company should operate more effectively. Accordingly, he suggested delegating authority for pricing decisions from the Council to the Governing Board. The Council decided at that meeting:

1. That the Governing Board should decide pricing policy for existing products and services, as well as the pricing of new products.

2. That the Governing Board should be granted the authority

158

to delegate the above-mentioned rights to the Director of the company. Once delegated to the Director, the rights could automatically be delegated further along the executive hierarchy, down to the Marketing Manager.

ANALYSIS

As shown above, in order to evolve maximum participation in decision-making, the Yugoslav self-management system requires by decree that an annual plan be accepted by the Workers' Council. However, in order to be approved by the Council, the plan has to gain a wide support base consisting of most of the members. Furthermore, the latest pressures to decentralize require that plans be made by the Economic Units and given only final approval (veto power is implied) by the Workers' Council as in XYZ. Thus, by law, plans are suggested by the executive body, debated by the general collective, approved by the *Zbors* or the Council, and implemented by the executives.

It was possible to plan this way in the past without creating dysfunctional phenomena, when the success of the company did not depend as much on the quality of decisions, as was true at the time of the research, and when planning was really no more than production scheduling because products were sold to a seller's market and uncertainty was low. (The technical and institutional subsystem were almost identical.[12])

With decentralization and with the change in the competitive situation, plans made through large participation and evolved through a wide support base turned out to be detrimental to the success of the company. Larger and larger divisions between the technical and institutional subsystems evolved out of the environmental changes. A stronger managerial subsystem was necessary in order to bridge the gap between the two subsystems and to

---

12. On organizational subsystems, see J. D. Thompson, *Organizations in Action* (New York: McGraw-Hill, 1967), p. 10.

absorb the uncertainty which faced the institutional subsystem and with which the technical subsystem could not cope.

The managerial subsystem was weak and it was expected to wither away; therefore, any tendencies on the part of management to strengthen itself were considered by the syndicalists as reactionary attempts against self-management.[13] Only those individuals who were professionally and politically strong, like ABC's Director, could oppose those pressures.

Planning is a way of handling uncertainty. However, plans were made according to the old practice of operating under full certainty and were thus based on production capability rather than market opportunities; such plans consisted primarily of production scheduling. What this chapter has described is the painful, frustrating alteration of organizational processes in order to handle uncertainty and to make unprogrammed decisions where the system was structured to operate in a programmed manner.

Both ABC and XYZ, and in this regard, all the companies in Yugoslavia, *had to* make their plans through general discussions in which even those who had no information about the market or professional knowledge on how to handle it *had to* participate. Those who were in daily contact with the environment and who had the professional knowledge to make the decisions were put into staff positions; they were prohibited from making them. The general membership, who had to make the decisions, could divert discussions to their level, thereby possibly reducing the efficiency of decision-making and reducing the time devoted to long-run problems. (Programmed decisions may decrease the time spent on non-programmed decisions.)

Furthermore, information on the state of the economy was rarely available because the economic tools employed by the government were changing erratically, and in both companies no one could predict the government's next move. In an environment

---

13. The strongest opposition was to the *Politikal Aktive,* which was considered an informal group that was retarding the process of maximum participation by confronting the legal decision-makers with a "finished act."

where the economic policy is based on prolonged experience, there exists a framework that enables even the non-participant in governmental decision-making to predict the government's next move on the basis of economic indications. Since Yugoslav experience in decentralizing was innovative, and since the country's economic policy was directly related to political conditions, prediction of government action was difficult (see Chapter 2).

As to the identification of means, cost figures of any company were unreliable because of the transfer price system which was abused when based on cost plus. Transfer prices which reflect market prices could have been used as a guideline for planning purposes and distribution of income, but they were not always available since the specific output of some units was not marketable. Even when market prices existed, they changed so often that the companies frequently needed to make appropriate changes.

Because of the system of establishing norms which were set at levels lower than those anticipated, it was known that the company or Unit would overshoot the plan. The question was: by how much? Furthermore, cost of production was also set in standards, but savings were subject to incentive pay. Since incentive pay was taken for granted and had to be distributed as part of salary, the standards for production cost did not represent the anticipated cost. Thus, the Planner was confronted with ambiguity as to what the market would buy, what his units would produce, and how much it would really cost him.

It would appear that the external uncertainty and the built-in information ambiguity generated several processes which are worth noting.

Bureaucratic red tape developed because apparently the system did not develop effective methods for planning under uncertainty. Furthermore, red tape developed because the system was not structured to absorb risk unless it was voluntary. Therefore, decisions were passed from one person to another until the situation itself dictated the solution, or until someone volunteered to effectuate a decision("the fanatic") and his leadership was accepted. In addi-

1 6 1

tion, red tape seemed to develop because the resulting bureaucratic conditions meant that plans would not be made, and only without a fixed plan could the flexibility necessary for the company's operations be attained.

Decision-making under these conditions also meant that many managers and workers felt discouraged by the fact that their plans and the reality of the situation no longer necessarily coincided. The component of risk, which always exists in a market economy, had its effect on their behavior. They had to adapt themselves to the new situation of risk bearing which many opposed because it introduced inconsistencies and uncertainty of a different kind than had prevailed in a highly regulated economy.

Making adequate non-programmed decisions under uncertainty requires experience, a frame of reference, and the freedom of action to choose among alternatives revealed by the frame of reference. The Yugoslav manager had little or no experience operating in a market economy; those individuals who had the experience and survived the war were eliminated by the system as capitalists, while the new managerial class grew up on the central planning model. In addition to having little experience with risk bearing, the new managers could act only by leading the members of the organization to choose what was hopefully the optimal alternative. Sometimes, optimal decisions, when made under conflict, required a compromise which could be achieved only if someone was willing to absorb both risk and the aggression of those adversely affected by the decision. Under the existing system of self-management, it was hard for the executives to absorb the increasing risk, because their power (which could be used for risk undertaking) was fully dependent on authority by acceptance, which apparently did not provide enough maneuverability.

In the state of tension induced by the conflict of organizational structure and environmental requirements, the meetings of the governing, executive, and socio-political bodies served a therapeutic purpose. People aired their grievances and frustrations, sought for a scapegoat, but continued to work. Group decision-

162

making served to absorb the frustrations created by the dynamic, unpredictable environment. A lone manager would not have been able to lead an organization under such conditions unless he secured the cooperation and commitment of his followers. Participative management secured this commitment even at cost to the planning process, and, as a result, to the immediate efficient operation of the company. Furthermore, it should also be noted that these lengthy meetings, attended by sixty or more people, served also to pool judgment and predict the state of the economy, thereby eliminating the chances of making extreme errors. (Group judgment, assuming that it distributes normally, will end up around the average and eliminate extremes.)

In analyzing the changes in the planning process, it was noted that, whatever the leadership pattern, in both ABC and XYZ pressure was created to move toward a vertical, hierarchical structure of individual responsibility throughout the organization rather than to the group responsibility characteristic of a horizontal, democratic structure. This would appear to indicate that responsibility is related to risk bearing, and that the vertical, hierarchical structure offers a more adequate means of absorbing risk through better identification of responsibility for decisions. The hierarchical structure segments environmental pressures, designates who is to deal with such pressures, and makes possible the tracing of responsibility for reaction to the pressures. The democratic, horizontal structure, in which all and thus no one in particular absorbed the risk for a decision, could not operate successfully under the new conditions, i.e., putting all the existing pressures on all members of the organization was overtaxing and ineffective.

The primary difference between the two companies lies in the behavior of the Directors in terms of risk absorption for decisions made. It appeared that the Director of ABC took upon himself the responsibility for company affairs—that is, he was willing to make decisions and bear the risk. In contrast, the Director of XYZ put all the burden on the governing bodies. A possible factor in this managerial reaction seems to be the amount of power that an executive possesses from sources other than those on whom he uses the power. This power then serves as a buffer when he makes decisions with which his subordinates do not fully agree; a weak Director will be unwilling to take risks because his followers' "zone of indifference" is narrow. ABC's concentration of responsibility in the Director, who had power based on external connections and professional knowledge and thus could afford to take risks, resulted in faster decisions but with greater dependence on the Director for decision-making, and many workers did not necessarily feel responsible for the decisions. When an economic crisis occurred, they reacted in a symptomatic manner which will be presented in the following chapter.

6.

Labor Relations

It has been indicated in previous chapters that executives' power in Yugoslavia is limited. Their power over financial resources is nonexistent because the Council makes financial decisions, and they have no power over other areas of concern like production or locations of plants, because such matters are also under the sole authority of the Council. In addition, executive power over subordinates is limited by law; hiring, promoting, disciplining, and firing are all within the realm of the elected decision-making bodies or their committees. This chapter deals with this lack of executive power in labor relations and the resulting repercussions.

The first part of the chapter briefly describes the law and practice on hiring, job security, firing, and disciplining, and compares these practices in XYZ and ABC. The second part offers three case studies, including two from ABC. Of particular interest is the case study which offers a description and analysis of a strike.

The Law and the Practice

The committees of the Councils of the Economic Units have the authority to accept workers into a Unit (hiring), assign them to jobs, discipline them, and terminate working relations (firing).

1 6 5

Similarly, executives are accepted to jobs, disciplined, and fired by a committee of the Central Workers' Council. The idea is that each Economic Unit is a social entity which should manage itself. Its leaders (the foreman and his assistants) may indicate what is needed and what ought to be done, but they should not possess ultimate power over the Unit—the group as a whole should make final judgments.

HIRING

In labor relations, a foreman may suggest hiring more people. Such hiring is then discussed by the Council of the Unit. If it agrees to the suggestions, the Council makes a request to the personnel service; the personnel service defines the job and specifies educational, training, and experience requirements; applicants must be sought through public notice in the newspapers so that all those who desire the job and qualify can apply. No one can avoid this process simply at his discretion, since it is established by law to enable the most qualified individual to get the job. It should be noted that in a society where ties of family and friendship play an important role, this legislation and the process of hiring minimize the chances of nepotism.

Each applicant for a job completes various tests and is interviewed by the company's social worker and the industrial psychologist to determine his qualifications. A file, which includes the worker's qualifications, recommendations, test results, and interview results is submitted to the Committee on Labor Relations of the Unit where he would work if hired. This committee, appointed by the Council of the Unit and composed mainly of workers, interviews the applicants and decides whom to hire. The foreman can comment or suggest to the committee but may not pressure for any applicant.

A person who is accepted is hired for a six-month trial period. At the end of the six months, the Council either approves the appointment or disqualifies the individual and seeks other appli-

166

cants. During the trial period the members of the Unit decide whether the new worker fits into their group in terms of his behavior, productivity, personality, etc. If a worker is lazy, he will probably be rejected because his low productivity affects the total productivity of the Unit, and, thus, the personal income of each worker. Also, because of the fact that when a person is hired, he becomes a decision-maker on an equal basis with the rest of the Unit, the workers are careful to note whether his personality and behavior are acceptable to them.

JOB SECURITY

Allocation of workers to various jobs also is done by a committee. The law on labor relations determines that each worker should be placed in a job that fits his qualifications, including his education and experience. The law also stipulates that if a worker has to be transferred to another job, he must fit its qualifications, i.e., he cannot be given a job requiring qualifications lower than his. It is not necessary to secure a worker's agreement to transfer if the new job fits his qualifications. Where the suggested job has lower requirements, the worker has to be consulted, and he cannot be transferred without his consent. However, this condition holds true only if his performance at a job meets the job definition; if not, his qualifications are reviewed by an ad hoc committee appointed by the Workers' Council. If his qualifications are insufficient, or if the job definition was inadequate, the worker is given time to study, train, and meet the requirements of the job. If he refuses additional training or cannot meet the requirements, he is either transferred, or the Workers' Council fires him.

Workers can be transferred temporarily from one job to another, but they cannot lose income as a result. For instance, if the weaving department has temporary surplus labor because of slack production, weavers can be transferred to the dyeing unit, where lower-grade jobs exist, while still being paid as weavers. The difference between the actual salary of a dyeing department worker and a weaver's pay is covered by a special fund for equalization of income. The fund exists because the worker should not receive lower income for reasons over which he has no control, and the dyeing department should not pay higher wages for jobs which qualify under certain rates simply because the weavers constitute the only available surplus labor.

It should be noted that there are certain circumstances in which workers can be relocated temporarily without their consent to a job not assigned them by the Council. This situation might occur in the case of a *force majeure,* such as a flood, fire, or earthquake, or if an unpredictable factor exists such as a mechanical defect which will paralyze the unit for an undetermined length of time, lack of raw material, or sudden absence of a worker. However, even under these circumstances, the transfer can be made only to a job which is *one* level lower than the job already held by the worker. Transfer to lower levels requires the worker's consent.

DISCIPLINING AND FIRING

Firing is a legal process which requires strong legal arguments as well. There are numerous laws designed to protect the worker and assure him maximum job security, and each company has a Manual for Labor Relations which defines the cases in which a worker is punishable and what punishments can be inflicted. Firing is used as a last resort.

Each Unit has an elected committee for disciplinary matters. Each foreman reports disciplinary transgressions to the company's legal counsel who then convenes the committee and serves as prosecutor and legal advisor. The committee hears the worker and determines which of the following disciplinary steps, listed according to their level of severity, are needed: warning, a public warning, last public warning, and a recommendation for termination of working relationship (firing). Fining can be part of the punitive action taken; its severity depends on the severity of the warning. The committee may also vote to free the accused from responsibility—that is, to acquit him. A recommendation to fire a worker is submitted to the Workers' Council of the Unit, which makes the final decision.

Throughout this process, the executive has to remain neutral. He cannot act as prosecutor and judge at the same time, as is the case in the hierarchical organization. His power is limited to reporting the worker to the committee and then testifying if asked by the committee. This power is not his exclusively; any worker can, and should if the conditions require it, report a transgressing worker to the committee. The Federal Law on Labor Relations specifically states that any individual can start a disciplinary action.[1] The committee members are supposed to use their judgment, based on personal knowledge of the foreman and the worker, as to how well the worker performs his tasks. It is claimed that such a process yields more justice than the actions of an executive who, in a momentary rage, may use managerial power against a subordinate without giving him a chance to defend himself. The foreman cannot discipline; he has to rely on workers' judgment on the issue.

That there must occur a management-workers confrontation in these trials may be a natural expectation. However, based on a review of all disciplinary cases that took place for three years in both ABC and XYZ, and on personal observation of two dozen, the researcher feels qualified to testify that such polarization is usually *not* the case. The committee seems to "put on the hat of justice and impartiality" during the hearings. Likewise, the idea that the committee members are workers and thus should side with workers does not occur, because, unless the members of the organization are disciplined, all workers will lose income as a result of the income distribution system.

Occasionally when the committee considers an executive's complaint against a worker, the complaint is held to be unreasonable

---

1. Paragraph 88 of the labor law according to: "Odgovorni radnik . . . ," *Savremena Praksa*, weekly magazine, January 29, 1968, Belgrade.

and is rejected. The executive has to continue working with that same worker found innocent by the committee—a situation many executives find very uncomfortable. Therefore, reports generally are made only on those cases where punishment is certain.

Under these circumstances the situation in the Unit may become unbearable because workers learn quite easily what they may be accountable for and what they may get away with. Difficulty in disciplining transgressions which are not clear-cut, compounded with the fact that subordinates know that the executive is powerless, generated an interesting reaction from the foremen. Those who were secure, or strong in their Units, possessed a good deal of authority through acceptance and seniority, and could afford to overlook or handle personally minor disciplinary transgressions, reporting only the important violations. The problem lay with the young, inexperienced foremen who had just graduated from the university. They found it difficult to lead in this powerless situation and, therefore, felt constantly threatened. Their reaction was either to give up completely on disciplinary matters, i.e., not to report anything, or to report every case no matter how minute. Others tried to create informal sources of power through various means such as not socializing with subordinates. In one case, a young foreman did not talk with workers on any matters but professional topics. By keeping a distance he deluded himself into believing that he had created a "fear of the unknown" which he could use as power to prevent minor disciplinary transgressions.

Participating in Labor Relations Decisions— *XYZ vs. ABC*

In dealing with participation in decision-making, the question arises as to who participates in the decisions on labor relations, and how different this process is from the other two types of decisions described in Chapters 4 and 5. In labor relations, the support base sought for a decision is limited and focuses on the official decision-making body—either the Council or its committee. There is no extensive discussion in the several bodies, groups, etc., as is the case with modernization or development of the annual plan. Extensive discussions occur only in the designing of the Manual for Labor Relations, which is a legislative action. The people who deal with specific transgressions number only the committee, the witnesses, the foreman, and in case of firing, the Workers' Council.

In certain cases where the disciplined person is a member of the Party, the political bodies become involved. These groups feel responsible for attempting to convince the worker to change his behavior or to discuss the inadequate relationship in a certain unit. The researcher's review of the cases did not indicate any instance where the Trade Union played any role in dealing with workers' rights in disciplinary matters. This group was active in the general discussions on the Manual for Labor Relations but not on specific cases.

In both companies the Governing Board seemed to play a crucial role in dealing with workers' grievances. Hearing requests to increase basic salary, requests for paid or nonpaid vacations, for scholarships, or complaints against executives, were its basic functions.

The difference between ABC and XYZ was as significant in labor relations as it was in the modernization and annual planning decisions. ABC was extremely strict in its labor relations. Workers and executives were brought before the committee for disciplinary transgressions on minute and almost meaningless matters. Being late to work without an acceptable reason was a disciplinary matter for which a person automatically was punished by losing 10 percent of his basic daily salary.[2] This regulation was institutionalized in the Manual for the Distribution of Income.[3] There were no time sheets or time clocks; the guard by the door registered the names of those who arrived late.

---

2. Two instances of tardiness of up to fifteen minutes *per month* were allowed. Beyond that, the salary deduction was automatic.

3. Paragraph 36a, Manual for Income Distribution, ABC.

At XYZ, the method was different. By the entrance was a large blackboard on which the latecomers' names, Economic Units, and times of arrival were registered. This presumably created social pressure on these individuals because members of their Units, noticing their lateness, were supposed to pressure them to contribute their fair share to the general effort. However, it was noted that for months the Finance Director of XYZ was late to work almost every day. His name, with the names of other workers on the line, appeared on the board regularly with tardiness of an hour or an hour and a half. To the best of the researcher's knowledge, no official steps were taken against him or the other workers.

Similarly, meetings of the committees for disciplinary matters in XYZ were rarer than in ABC. The number of people fired was zero. The 30 people listed as "fired" were those who left for Germany voluntarily, and, because they did not appear at work for a certain period of time, they were required by law to be classified as fired. During 1966, the disciplinary committees in XYZ heard 144 cases. Only 102 were completed. The rest were either still under investigation (33) or in the process of being tried (9). Most of these 144 cases dealt with unexplained absence from work, leaving work before the end of the shift, or, in about 20 cases, refusal of the worker to follow the order of an executive. The disciplinary steps taken were:

warning	31
public warnings	27
last public warings	6
firing	30
freed from responsibility	8

ABC's data differ considerably from XYZ's. In January, 1966, *alone,* a total of 104 cases were submitted to the committees; in February, 104; and, for the rest of the year, an average of around 70 cases *per month.*

Refusal to accept an order from an executive was not much more prevalent at ABC than at XYZ (37 cases during the first ten months), but the violations were generated primarily by a few foremen. As mentioned above, other foremen would not submit complaints; thus, this figure is hardly representative. Sleeping during work (third shift)—23 cases; fist fights—32 cases (for the first ten months); "inadequate attitude"—21 cases; lack of conscientious behavior—49 cases; leaving the job before the end of the shift—75 cases; drunkenness at work—6 cases; smoking where not permitted—12 cases; taking food out of the cafeteria (eating is permitted only there)—2 cases; stealing—16 cases; requesting sick leave and not reporting it to the company's health service—6 cases; remaining in the company after working hours (presumably obstructing other workers)—2 cases; changing shifts without the knowledge of the foreman—3 cases; avoiding work—5 cases; not carrying out orders—4 cases; not reporting lateness—2 cases; abusing a hierarchical position (this must be an executive)—2 cases; entering the company outside of working hours without a permit— 1 case; undisciplined behavior—9 cases; false reporting of sickness —1 case; not wearing the company's work uniform—2 cases; these comprise the various transgressions brought to trial with decisions as follows:

warnings	222
public warnings	65
last public warings	47
fired	17
freed from responsibility	114

The above-mentioned measurements illustrate the difference between the two companies in labor relations.

The following case studies illustrate the process of disciplining and firing a worker in ABC and XYZ, and include a description and analysis of a strike that took place at ABC. The purpose of these illustrations is to impart to the reader a real feeling of how decisions on labor relations are made and what potential advantages and dangers exist in democratic disciplining.

The two cases following represent *extremely different* situations.

It is believed that these descriptions will provide the reader with information which will facilitate his understanding of the more common cases which fall somewhere between the extremes.

Case Studies

BORA, JUNIOR MAJSTOR

Bora worked in ABC as an apprentice when he was a teen-ager Later, he was drafted. During his military service one of his friends was killed, and an investigating committee interrogated Bora as to whether he had anything to do with his death. As a result, he was hospitalized with a nervous breakdown. When he was released, he returned to ABC and he was accepted, because the law assures the worker that he may return to the same job he had before his induction into the military service.

Bora was found to be a difficult person to get along with and displayed a tendency to get into frequent fist fights with his fellow workers. The first time he used his fists occurred when a worker had a transistor radio on too loudly in the cafeteria. Bora suggested he turn it down. The other man refused, they exchanged curses, and in the end they fought. The committee for disciplinary matters gave Bora a public warning. Next he fought with another *majstor* who did not deliver repair parts on time. The committee then gave him a last public warning. At this point, the Party talked to Bora in an attempt to show him that his behavior would cause his dismissal, and that employment conditions were such that he might find it difficult to get another job particularly since firing meant "being rejected by the society of ABC." Bora promised to behave himself.

During the period of this study, Bora was brought to trial for the third time—in this instance, for hitting a worker on her hand with a wrench. The researcher attended the trial, and the following material presents his observations of the proceedings.

At the trial three members of the Economic Unit to which Bora belonged sat behind a table. (The researcher sat behind the committee so as not to appear conspicuous.) The head of the committee was a *majstor* who happened to have been Bora's *majstor* during the defendant's apprenticeship six or seven years before. The two remaining workers were women—weavers. They seemed to feel the importance of their position and were a bit scared of the power rendered to them. They constantly looked at the lawyer for clues to what was right or wrong. The lawyer, who was a referee for disciplinary matters at the company's legal department, was supposed to give legal advice. In addition, the stenographer of the legal department attended the session to record the proceedings. She happened to be a very active member of the Communist Party, whose whole life centered around the company. She was feared by many because she had direct connection to the Director through the Party meetings. In a number of hearings she made comments which, in the researcher's opinion, affected the committee's decisions. These comments were made invariably in the name of conscience, Party responsibility, etc.

Bora was called in. The lawyer read the report and, among other things, said: "You have hit a worker in the cafeteria, and later a *majstor*. Now you are accused of hitting a woman on her hand with a wrench. What do you have to say?"

Bora explained that he had been repairing a machine for three hours. The woman approached him and, pulling his hair, accused him of oiling her jacket. He pushed her away, and since his hands were oily, the wrench fell from his hands and hit her arm. He claimed that all the witnesses were against him and were assisting in an attempt to fire him from the company.

The complaining worker was called in. She accused Bora of lying and claimed that he did hit her.

Witnesses were called, and Bora attempted to disqualify each of them. He claimed that they could not have seen or heard what was happening because the looms are taller than men, and the noise is so great that no one could hear a conversation.

Bora and the woman were asked to wait outside, while the committee deliberated the case. Knowing both Bora and the complaining woman personally, the committee commented on Bora's nervous behavior, but stated that since several people had talked to him (presumably the Party), he had begun to concentrate on his work and seldom had associated with anyone. The committee then declared that the woman had no right to pull Bora by his hair. The lawyer, who played an important role in establishing the validity of the evidence, mentioned that Bora came near to being fired earlier when he had hit the *majstor*, but that when some of the witnesses realized this, they changed their incriminating testimonies.

An important question in the committee's consideration was whether Bora was a good worker. The chairman testified that his work was satisfactory—a statement considerably in Bora's favor. The lawyer then said that Bora had admitted to the head of the shift that he had hit the worker. Immediately, a raft of criticism against the head of the shift was launched by the committee members: "She really does not try to keep good relations among the workers," "She only complains" (she would report every single problem to the committee). Nevertheless, the conclusion of the committee was to suggest to the Council of the weaving unit that Bora be fired. It is interesting to speculate on how this decision was reached. The members of the committee could not make up their minds: to give Bora another last public warning seemed to be insufficient because, as the lawyer said, the workers would see that Bora was not being punished even though he had hit a third worker and already had one last public warning. Therefore, the next step had to be to fire him. The committee deliberated the decision, looked at each other, and one of them said, "Well, let God help him in the Council.[4]

Bora, holding his cap in his hands and with his head lowered,

---

4. Once again we noted, as in the decision on modernization, that when a group had difficulty in making a decision, relief was felt that it could transfer the responsibility somewhere else.

was summoned, and everyone rose. The chairman read: "The disciplinary committee of the weaving Economic Unit has decided to recommend you to the Council for termination of labor relations because of major disciplinary transgressions."

When it was noted that Bora was very surprised, the lawyer said, "You admitted it." Bora said, "I did not." The lawyer retorted: "Yes, you did, to the head of the shift."

"I did not! When she asked if I had hit her, I said 'I hit her?' questioningly and not affirmatively. I am going to get a lawyer."

Bora asked the committee to give him time to leave the Company voluntarily rather than be fired, knowing that approval of his request would help him get a job elsewhere. In the meantime, before the next Council meeting, a wildcat work stoppage, of which Bora was one of the ringleaders, occurred in the company. This strike affected the mood of the Council and its willingness to let him withdraw rather than be fired.

STRIKE AT ABC

The following description of ABC's strike is presented to illustrate a reaction to managerial problems. Since this particular strike was generally characteristic of those in Yugoslav industry, the following discussion offers as background material Bogdan Kavčić's analysis of strikes in Yugoslavia,[5] as well as the researcher's contribution to this analysis. Finally, the strike at ABC is used to illustrate the analysis.

1. The Character of Yugoslav Strikes

Strikes appeared in Yugoslavia by 1958, and the rate of work stoppages has increased since 1961, and particularly since 1965. Yugoslav stoppages are different from those which are more familiar because they are not organized, i.e., they are not announced ahead of time after a specific leader has attempted to bargain with management and failed to come to terms.

---

5. Bogdan Kavčić, "O Protestnim Obustavama Rada," *Gledišta* (Belgrade: February, 1966), p. 202.

The usual pattern is that as a result of various causes to be discussed below the workers spontaneously refuse to return to the machines. A stoppage usually involves from five to fifty workers, generally the minority of the membership of an organization, rather than the whole company. Those who strike are probably the low-qualified workers who are not members of the governing bodies. An average work stoppage last several hours. Most of the requests made by the strikers deal with dissatisfaction with low income or a request for the removal of certain *majstors* or executives from their positions.[6]

Kavčić indicates that most stoppages are caused by lack of adequate communication between governing bodies and the general membership. Because of this gap, the members are not informed on decisions. They find themselves isolated; their opinions are not heeded by their representatives, and they become dissatisfied with the prevailing conditions.[7] Thus, work stoppages should be understood as a reaction against the lack of participation, as a display of rage against a system which seemingly gives the workers powers which in reality, however, they do not possess. Usually, the immediate reason stated for a strike is low income or major disagreement with certain executives. The Yugoslav strikes are designated as "protesting work stoppages," because, as Kavčić put it, "they are a spontaneous exhibit of lack of satisfaction."[8]

Kavčić's analysis includes most work stoppages in Yugoslavia, but mention of some of the researcher's observations may contribute further to the reader's understanding. As with decisions earlier discussed and analyzed, the leadership pattern in labor relations is an extremely significant factor—in this case, even a critical one.

------

6. In Slovenia, we were told, one of the reasons for striking was that the executives ordered machines for modernization, and the workers discovered that the competition obtained better equipment.

7. Kavčić, "O Protestnim . . . ," p. 206.

8. *Ibid.*, p. 203.

"Well, is this supposed to be a work stoppage? Or just a coffee break?" *Jez* (Belgrade), November 11, 1966.

Administrators who are oriented toward decision-making efficiency, the type who concentrate several executives and other "activists" around themselves for that purpose and thus operate with a comparatively narrow support base from the total membership, are likely to create the information gap which may lead to the protests mentioned above. This situation will occur if there are critical conditions which test the informal support base of the decisions. For instance, low income during certain months will lead workers to test executives' leadership and professional authority. A work stoppage may be the manner by which the informal decision-makers will be reminded of where the formal authority lies. Therefore, it would seem that the work stoppage is an exhibit of the dissatisfaction created by the difference between the level of reality—who really makes decisions—and the level of anticipation—who *should* make them.

Theoretically, the workers do not need to strike; in a sense they are striking against themselves. Officially, they have the authority to make all decisions on wages, hiring, and firing. Even if they are a minority, they should be able to convince others of their ideas.

179

Again theoretically, they have only to convene and vote to achieve their goal. However, if a Director is oriented toward pure economic efficiency and is not willing, in the short run, to spend the time and resources necessary to retain a wide support base; and if, because of educational differences, the members of the governing bodies are divorced from the general membership (i.e., technologists and *majstors* are elected, so the low-qualified workers are not represented), then the gap between the support base and the general membership widens to the point where any spark can ignite the fire.

2. What Happened at ABC

The company was strongly oriented toward economic efficiency. The Director had a forceful personality. As one worker said, "He [the Director] has that quality that when you talk to him, he seems to put his ideas into your mind and you fully agree with him. Only when you get out and think again, you see he is wrong. But, if you confront him again, you doubt whether he is wrong or not."

The Director had his way in choosing his executives, although this prerogative was not granted formally. In the United States, each supervisor has a voice in the selection of his subordinates. In Yugoslavia, the Council hires executives and the Council as a group determines the hierarchy. Thus, if certain Deputy Directors are appointed, the Director has to comply with the nominations. A weak Director, who has no political backing and who yields to political pressure toward maximum democratic hiring processes, may comply with all Council nominations. Stronger Directors may influence the Council on the question of who should be appointed. Both practices are legitimate within certain limitations; however, these limitations are not clear. Manipulation of power by the Director in order to have someone appointed is illegitimate because he is abusing his position, but the use of arguments to convince the workers that one person is better than another is acceptable.

At any rate, the Director of ABC, because of his personality, his strong political backing, and/or his professional knowledge, has managed to gather around him what seemed to the researcher to be a tightly knit group of executives. This group worked together under the Director's leadership to formulate alternatives which were suggested to the governing bodies for decision-making. However, the general membership did not seem to be interested in the decision-making process, perhaps because the executive function was so strong that it overshadowed workers' participation.

Two factors generated the information gap: first, apparently less information was supplied to the general membership at ABC, because it was assumed that the existing governing bodies operated as necessary; second, and this was affected reciprocally by the first factor, the general membership did not seem to be interested in the proceedings. Reports of the Council were sent to the Economic Units, but few people looked at them or read the notices on the bulletin board. The lack of internal communication and wide participation were not sufficient alone to initiate a strike. The lack of communication had existed for a long time. For a work stoppage to occur, the situation had to deteriorate to such a point that the communication gap would force a confrontation.

Economic conditions in the company were not encouraging. Inventories were climbing and consuming cash balances. Sales were low and so were profits. When the beginning of the month came, and the accounting unit staff passed from department to department distributing salary checks, the spark for the fire was provided.

It should be emphasized that a Yugoslav worker does *not* know his final salary for a certain month until he sees that check. He knows his basic salary, he knows how much work he has done on the machines, but he does not know how well his Unit or the company have done. The variable part of his check can amount to a maximum of 60 percent. When business results are good, profits are distributed several times during the year, providing unexpected boosts in income. In this specific month, March, 1967, the conditions of the company were such that there was no company profit for distribution, nor were the profits of each unit distributed. Furthermore, the federal government had changed the law on child support; and this sum was now taken out of the worker's paycheck.[9] For different reasons, the company's usual contribution for traveling expenses was omitted as well. Several workers had bought books and other products on credit while their income was high. Now their deductions amounted to quite a substantial part of their paychecks. Thus, many workers were paid a net of only 25,000 dinars, or less than $20, which would not suffice even for food. One weaver netted only 4,000 dinars for that month (about $2.50). It should be made clear that, because personal income varies this way every month, it is difficult for an individual to plan his expenses, especially if he is a low-qualified worker who is unable to predict the state of the economy, the profitability of his company, and the probability that his group will decide to distribute certain amounts as personal income. He is confronted with a varying income which he has to take for granted.

A large reduction in personal income can have various repercussions. Many workers could not save any income because their salaries were low. In 1964, in Belgrade, for instance, the average family of four spent more than it earned, according to data issued by the Belgrade Institute of Statistics.[10] If the worker received a lower income he had to seek loans. Personal loans were hardly available in Yugoslav banks; therefore, the only course of action open to the worker was to take a loan from family or friends, and many did not have anyone to turn to because their acquaintances were equally poor. Thus, when payday came, the researcher noticed many pale, tearful faces; people stood with a paycheck in one hand, with faces lifted and eyes glassy.[11]

---

9. Until then, the government paid certain amounts of money to each family for each of their children.

10. *Statisnički Godisnjak Beograda,* 1965, p. 106.

11. The executives were supposed to enclose with the paycheck an explanation of why the income was so low. They did not do so, which frustrated the workers because they expected the explanation.

The protesting work stoppage took place in the third shift in a specific part of the weaving unit, the slasher, where Bora was working as a junior *majstor*. Two other workers in that unit also had received a last public warning. Bora was to be recommended for firing at the Council meeting on Monday. On Friday night, pay envelopes were distributed. The Director was in Leipzig attending an exposition. Of the remaining executives, only the head of the third shift was present, and she was a young girl who reported every small transgression to the discipilnary committee. She apparently had no authority by acceptance.

The second shift received their checks, grumbled a bit, and left. The third shift received their checks before starting to work. Bora began an attempt to convince the shift not to start working, and was joined by the other two workers who had also had last public warnings. As a *majstor,* Bora had the status of a leader. His agitating caught on, and 46 of the 70 workers present did not take their places by the machines. These people tried to convince the remaining 24 to join the majority, but failed. There were *no* fist fights or accusations, only some of the women wept.

It is of interest to analyze those who continued to work. All the other departments around the slasher, although they received the same low pay, continued to work; the finishing department, indicating its disagreement with the work stoppage, began to sing while they worked. The 24 who kept working in the slasher included: 8 service and maintenance workers of the weaving department who *had* to work for those who continued working in the other units (workers in other units appeared to press these 8 to continue working), the head of the shift, 2 *majstors* who were Party members, the warehouse clerk who was a Trade Union leader, the janitor, 2 support workers who had to work because of those who remained by the machines, and 9 weavers who went to work on the line. Most of the last 9 were women who were involved in governing bodies or committees. One of them was a member of the disciplinary committee, and they all tried to convince the striking people to return to work. No Party member struck, nor did anyone active in the Trade Union or Youth Brigade. The common denominator of the 46 workers who did strike was the fact that except for one weaver, they were not members of any governing body nor its committees, and that they were relatively new in the company (six years). Those who continued working had been in the company fifteen to twenty years, and were active in governing bodies. Those individuals who were involved in the company's affairs seemed to feel responsible for its well-being and were willing to continue working. The others felt they should protest. Furthermore it would appear that dissatisfaction alone was not enough to create a "sit-in" Yugoslav style; necessary also was an informal leader, such as Bora and the two others, who had much to gain and nothing to lose from the work stoppage.

Immediately after the action took place, the agitators went to the night editor of the leading national newspaper to report a work stoppage at ABC. They aired their grievances as well. Apparently in an effort to gain some political backing, they attempted to play the role of "fighters for self-management," battling the oppression of the Director.

During the night, the Deputy Director and the head of the weaving department rushed to the company. They spent the night with the workers, but attempts to convince the strikers to return to work failed. No bargaining took place either, because neither the Deputy Director nor any other executive could promise anything. Acceptance of any request was up to the Workers' Council. It should not be forgotten that the 46 people who struck were only a small percentage of the 2,600 workers of ABC. The next morning, the first shift reported to work as usual, angry and ashamed that a stoppage had taken place. At 6:30 A.M., the striking group convened and the members of the *Collegium* reported to this meeting. This was the first instance where the researcher noted a management-worker confrontation. It would seem that this confrontation took place because the workers could focus their complaints on the executives.

As Kavčić pointed out, lack of communications is a central cause of the stoppage. In this instance, the workers complained that they were not informed about situations in the company. "If I knew what you are telling us now, I would not mind eating bread and salt all my life," said one of the weavers. Furthermore, they complained that the Council members did not report the proceedings of the meetings to them. The executives replied that the workers did not pick up the minutes of the meetings, which were available, and that they did not read the notices on the board. The reciprocal accusations continued, but, to the researcher, there existed indications that in this democratic structure, leadership had a responsibility to keep its followers informed whether or not they showed an interest in the situation. *In the long run,* lack of information and involvement will yield undesired results. Thus, even though the workers seemed uninterested, *keeping them interested by all available means* had a very significant, positive value.

The workers complained that the company spent money on luxury offices, on television advertising, and on installing a costly computer, while they had no money to live on. Management answered that contracts for the offices were made when there was a boom in the market and that the same was true for the advertising budget. No one could anticipate the magnitude of the reform. The computer order had been placed in 1965, before the reform occurred. The workers accepted these explanations without further complaint.

In the afternoon, a meeting (*Zbor*) of the weaving unit was called. The strikers were condemned as "people who lack conscience." Managerial involvement in this condemnation was minimal. The researcher noted that the leaders in this process were familiar to him from the various committee meetings he attended; namely, people who were active in various governing and socio-political bodies of the company. These individuals served now as a countervailing power to the strikers, acting in the researcher's opinion, according to a managerial role, i.e., taking into account the company's problems rather than the individual problems of the workers. Despite the fact that there was no money in the company and salaries were low, a feeling of "togetherness" was exhibited by these people. Although the Director, according to Yugoslav self-managerial criteria, was authoritative, the participative structure created enough of a support base to buffer internal crises and "extinguish sparks of fire." The *Zbor* decided not to fire those who struck, even though this action was suggested by some workers, but only to withhold their salaries for that night as well as the bonuses they had earned.

The next day, Sunday, the Director arrived from Leipzig. On Monday a new strategy was undertaken to engage the membership in the difficulties faced by the company. Dozens of meetings were called. *Zbors* convened as did the Party and the Trade Union. One of the solutions arrived at was that each Unit should have a meeting a week, each Party cell two meetings a week, etc. The Director seemed to have hit the problem on the head. If the source of the trouble was lack of information, by achieving a decision to meet weekly, he eliminated at least this problem.

On Monday afternoon, the Council of the weaving department was convened to discuss Bora's fate. The general consensus was that he *had to go*. The Deputy Director was at the meeting (presumably to see that this action would be taken), but he did not have much to say. The Council, however, expressed its dissatisfaction that the personnel office, headed by the Deputy Director, was willing to give Bora time to leave voluntarily rather than be fired. Had the Deputy Director given him the time, it would have meant that the Council was being bypassed in exercising its authority to punish.

This meeting saw the end of the strike and Bora's membership in the company. One result of the strike was that the executives became involved in participating in *Zbors,* soliciting ideas, and transferring the burden of responsibility for a difficult situation to the workers rather than trying to find a solution by themselves.

Thus, to return to Kavčić's analysis, an information gap was not enough to initiate a strike. This was a necessary condition, but additional conditions included the deterioration of economic or internal social conditions, which would make this gap felt. Then, there had to exist the "atmosphere" which had to be ignited by a spark, usually by an informal leader who had little to lose from agitating for a work stoppage. How many workers joined the stoppage depended on the degree of interrelation in the technical process, i.e., the interdependency, the organizational and physical distance between the Unit initiating the action and the other workers. An additional factor, which determined the "affected area," was the people who opposed the strike, such as those involved in governing bodies and other company activities. Therefore, while the self-management system destroyed one "managerial" group—the executive elite—apparently, it created a different group which was wider, more scattered, and spread throughout the organization, and which shared managerial orientation even though its members were not in classical managerial positions.

XYZ'S PERMISSIVENESS

As indicated earlier, XYZ faced similar economic difficulties. But the membership's reaction was mild. Its greater permissiveness in labor relations is illustrated in the following case which took place in April, 1966, when economic conditions were much better. This may have affected the course of the discussions, but, having visited the company in 1967, the researcher believes that the "organizational atmosphere" was such that it would have yielded the same results even though the course of the discussion might have been different.

Below is the researcher's translation of the minutes of the meeting of XYZ's Workers' Council, which took place on April 4, 1966, and dealt with the case of Vera.

President: On the agenda is the case of Vera, who was punished several times by the disciplinary committee for: absenteeism from work one day, not wearing protective clothing (overcoat), and coming to work several times in a drunken condition.

A Worker (not a member of the Council): She is under very difficult economic conditions at home. However, it is time she eliminated her bad behavior. She promised the members of the disciplinary committee to stop drinking, and several days ago she came to work drunk.

A Typist (member of the Council): I suggest we postpone discussing this matter and reevaluate her case.

Social Worker (not a Council member; serving a staff function): It is unfortunate to discuss this case in such a large meeting, but it seems that I have to inform you that she is mentally retarded and she cannot be held responsible for her behavior. After the ten years she has worked in the company, she should not be thrown into the street because in that case she will become a problem to society. I think we should transfer her to another Unit where she does not have to work on machines, so she can go to the doctor more frequently to be helped. She gives results at work and she is a good worker.

Junior Executive (member of the Council): It would be really uncomfortable to make a decision on firing someone who is not healthy. We should delegate the duty of curing her to the health unit in our company.

Another worker (a non-Council member): She is really a problem in the spinning unit. Her intelligence is rated at around 60 or 70 percent as determined by the Institute for Mental Health. Her life at home is very hard, and furthermore her personal life (sex) is not within the normal boundaries. In addition to this, how can we keep her in the Unit because the workers say, 'She is the smart one; we are crazy.' However, I also don't think we should leave her on the street.

Decision: The Workers' Council unanimously votes that taking into account the health condition of Vera, *to reject* the suggestion of the disciplinary committee of Economic Unit No. 1, plant RN, to fire Vera from the company. The responsible health unit of XYZ is delegated to undertake the necessary steps to have her adequately cured, and to transfer her to another Unit where there is no direct danger of her being hurt. [Italics mine]

Analysis

LEADERSHIP PATTERNS AND LABOR RELATIONS

In comparing the case of Vera to that of Bora, the researcher had an impression, substantiated by observation of *numerous* other cases (not presented because of space limitations), that the horizontal structure, in giving the power to discipline and punish to the general membership, can be both cruel and kind. For instance, there were numerous cases where the group's mood was hostile and ostracism prevailed. In contrast, there were cases like that of Vera at XYZ, where the group decided to help rather than fire her, although the latter action might have meant higher profits and greater comfort.

On the one hand, the horizontal structure developed cohesiveness and care for the weak, which might have been limited under an individualized and powerful decision-maker with strong economic goals. On the other hand, group decision-making created ostracism if a leader in the group could direct emotions in that direction, and if the atmosphere were hostile as a result of various external or internal pressures.

Only a few instances in which there existed a hostile atmosphere, such as the one described at ABC against Bora, were noted in XYZ. The reason may be that with an autocratic leadership like ABC's, when the system came under pressure (unsuccessful business results affecting the personal income), there was a tendency for the workers to search for a scapegoat for their frustrations. Under self-management, the group could turn in this search against its members rather than against only executives and the company at large, as was true in the strike (i.e., it is possible that those who participated in the strike had been serving as a scapegoat for the other workers).

It is interesting to note that while XYZ rarely freed anyone from responsibility, ABC gave many warnings which were only mild punishments and dispensed numerous "freed from responsibilities."[12] This might be a function of the magnitude of the reported transgression; at ABC, as mentioned earlier, even minor cases were submitted to the disciplinary committee. It could also be a manifestation of a worker's opposition to executive disciplinary pressure, which may indicate that there are *limitations* to the managerial role undertaken by the workers. When business conditions deteriorated, frustrations gave way to aggressions and the direct outcome may often have been a search for a scapegoat or simply the freeing of workers from executive accusations.

Thus, while risk absoption by ABC's leaders led to faster decisions, it also led to less involvement of workers in decision-making, more aggression in disciplining, and more dysfunctional behavior in labor relations.

In XYZ, spreading the responsibility led to slower decision-making and lower economic efficiency, but simultaneously absorbed the aggressions for the unsuccessful operations in a manner that did not manifest itself in a highly dysfunctional manner. Furthermore, the friction which was observed at XYZ was on the surface, easily identified, and, therefore, perhaps easily resolved. The aggression at ABC was subdued; on the surface the company seemed to be a smooth-running organization, but dissatisfactions showed up strongly at crucial moments.

However, it should be noted that aggression in ABC *was limited*. Dysfunctional activities were isolated by the general membership. Even in the difficult situation created by the strike, with all the aggression it generated, total management-worker polarization was not reached. The participating workers acted in a managerial role; their limiting the strike and punishing the strikers illustrates this fact. Thus, even with authoritarian leadership, the horizontal structure created desired results comparable to results achieved by permissive leadership in vertical organizations.

---

12. See pages 172 and 173 in this chapter.

190

GROUP DISCIPLINING

Disciplining requires tact and discretion, which group decision-making may not engender. Exposing an individual's weaknesses to the people with whom he works may have a greater effect than any of the formal punishments the committee can inflict. It was noted that if this exposure was repeated too often, an apathetic, "so what if you fire me!" attitude could result. The individual lost any fear of those who had the power to discipline him.

It was also noted that in this system of labor relations there was no one to take the worker's side if the Council or the committee "put on the managerial hat." He could seek a lawyer, but this was a step some workers could not afford or did not have the educational background necessary to initiate. To whom could the worker turn? The Council was composed of workers who sometimes could be more extreme in their attitudes than the executives themselves. The Trade Union took general stands like the Party, and seldom fought for a single worker unless there was a major injustice involved. The worker was protected by numerous laws, but once he was brought to trial and his guilt was proven, even if somewhat ambiguously, there was no institutional mechanism which could represent him.

While the above description may indicate that the worker is helpless in this system, it is desirable to note that there are cases where even major transgressions are not punished. In such cases, the workers take the accused's side, and it is difficult to convince them to punish him. Whether the group with the power to punish takes one stand or another depends on the internal relations in the company. Group disciplining, therefore, apparently does not lead to more justice, but exchanges individual discretion, which may be abusive, for the unpredictable behavior of a group, which may be abusive as well.

If disciplining is necessary to control people's activities, group disciplining by peers in both ABC and XYZ had a very interesting effect in achieving a highly predictable worker behavior necessary for smooth operation of company affairs.

The researcher noted while visiting some shops in both companies that many foremen were not in their Units, but were at various meetings. Asked if the workers would work without supervision, one of these foremen replied, "They control each other. They don't need me for that." The supervisor's function was not that of a policeman but simply of a coordinator of activities.

In some Units, if there was no need for coordination there was no supervisor. In one company we visited, in the absence of a supervisor in a certain Unit, the workers themselves made the decision to fire two of their fellow workers because they were late to work once too often. Such action is not surprising because of the reward structure in which each individual's salary depends on the group's achievement as well as his own. He cannot decide to decrease his efforts beyond a certain point, because the collective at large will be affected.

In the process of the withering away of the state, the hierarchical power imbedded in control has to disappear—an individual must learn to work without being watched by a "boss." The "bosses" should be his peers. This situation existed in both ABC and XYZ and seemed to develop a consciousness of togetherness and a gain in the worker's self-respect. *Majstors* came to work on Sundays to repair machines, and executives could devote time to developing subordinates rather than disciplining them. The researcher spent several hours in one Unit observing the foreman (selected at random) at his work. Several workers were resting by the machines; when the foreman came by, they made no move to get up, nor did the other workers increase their work rate. The same thing happened in other Units where the workers themselves reported serious transgressions to the *Zbors*.

Thus, the group disciplining method made the participative system potent. If executives had power to punish and reward, the hierarchical system would prevail regardless of the philosophy behind the organizational structure. Since this power was withheld from the executives, they actually had to seek support from the workers and rely on them for the adequate management of the company.

These desired ends were not achieved without cost. Fist fights, quarreling, and not talking to fellow workers were known phenomena of this peer-group disciplining. There was no "boss" on whom a subordinate could pin the frustrations caused by what he considered an unjustified disciplinary action. We seem to accept the fact that part of a supervisor's job is to absorb aggression, and, as a result, some of the pressure on the subordinate is relieved. This release was not available in the system of peer discipline. The aggression had to be directed against the whole system or against a scapegoat, a condition which was often more conducive to apathy or aggression than to participation.

This disciplinary system could work adequately if all transgressions could be predicted and regulated by a manual. The result would be objective disciplining, since the committee's function would be only to determine whether the transgression occurred and to find the appropriate punishment in the manual. However, such objectivity was impossible; therefore, subjective judgments had to be made. When subjective judgments take place, *someone* has to absorb the aggression of the affected, dissatisfied person. There is no such "someone" in this disciplinary system, so the aggression manifests itself in dysfunctional behavior against the whole system.

Treating major and minor transgressions in the same manner diminishes the effectiveness of disciplining major cases. All transgressions could be treated alike if very minor cases could be handled outside the committee, as is possible with senior, self-confident executives. Unfortunately, those executives who were the most insecure had to resort constantly to the committee, which then further eroded their authority by dismissing many minor complaints.

In addition to the above-mentioned difficulties in disciplining, the group method of handling labor relations hampered labor mobility. Hiring or firing was a very complicated, time-consuming process. Hiring was constrained by the question of the group's acceptance of the new worker. Firing was constrained because people were afraid that they might set a precedent and then be the next in line to go; thus, they tended to oppose firing. Therefore, when modernization occurred and major changes had to be made in the labor force, it became extremely difficult to make the painful decisions of firing one group and hiring another one.

In the future, assuming that the market economy will develop and that competition will increase, the pressure for short-run economic efficiency may increase as well. As the pressures connected with discipline may increase also, the problem of workers' representation may become crucial. The governing bodies do not represent only the workers, but are supposedly the governing bodies of the whole company. The Trade Union takes care of social responsibility rather than workers' *specific* interests. Given this lack of representation, work stoppages may take place until a formal means of representation crystallizes. Furthermore, the maximum job security now offered by the system will have to be relaxed. As the economy becomes more competitive, more labor mobility will be needed whether through positive means like luring workers away from a company, or through negative methods like firing the surplus.

It would appear that if the process of political thawing continues, its next phase will take place in labor relations. Executives will be given the power to hire and fire in contrast to its being delegated exclusively, by federal legislation, to group decision-making.

Self-management in its primitive form, as described in Part I of this book, cannot survive as a normative system. The environmental pressures presented in Part II are too demanding. A system which is a compromise currently may be evolving in Yugoslavia.

PART III

The Environment and the Organizational Structure

The preceding parts of this book familiarized the reader with the environment and with the self-management system at work. Part III of the book ties the changes in the environment to the organizational behavior observed (Chapter 7), and compares the American environment and its vertical organizational structures with the Yugoslav environment and its horizontal organizational structures (Chapter 8). In addition, a summary of the researcher's findings is presented, and, based on the above analysis, some possible contributions to the existent body of knowledge in organizational theory are indicated.

Part III may repeat ideas expressed earlier, but this repetitiveness is inevitable since relationships between previously drawn conclusions are discussed.

7.

The Self-Management System
and the Changing Environment

While the previous parts of this book have dealt only with companies XYZ and ABC, this chapter expands the researcher's observations and attempts to present some generalizations based on the experience of the two companies and on additional interviewing done throughout the country during two years of research.

The chapter is divided into four sections. The first describes the changes in the environment and their effect on organizational authority structure, executives' positions, leadership qualities necessary for effective operation in the new conditions, and the unintentional results yielded by the changes in the environment.

The second section describes and analyzes a new development in managerial practice in Yugoslavia, which seems to be an outcome of the environmental pressures and organizational realities.

The third and fourth sections present analyses of the process of goal displacement taking place as a result of environmental changes and their effect on organizational behavior and managerial processes in Yugoslav companies.

Recent Developments in the Yugoslav Managerial Structure

As indicated in Chapter 2, the Yugoslav economic and social environment has been characterized by accelerated change. As a product of these changes, a genuine "bottom-up" organizational authority structure developed, and this new system had to operate in a relatively more competitive market. It had to adapt itself to the new environment, a necessity which created great anxiety and dysfunctional phenomena in many organizations. The following discussion analyzes these changes and the behavior attributed to them.

During the pre-1965 period, the government, through its power to allocate investment funds, to absorb a large part of company resources through high tax rates, and to determine rates of exchange for dollars exported, was instrumental in the success or failure of a company. The effectiveness of a company was highly dependent on government intervention. The major goal and controllable variable of a given enterprise was to maximize its production. This situation was partially encouraged by the fact that the Yugoslav market was a seller's market where diversification of products and their quality did not mean much to a company's economic success. The Directors of the various companies and most of the members of the Party qualified for their respective jobs more by virtue of their loyalty to the Party than by the degree of management skill they possessed. As long as a Director's political affiliation was secure and his ties with government officials favorable, the economic success of his company and his position within the company were assured. Under these conditions, the sources of authority were external. Management operated with a comparatively high level of certainty which existed not because the environment was stable (Chapter 2 indicated the reverse was true), but because the elements which affected a company's results were primarily noncontrollable. Operating for the most part in a noncontrollable environment where the law of the situation dictates the course of action apparently generates the same response in decision-making as that which occurs in an environment of certainty. The certainty was even higher before 1950, when central planning was in operation and all courses of action were determined externally.

CHANGES IN THE ENVIRONMENT

With the trend to decentralization, management had to operate under conditions of high uncertainty. The "success determinants" became more complicated than merely the achievement of large production, factors affecting results became controllable, and the sources of managerial authority became more internal than external. The effect of these changes on organizational behavior were manifold and demanding.

The reform was two-fold, socio-political and economic, and was designed to foster and accelerate decentralization of both economic and political powers. This dencentralization was supposed to increase the mechanism of competition and, thus, create pressure for higher productivity which Yugoslavia needed in order to sustain its rate of economic growth.

The socio-political aspect of the reform consisted of a formal withdrawal of the Communist Party's interference from the decision-making process within the companies. The Party formally established its function as a discussion group, where only recommendations were to be formulated. Theoretically, the Party could not request acceptance of these recommendations. "Kitchen cabinets," where Party members made decisions and designed strategies to force the decisions on the Workers' Council, were publicly criticized. The Party would question the responsible individuals and publicly refute their managerial style.[1] Furthermore, the right of workers to strike as a means of expressing dissatisfaction with the way the company was being managed was granted publicly

---

1. Slobodan Stankovic, "Yugoslavia's Critical Year," *East Europe,* 16 (April, 1967), pp. 12-17, says Tito explicitly "suggested that Party members needed to stop commanding, as was once necessary, and instead begin to direct [guide]."

in a television program by the Secretary of the Trade Union, himself a high official of the Communist Party. Individuals who struggled against the decentralization of political powers were purged from the Party. One of those ousted was Ranković, Minister of Internal Affairs, and as such, in charge of the Secret Police.

These socio-political developments increased the workers' freedom to express dissenting opinions, to challenge executive judgments, and to widely utilize their legal powers, dormant until this point, to reward and punish.

The economic part of the reform manifested itself in the transfer of more evonomic powers for decision-making to the companies and to the market forces. This transfer was accomplished by the relaxation of price regulations, the transfer to banks of authority to allocate investment funds, and the elimination or reduction of barriers to imports in order to induce competition. This reform, therefore, extended the transfer of economic powers, which had begun with the first reform of 1950. Decentralization on the macro-level was carried into the enterprises themselves; in the name of the reform, a request was made for the delegation of maximum feasible power to Economic Units and the *Zbors*. Centralized companies were considered to be opposed to the reform and thus politically undesirable.

THE EFFECT OF THE CHANGES ON ORGANIZATIONS

As a result of the changes, the lowered trade barriers increased pressure for greater productivity needed to survive the onslaught of competitive imports flooding the Yugoslav markets. Furthermore, investment funds which previously could be acquired through political pressure, had to be obtained through economic justification, mainly because the banks became profit-maximizing and profit-sharing institutions. To this should be added the fact that the Yugoslav market arrived at a level of saturation and turned from a seller's market into a buyer's market, which imposed greater pressures on the companies to make competitive decisions.

200

These changes required market orientation of management rather than a Government-Party orientation. Executives had to possess professional managerial skills, rather than Party ties. Rapid decision-making, characterized by uncertain results, was required, as well as a new structure of authority-responsibility in which individuals assumed responsibility for decisions. In other words, the timing of decisions became crucial and the "entrepreneurial spirit," which involved willingness to absorb risk, had to be given full opportunity to express itself.

The existing organizational structure, the prevailing laws defining the ways in which the system should operate, reinforced by the socio-political aspects of the reform for decentralization, was incongruous with the new market needs introduced by the economic aspects of the reform. The organizational structure, with its legal definition of decision-making, and the pressures for further decentralization of decision-making required by the reform permitted, and in a sense encouraged, long discussions on all levels of organization until a democratic consensus developed. Red tape, which had been a latent phenomenon, appeared on the surface in full bloom, since a consensus had to be achieved within a given time, which could not be accomplished because of the ponderousness of the system. Entrepreneurial spirit could not express itself fully because it was so highly constrained by *group* decision-making and *group* responsibility; the individual had difficulty affecting the course of action of the company and, thus, finding an outlet to his personal drives.

The Party's withdrawal of support from the Directors and the transfer to the companies of economic and political power to manipulate the crucial variables for success altered the authority structure within each company from "top-bottom" to "bottom-up" organization, i.e., to a comparatively pure authority-by-acceptance structure. Previously, the formal organizational authority structure was not necessarily correlated with the power structure. Even though the political organizational authority should have been "bottom-up," the informal sources of power such as the Ministry

"He's not used to doing it without the party net." With responsibility and plan fulfillment as a balance, the manager walks the tight rope.

Ludas Matyi (Budapest), March 4, 1965.

of Trade and the Ministry of Internal Affairs determined an essentially "top-down" hierarchical organization. With the socio-economic reforms, these external sources of power diminished in importance, and the legal definition of the decision-making process became the crucial factor in determining the way decisions were to be made.

1. The Effect on Executives' Position

The changes which affected the executives' operations were quite rapid and extensive, and apparently did not allow adequate time for attitude adaptation.

Prior to 1950, management had been all-powerful because it represented the state and its planning bodies. After the 1950 reform, management lost its absolute external support, but still derived power from external ties. With the decentralization trends and especially the economic reform of 1965, the process whereby management had to rely mostly on authority by acceptance rather than on external ties was completed, and a full "bottom-up" authority structure was the result. Thus, after fifteen years of assuming an autocratic position, the Director was now required to operate as a permissive leader, whether he was ready for it or not.

In the past, due to his possession of power from external sources the Director did not seem to mind the severe formal imbalance between responsibility and authority (analyzed in Chapter 2) with which he had to comply. However, with the changes in the environment, the Director lost the external source of his power and did not gain any new material or social status, because the self-management ideology continued to consider management as a necessary evil which should wither away along with the state. The competitive market, however, increased the pressure on executives to realize competitive results, and required undertaking responsibility, undertaking risks and hard work in permissive leadership of the company. Those executives who could not adapt themselves to the new conditions whereby they had responsibility without authority or whereby their authority was highly limited (since it was based exclusively on acceptance) either quit or continued to work, displaying definite dysfunctional behavior.

The executives who found this transformation, with its new demands, beyond their ability, seemed to be those who did not possess the professional knowledge necessary to undertake a scientific analysis of the market forces. Such professional managerial knowledge could have served as a basis for the professional authority so essential for authority by acceptance which they could have used instead of the external power they lost. Furthermore, these executives had attained their positions previously through political affiliations, and frequently, their attitude, training, and past experience were not geared to permissive leadership. With time, the squeeze on such executives could be quite potent since the pressure on them mounted when the feedback on decisions started pouring in. Because the system rewarded the members of the organization directly for the successful operation of the company (see Chapter 2), the workers began to compare their salaries (total, variable, and fixed) with those of workers in comparable jobs and with comparable training in other industries. When wide discrepancies were discovered, management was challenged to account for the company's performance. Executives who could not explain and pacify the collective found it harder to maintain their position in the company.

2. Survival of the Fittest (?)

The trend that should have emerged from these developments was one where the more capable Directors, those with both leadership ability and professional knowledge, would be able to survive the pressure. They would be able to design acceptable strategies within the given constraints and to secure the workers' cooperation. Those Directors who were not able to bridge the changeover by virtue of their own abilities would necessarily be dropped with time. However, that such a trend did emerge is not completely clear.

In 1966, during the month of April, reelections for Directors were held. Although it was expected that a large number of Directors would not be reelected and that the workers would elect those with high professional training, the results did not bear out these assumptions. The workers typically maintained the old Directors. From 353 elections in the industry, only 71 new Directors were elected. Eighty percent of the old Directors were retained. Of the 71 new Directors, only 41 percent had a high level of educational training. And of the 282 Directors who were reelected, only 18 percent had a high level of education, whereas 26 percent had a medium level of education, and 36 percent had little training (elementary school). Seventeen percent of the Directors who were reelected had no education at all.[2]

There are several possible explanations for these results. One is that the Directors succeeded in creating an informal power position in the company which enabled them to manipulate the desired job definition in a manner that qualified only themselves for the job. Another explanation may be that the companies went through numerous and intensive tremors caused by the environmental changes, and the workers simply wanted some feeling of continuity, some feeling of security. A change in management would have started a new series of adaptations which, in the view of many workers, perhaps, would have been undesirable. However, it would seem that, in the long run, the "bottom-up" authority structure, with pressure from outside and inside, should lead to the survival of only those executives who have both professional authority and permissive leadership. Only a combination of these two qualities can assure a stable executive-leadership position in the evolving Yugoslav competitively market oriented environment with the legally required, industrial, democratic system of its enterprises. This effect is anticipated because the external environment requires competitive decision-making and efficiency while the internal mechanism enables and encourages dropping those executives who cannot effectively demonstrate democratic leadership.

3. The Importance of Leadership Qualities under the New Conditions

It has been asserted that professional managerial knowledge in itself is not sufficient for a company's successful operation and an executive's survival in the system. Permissive leadership abilities are essential for a company's success under the self-management system, because the ideology of industrial democracy is an accepted dogma and a required method of social conduct. Before an execu-

---

2. These data were provided by a letter from an associate of the researcher.

tive can implement a decision, he must convince the workers of its adequacy and secure their approval. Those executives with outstanding leadership abilities based on technical knowledge or charismatic qualities can satisfy the workers' self-managerial rights by means of a simple presentation and summary of actions to be taken. Those who have not established their leadership, or engendered enough trust, are compelled to pursue lengthy discussions and explanations. Such an approach is quite frustrating and inefficient, and speeds the process by which these companies become involved in financial difficulties and possible bankruptcy.

What this study of leadership and organizational behavior in Yugoslavia seems to indicate is the fact that a leader must be permissive in order to be able to guide a company. Furthermore, he must be professionally qualified in order to achieve results. If he is not worker-oriented, he can create an information gap which may yield worker unrest. If he has no professional knowledge, his inability to achieve satisfactory economic results also may generate worker unrest.

The question is: how permissive should a Director be? ABC's Director was permissive; he attended meetings, frequently spoke to workers on the line, and was interested in their welfare. But it was clear to everyone that he took the responsibility for the company's affairs on himself and acted forcefully in the directions in which he thought it would be best for the company to proceed. The Director of XYZ did not assume responsibility; rather, he let those who had the legal authority make the decisions. These two styles generated two different patterns of behavior. In XYZ, a group of middle managers could take over the Director's position if he had to quit. At ABC, the Director's absence would have been a major setback for the company.

At XYZ, more participation was evident, although there was less efficiency in decision-making.[3] This participation existed only

---

3. For more details on this topic, see I. Adizes, "The Effect of Decentralization on Organizational Behavior: an Exploratory Study of the Yugoslav Self-Management System" (Ph.D. dissertation, Columbia University, 1968), chapter 7.

to the degree that "painful" decisions, such as modernization and full technical integration of the various plants, took place very slowly and were dictated more by the law of the situation than by the Director's leadership. At ABC, "painful" decisions, such as rapid modernization, which consumed large amounts of resources that otherwise could have been distributed as personal income, were effected by the Director's leadership. However, also noted at ABC was an information gap that in moments of economic difficulty turned out to be a credibility gap and a source of large dissatisfaction.

Therefore, an argument for either leadership pattern is inconclusive. What in fact is needed is an individual who is confident enough to assume voluntarily the responsibility for a company's affairs. However, he should not be too efficiency-oriented even if he feels responsible and has the drive to achieve the highest results. He should be able to act as a teacher who stimulates others to do what he wants without making them feel that their actions result from his wishes or that what is happening is his sole responsibility. Thus, he should be like the Director of XYZ in letting others make decisions; at the same time, he should be like the Director of ABC who felt responsible for decisions even though he only led the way to their evolution.

The researcher noticed that, as in vertical organizations, there seemed to be a tradeoff between economic results and human capital results. XYZ had lower economic results, but its human capital results were better in the short run; at ABC the reverse held. This is of interest—the more vertical organization achieved better economic results than the more permissive one. (This conclusion should be compared to the improvement in results obtained from making a vertical organization more permissive. It would seem that movement from both ends of the spectrum of vertical-horizontal structures toward the middle improves results.)

Further differences between the two companies lie in the amount of time required for decision-making. Under the permissive leadership of XYZ, major decisions took longer to make than under the authoritative leadership style of ABC. Permissive leadership encouraged more genuine participation by offering more channels through which the participants could affect decisions. The authoritative style required less time to make and implement decisions, but this may be because participation was limited. However, constructive suggestions were fewer, as were the constraints imposed on decisions such as modernization.

DYSFUNCTIONAL RESULTS[3a]

The change from a "top-bottom" to a "bottom-up" authority structure without previous changes in attitudes and training, and without a critical reappraisal of the legal constraints on decision-making, had some dysfunctional effect on organizational behavior.

Even for those executives who were able to operate under the permissive leadership system, success was not without its frustrations. Many of these individuals considered it a waste of time to spend hours in a meeting with professional inferiors discussing alternative actions, since they already felt they knew which course would be best. As one frustrated executive said, "I don't tell workers how to work on a machine because they know best how to do it. Why should they tell me what price to set for a product? They don't know the markets. They don't know the state of competition." Nevertheless, it was their job to convince the workers of the effectiveness of the suggested alternative. This problem was aggravated by the fact that the discussions at these meetings frequently centered on trivial problems, about which workers had more understanding and were more concerned.[3b] As a result, many plans formulated by the executive staff were transferred to an ad hoc committee or selected for a review, not because of critical faults, but because some insignificant aspect, as perceived by the executive, was found to be unacceptable, or because a meaningful disussion could not be achieved in these large meetings. It was not uncommon for executives, weary of slamming tables and

---

3a. For suggested functional results see pages 221-223.
3b. See Adizes, Chapter 7.

delivering tirades over certain points, to become withdrawn and apathetic to the frequent, irrelevant, and trivial objections made from the floor.

The communication so crucial for effective decision-making was observed to be frequently inadequate in the meetings of the decision-making bodies. While disagreements would occur in the meetings of the *Collegium*, they were minor compared to the power-fully vociferous disagreements as well as the dysfunctional phenom-ena such as apathy, withdrawal, and nervousness which were common occurrences in the Workers' Councils and Governing Board meetings under XYZ-style leadership. In the *Collegium*, which was attended only by executives, the "transmitters" and the "receivers" were apparently more on the same wave length than in the governing bodies just mentioned.

In the opinion of the researcher, the causes for many of the organizational difficulties in the Yugoslav system—inadequate time allocation for decision-making, inability of trained managers to communicate fully with the decision-makers, imbalance between authority and responsibility, and between contribution and induce-ments for executives within a competitive environment requiring competitive decision-making and risk-taking—have contributed to a wholly new phenomenon in Yugoslav management, "contractual management."[4]

"CONTRACTUAL MANAGEMENT"[5]

In Skoplje, the capital of Macedonia, a certain company on the verge of bankruptcy received an offer of assistance from a pro-fessional manager. He proposed to manage the company under the condition that the Workers' Council not be permitted to dictate operative daily business decisions. Such an arrangement could be established if the workers would delegate to him, through the *Statut,* the necessary powers. The Director committed himself to

---

4. This term was coined by the researcher.
5. All the data submitted below were gathered in the course of interviews.

increase sales and profits by a stated amount of dinars within a given period of time. If successful, the manager was to receive a salary bonus. Realizing that the company would soon be bankrupt and that, as a result, they would be unemployed, the workers accepted his proposal.

This incident typifies a pattern of "contractual management" which seems to be emerging in Yugoslavia. The Director would offer his services to a company and would state what he felt he could contribute and the amount of monetary reimbursement he desired. This offer partially eliminated the conflict created by the ambiguity surrounding the question of where the decision-making and executive powers actually resided; the Director requested the operative decision-making power, while the Workers' Council maintained the power to hire or fire him, approve his budgets or projected income as well as the general policies he might undertake in order to carry out "the contract." Furthermore, the reimbursement required by the executive appeared to cover the risk he was taking in making his suggestion. Essentially, the executives were altering their strategy of acquisition of power from "behind-the-scenes" maneuvers to straightforward proposals in the form of contracts, indicating their competence to manage and their wish to do so without hindrance. This process was indicated in Yugoslav newspapers as the desired method by which an existing Director, or a new one, could seek his position; he would be stressing his abilities and suggesting the contributions he could make, and therefore, would assume the responsibility without decreasing workers' control over the company.

A problem arose, however, in connection with the above-mentioned contract. The Party and the Trade Unions felt it might be unethical for the Director to collect his bonus, since they claimed that he was obtaining surplus remuneration by exploiting the workers with his professional knowledge. The question was whether the Director should not have offered his services without requesting any bonus. The discussion over the Director's contract eventually was aired on television and radio and became the focus of public interest. Ultimately, the Director voluntarily returned 50 percent of his bonus and, with a portion of the remaining half, bought the city of Skoplje an ambulance. He retained only a small amount as his own income.

A similar attitude was reflected during an incident in Niš. The Director of Yugoslavia's largest electronics industry threatened to resign. He felt that the Workers' Council and the Community of Niš were pressuring him to carry out unwise decisions, particularly those concerning local interests. Because he was reputed to be one of the top electronic engineers in Yugoslavia with almost unlimited possibilities of employment, he could easily succeed in demanding changes in his working conditions without fear of unemployment. As a result of his protest, the Workers' Council remained the formal, all-powerful, decision-making body of the company, but delegated extensive daily decision-making powers to the Director.

In a third company visited by the researcher, a manager who was applying for a Director's job, and who was strongly supported by the Party, had requested the Council to slash his proposed salary to a point where it equaled the opportunity cost of his employment as a lawyer in another company. In fact, the resulting figure was 30 percent lower than what was offered to him. This act amazed the Council, but can be understood from the Director's statement to the researcher. He said, "I want them to realize that it is they who need me and not I who need them. I can always leave!" When considered for appointment, the Director summarized to the Council his education and experience, pointing out the relevance of both to the success of the company. He also presented his plans as to what could be done in the company and how, but he expressed the desire to serve as an independent leader rather than as a puppet-Director. He indicated that the Council should establish the guidelines and make major decisions, but that he should be able to act freely within these guidelines.

The researcher talked freely with several workers in the company. They were aware of both the real necessity for the Director's services, the fact that he could obtain a higher salary elsewhere if he wished. This awareness created admiration and willingness to follow the Director and served as a source of authority for his decisions. (In 1968, when his immediate assistants staged a coup d'état to overthrow him, the workers signed letters of support for him and fired the rebellious minority.)

What these three cases appear to indicate is a reinforcement of what is already known from management theory: there can be no effective duty implementation without authority to carry it out. Responsibility to carry out decisions, without the authority to shape either the decisions or the manner of their execution, is meaningless and ineffective. Executives found it necessary to create this authority either through a given legal contract (case #1), or by threatening to resign (which might affect the company adversely), or by making their threat potent through choice of an adequate salary (cases #2 and #3). All three cases, however, illustrate the generation of authority by acceptance; in essence, authority by acceptance was tested, and once the test was passed—i.e., the Director was appointed—the acceptance rendered the authority which the Director needed in order to manage the company.

There were other sources of authority used or created by the Directors, but, in comparison to the effect on the process, described above, the others seemed to be dysfunctional. These additional sources of authority appeared to be achieved not through active acceptance but rather through sufferance by the subordinates. Several illustrations of this phenomenon may be cited. Executives would submit the information necessary for decision-making in such a complicated manner that the decision-maker would accept it without further question. Or, the decision-making meeting would be made so festive, large, and formal that the workers on the line felt out of place and would accept automatically what they were being told. A third way of acquiring this type of authority lay in the executive's making himself the center of information networks, i.e., all correspondence had to go through him. This behavior was dysfunctional with respect to the long-run effectiveness of the company, but it seemed to be the short cut taken by executives for the purpose of acquiring the desired authority to carry their ideas through, when the other alternative, acquiring authority by acceptance, did not appeal or was not available to them.

The Displacement of Goals and Its Effects on Yugoslav Enterprises

In addition to the effects described above, we suggest that the environmental changes had an effect both on the goals pursued by Yugoslav companies and on the processes designed to achieve them.

THE DISPLACEMENT OF GOALS[6]

Company goals displaced by the changes in the environment were: (1) the importance of maximum production, and (2) the involvement of the collective in the decision-making process. The goal displacement has affected, among other things, the importance of the status of individuals within a given enterprise. Status can be viewed as a social means of distributing rewards to those attaining or forwarding social goals. A discussion of this process follows.

An important goal which underwent a change was the notion of achieving maximum production. Profit maximization, which is not necessarily related to production maximization, took its place. Production maximization could be undesired because it could

---

6. Goal displacement in an organization may include making a previous means the new goal, and the previous goal a means to the achievement of the new goal. A. Etzioni, in *Modern Organizations* (Englewood Cliffs, N.J.: Prentice-Hall, 1967), p. 10, claims that it should be a replacement of a legitimate goal by some other goal for which the organization was not created. We relaxed the last part of Etzioni's definition in this book.

pile up inventory and consume cash balances. In the past, *"udarnici"* and *"heroji rada,"* the work heroes who like the Russian Stahanovich, could double and triple the norm, were given special recognition and privileges. The companies' goal had been to complete a specified plan as early as possible, and the heroes were instrumental in this effort. With obvious sorrow in their voices, several workers told the researcher of the era of festivity (dancing, embracing, etc.), when the company's siren would announce that a production plan had been not only realized but surpassed. People no longer felt pride in such accomplishments or in their production heroes. Those individuals who began to gain status were the technocrats who could show degrees, diplomas, and formal knowledge and who could determine how much should be produced and how the products should be sold. The shift in status stripped the worker from the potential glory to be derived from hard work on the line, a glory that, earlier, was part of the culture and a symbol of workers' dominance.

Other dogmas were affected, too. As one of the interviewed Directors said:

We are being freed from dogmas. In the past the goal was maximum employment. . . . If a person worked, it was good and desirable. Now working is not enough. Now it has to be producing a product that is acceptable by others. It has to be a profitable work. Those that are not good, whose work is unacceptable by the market should disappear. Thus, maximum employment lost importance and maximum efficiency took its place.

Maximum labor production was not necessarily akin to maximum organizational efficiency. This factor seemed to affect adversely the spirit of many individuals within the companies, since it became more difficult to evaluate the crucial inputs and outputs for organizational success. In order for results to be recorded, production had to be sold, which meant that the time period within which organizational effectiveness had to be accounted for had to be prolonged. This situation increased the ambiguity with respect to the appraisal of organizational effectiveness and individual contribution to the company. Those who handled uncertainty gained in status, e.g., economists and technocrats. The work heroes from the production line, although they still were rewarded comparably to the economists and managers, saw their status diminished.

The second component of the goal displacement was connected with the results self-management was supposed to yield. The goal of self-management had been participative decision-making, i.e., involvement of the collective in the decision-making process. The system was an educational experiment where involvement in company management was considered a means of educating the peasants of yesterday to become the industrial workers of tomorrow. Those companies which achieved high participation levels through a high rate of governors' rotation, as well as high levels of discussion of matters crucial to a company's performance or policies, were regarded as successful, progressive organizations. They elevated the collective; they fulfilled self-management's norms of involvement. Since profit creation was independent from the managerial process, and was dependent for the most part on government regulations, both acceptable economic results and participative management could be achieved. The introduction into the system of competitive market forces and the diminishing of government intervention altered the function participative management was expected to perform; it was now expected to lead to profitability through rational decision-making. Since, in the short run, there is no necessary, direct relationship between participation and profitability, this change seemed to be significant as it created numerous frustrations and problems which plague many Yugoslav companies today. In many companies, the participative system, which turned out to be ponderous and thus hindered the efficiency of decision-making, did not contribute to profitability or harmonious internal relationships, but rather to declining business results and various internal frictions.

In essence, the Yugoslav companies were experiencing the inevitable, chaotic interim period when one standard of conduct was discarded and another was taking hold. On the one hand, Yugoslavia was still operating under a system involving maximum participation in the decision-making process, involving rewards calculated to induce maximum production and minimum layoffs of workers, and involving powerless management to further the democratic managerial process. On the other hand, the evolving market system required an organization to create profits by operating rationally, decisively, and knowledgeably; it required that decisions be made by professionals; and it required a certain optimum size, inevitably smaller than the Workers' Council of 60 members or more, as a decision-making group.

For any degree of success in the competitive market, flexibility must be present in the decision-making process, especially in relation to production plans. However, the democratic process, appropriately adhering to the system of maximum participation, made flexibility almost impossible. Part of this inflexibility was the result of involvement of the collective in decision-making.

How much involvement was being sought and in which areas, is the third facet of the goal displacement process described here. For a long time, the Yugoslav system focused on the collective rather than on the individual. The elevation of the entire collective, rather than the individuals within it, was a Communist doctrine, and Communist egalitarian concepts formed the ideological basis for this approach which, in the "take-off" period of the Yugoslav economy, seemed to be effective. Through "togetherness," sacrifices could be achieved from the existing generation to rebuild and improve on the destroyed economy. However, this philosophy of egalitarian-collectivism advocated certain paternalistic standards of conduct which were inconsistent with the new needs of the post-economic reform period. Higher labor mobility was needed. The companies under economic difficulties had to free the surplus labor which had to find employment in those areas where the market indicated the existence of great economic opportunities.

Labor mobility appeared to be hampered by the standards of collectivism and the involvement of the collective in decisions on hiring and firing. When the economic conditions of a company worsened, a decision to fire part of the labor force was necessary. However, the members who were empowered to make the decision were reluctant to implement it, since such a decision might mean that any one of their group might have to go. Furthermore, there was a question of ownership—people invested their potential income in the company by foregoing personal income in favor of investment. Firing these people would have deprived them of future income derived from this investment.[7]

The process of hiring also was hampered by collectivistic decision-making. If new opportunities existed which required either expansion of one company or establishment of a new one, expansion of the labor force of a company was hindered by collective decision-making, since the decision-makers seemed to be reluctant to let more people enjoy the "growing pie" of income. Increasing the labor force, at least in the short run, may have meant decreasing the rate of growth of personal income enjoyed by the existing members. Thus, although there was a need in some organizations for structural changes in the labor force, i.e., firing the unqualified and hiring more existent trained manpower, such changes could not be implemented because of the system of decision-making. In the post-reform unemployment, a large percent of those seeking positions were newly graduated engineers or other technocrats.

Establishment of new enterprises was hampered by the collectivistic approach to decision-making, since the entrepreneur who could have put together resources to exploit opportunities was discouraged from doing so. Only the federal or local government could establish new companies and these companies had to be

---

7. To permit labor mobility hampered by the ownership dilemma, and to encourage investments in the company, the Yugoslavs are considering certain means for providing capital markets: one illustration would be the issuing of company bonds, as was true in the case of *Crvena Zastava* (see p. 227). We should not be surprised if Yugoslavia establishes a stock market in the near future; however, its name, as Kenneth Boulding remarked in a talk at UCLA, would not be the "Wall Street" Stock Exchange, but perhaps the People's Stock Exchange.

managed by Workers' Councils through group decision-making. The entrepreneur who supposedly wanted higher rewards for higher risks in establishing and running a new company and for the larger amount of energy required by a new enterprise, was limited in his endeavors. The rewards he could derive via the egalitarian group decision-making process were few (see Ch. 8).

The pressures indicated above were apparent, and adaptations were made to enable more freedom of action. The changes were small, but they indicated a trend. A recent change, resulting in an increase of managerial freedom as opposed to group decision-making constraints, occurred in the enlargement of the size of enterprises exempt from the self-management decision-making process. The new regulation stated that entrepreneurs could open *their own* companies[8] and manage them in a hierarchical manner rather than through Workers' Councils, if the size of the labor force was not above ten people. Previously, the maximum allowable size had been five people. In terms of the hiring and firing process, strong pressures were exerted on the federal government to change the laws to allow for more freedom of the executive function. In June, 1968, these pressures resulted in the introduction of new laws which permitted more managerial freedom in labor relations.

THE EFFECT ON ORGANIZATIONAL AFFILIATION

The transition from the political goal of participative decision-making to the economic goal of profit maximization apparently had a significant effect on the social hierarchy and general morale within the organizations studied by the researcher.

As a result of the new emphasis on professional competence, the status of the professional political leader deteriorated. Infor-

8. For a discussion on the developments in Eastern Europe in general, M. Gamarnikow, "The New Role of Private Enterprise," *East Europe,* 16 (August, 1967), pp. 2-9, and on a separate phenomenon, "the agency system," see M. Gamarnikow, "Another Step toward Private Enterprise," *East Europe,* 17 (January, 1968), pp. 2-9.

mally, he was now considered a "big mouth," one who could manipulate words beautifully but could make few worthwhile contributions toward profit making. Similarly, the Trade Union lost most of its glamour as the leader of the proletariat, having been replaced socially by the technocrats.[9]

This overall shift in power greatly affected the quality and necessity of various meetings[10] which had previously constituted the backbone of the participative decision-making system. Because management, and actual decision-making power, was being handled increasingly by specialized professional managers, many meetings became a meaningless formality, devoid of any actual influence except for formal voting. The workers were aware of the difficulties of managing under uncertainty; many appeared all too willing to abolish the old system. As one individual said, "I wish someone would tell me what to do and I would not have to worry why." "Let someone else manage; I want good pay." Several workers even intended to quit the Party, since they felt that it was consuming endless hours of their time for what were now felt to be impotent discussions. Some workers said to the researcher: "Those who can't do, become political leaders." For instance, a person who was interviewed for a job in one of the researched companies was asked about his education. When he replied that he had graduated from the Superior Institute for Political Leaders, the chairman of the committee, a worker, answered jokingly, "This is for the afternoon [i.e., for the political meetings], but what can you do during the day?" The person was not accepted for the job, whereas in the past, the researcher was told, he would have been accepted because of his political ties.[11]

Since the Communist Party lost its major attraction as a source of rewards and became a liability requiring endless time for meet-

---

9. For a discussion on the general trend in Eastern Europe, see M. Gamarnikow, "New Tasks for Trade Unions," *East Europe*, 16 (April, 1967), p. 18.

10. More in other companies visited than in XYZ and ABC.

11. For a discussion about this trend in Eastern Europe, see M. Gamarnikow, "The End of the Party Hack," *East Europe*, 14 (November, 1965), pp. 3-8.

Dr. Tito prescribes for his patient (the "Party"): "With the shape you're in, you have to become more active—start moving around!"   Jez (Belgrade), May 26, 1967.

ings, the membership in the Party began to dwindle. Many people left the Party voluntarily and at an increasing rate: in 1964, a total of 2,273 members left; in 1965, the number more than doubled to reach 5,762, and, in 1966, it reached 7,640. In 1967, during the first six months alone, 4,321 returned their membership cards. Sixty-one percent of those who left were highly qualified workers who apparently had a better use for their time; a total of 65.8 percent of this group were 26 to 40 years old and, thus, at the prime of their productivity, and 68.9 percent had been in the Party not more than six years. Unlike the older Party members, they apparently did not have the deep, pre-war affiliation with Communist ideology.[12]

This phenomenon is considered desirable by some theoreticians,[13] because they claim it is time to get rid of the opportunists in the Party. The membership should change to contain those who want to affect the course of events without pursuing their own immediate interests. Thus, the Party members should perform in the same manner and under the same rules of the game as the executives in the companies: as leaders who use their integrity, professional knowledge, and personal conviction in order to induce certain activities without seeking their own immediate personal benefit. What long-run effect this strategy, based on ideological interpretation of human nature, will have on the role of the Party in the country remains to be seen.[14]

It is interesting to note that the Yugoslav social scientists interviewed in the United States by the researcher claimed that many political developments were made possible by the self-management experience. People learned to be open, to question, to challenge. In industrial organizations they were free to speak up and were taught to be led democratically; yet, in the Party or government ruling bodies, they were restricted in the expression of their opinions. The discrepancies in the system developed to a point where one side had to yield. It was Tito who tipped the balance toward further democratization of the Party in order to bring the political institutions in line with the industrial management developments.

Thus, it will not be overly speculative to conclude that the self-

---

12. The figures are derived from "Ko i Zasto Svojevoljno Napusta Skj," *NIN*, weekly magazine, April 7, 1968.

13. *Ibid.*

14. For a similar observation on the rising status of the technocrats and the decreasing importance of Party affiliation, see Jan F. Triska, "The Party Apparatchiks at Bay," *East Europe*, 16 (December, 1967), pp. 2-8.

management mechanism eroded the highly frozen and centralized Party authority. It trained technocrats, the so-called "economists," whose reasoning and goals were different from the dogmatists, the so-called "Communists" or "syndicalists" (see footnote 18 on page 229). Self-management served as a springboard for the technocrats, whose status it elevated, and gave them the strength to fight within the Party. Starting with the individual organizations, the system trained people for democracy, preparing them for participation on the national level. This experience was of value for the Yugoslavs because democracy and participation were the exclusive assets of a narrow elite in pre-war, agricultural, monarch-ruled Yugoslavia, and were non-existent during the centrally planned phase of the post-war period.

With all the dysfunctional behavior described in Part II, it should be borne in mind that self-management generally yielded amazing functional results in the long run. It made possible uncertainty absorption while the country was being decentralized, a process which generated unpredictable turbulences with conflicting trends. Self-management, by making participation obligatory, created communal commitment, and people apparently felt comfort in being "in the same boat." If a hierarchical organization had existed and only management had absorbed the uncertainty, the erratic environment would have led to destructive polarization between those who have to decide (management) without being able to predict what will happen, and those who have to implement (workers) without understanding the reason for the inconsistency between decisions and their anticipated and realized results. Obligated to be managers, the workers had to become involved and to accept the uncontrollable developments and their repercussions.

However, this democratic self-management structure needed a strong leader, willing to absorb uncertainty and able to convince the membership to delegate him certain powers. Otherwise, the democratic structure could easily become an anarchy where no one enjoyed either the results or the process of democratic management. Furthermore, the structure apparently required that management not become too autocratic, since there could result a "credibility gap" in which workers were taught to participate but were not given an opportunity to do so. Therefore, it was desirable that the leadership should assume responsibility; simultaneously, the general membership should become involved in decision-making, although such involvement might restrict leadership's discretion—the number of choices open for decision-making for which leadership assumes responsibility.

At the time of this research, self-management was, and still appears to be, a major national educational project. If they are compelled to manage, workers have to learn to read, to compute, to account, to forecast—in other words, to acquire a certain amount of sophistication. The peasant of yesterday has to learn for a good reason: his paycheck will grow as he shares the results of the company's efforts. Hence, self-management may be a desirable mechanism for developing countries undergoing the industrialization process. However, apparently there are limits to this educational effort.

The researcher was told that the membership composition of the Workers' Council altered throughout the country with the decentralization trend. As top executives were excluded legally from formal membership in order to maximize workers' participation, a growing percentage of junior economists, technologists, and junior engineers who served as foremen were elected to the Councils. The consensus seemed to be to "keep the big mouths out." Thus, in certain cases, Party affiliation, or being merely a worker on the line, was not helpful for Council election, unless the person was professionally qualified as well. In the past the opposite trend was encouraged: a maximum number of workers from the production line should be on the Council.

Council membership itself began to lose its attraction. Many workers no longer wanted to be in self-managerial bodies. Those with whom the researcher spoke indicated that fifteen years of managing had been enough for them and that the self-management process had been harmful to their family life. Meetings were

Campaigning in Nish, Serbia: "Of 99 registered candidates, one is actually a worker. Incredible, you say? Look at his hands!" *Politika* (Belgrade), February 12, 1967.

usually lengthy (even up to eight hours) and were held after the normal working hours, including Sundays. Thus, in a number of families in Yugoslavia, where the wife was employed as well as the husband, family gatherings were decreased by these frequent meetings. One worker told the researcher that she accepted a position in a company at half salary on one condition: that she would not have to attend or partake in any meetings or political activities. The value she placed on having leisure time to spend with her two children was higher than the opportunity cost of her salary. Some of the young people interviewed preferred to invest the time in studying in order to get ahead professionally, rather than wasting time in impotent meetings.

In addition to the above-described changes, the researcher noted pressure to realign the ideology and its dogmas to fit the reality of the situation. The emphasis in this new interpretation was on redefinition of the contribution of capital in the creation of value, as well as on redefinition of ownership rights.

In the past, only labor contribution qualified as a basis for distribution of created value. With the market economy, capital mobility was imperative. In the past, capital had been channeled by the government, which was not a profit-maximizing institution. Therefore, there was no pressure to allocate part of the profits to the contributors of capital. When the banks took over the distribution of investments, and when they attempted to maximize their profits, pressure to allocate dividends to capital was created.

A bank is formed out of capital resources contributed by each of several companies. The bank screens applications for loans and allocates funds to those which appear most profitable. It has to act in this manner because its partners, the companies, press for maximum income from their contributed capital. Thus, the companies receive dividends for their capital rather than fixed interest on savings.

One case may illustrate some of the very interesting processes which began to evolve as a result of the drift to a market mechanism. For a long period of time, one large company in Belgrade has enjoyed a monopolistic position in the industry. When competition pressed, the company applied for a loan to the Belgrade Economic Bank. The Bank, claiming that the existent management could not handle the competition, refused to grant a loan until top management were fired and new administrators hired. The company, after much fuss, complied.[15] The case was a break from previous experience, since, in the past, managerial appraisal was carried out within each company and was affected by external political factors. The value of management as a decision-making component was ignored. The Bank's insistence on new management raised the status of executives, as well as the salaries they obtained, and crystallized the developing notion that good manage-

---

15. Interview with Associate Professor Vasić of the University of Novi Sad, May, 1969, at UCLA.

ment is crucial in competitive markets. Because it was profit-oriented, the Bank played a significant role in this development.

An illustration of pressures on the dogma with regard to capital as a creator of value may be seen in an incident from a question-and-answer television program.[16] Roman Albrecht, a member of the Central Committee of the Communist Party, was asked by a Workers' Council the following question: "We have capital for which we have no immediate good use, while a company in our neighborhood badly needs capital for its operations. Can we lend them the money and share their profits in the future? We are Communists and they are Communists. Is it acceptable practice for us to receive part of their profits without literally laboring for it?" The answer given was that such an arrangement was acceptable and should be accomplished by bargaining for a "just" return on the capital.

It should be borne in mind that, at that period, a law for the encouragement of foreign capital was being considered by the Yugoslav Parliament. No foreign capital would have flowed into Yugoslavia unless there existed a willingness to distribute competitive dividends (not interest) to the foreign investors. The Communist hierarchy could not justify as correct practice the distribution of profits to foreign capitalists and at the same time reject this practice inside the country. However, individual capitalists were, and still are, discouraged. In other words, an individual cannot lend money to a company and anticipate dividends without laboring in that company; however, an *institution* can do so and then share the acquired dividends among its members. Thus, a compromise is achieved in which capital can flow from one use to another, but an individual who does not actually labor cannot gain from this process. Decisions on where to transfer one's money are not yet considered as valuable labor but as speculations which should be eliminated.

---

16. *Aktuelni Razgovori*, February 23, 1967, 8 P.M., TV, Belgrade. Recorded by the author.

It should be noted that even this dogma is being further eroded. A market economy needs mobile labor and capital markets, both of which are just developing in Yugoslavia. For instance, *Crvena Zastava,* the Yugoslav Fiat branch, raised capital needed for expansion through the sale of bonds to the market. The bonds yielded 7 percent, which was more than banks offered on savings, and were redeemable in the form of a car, an item for which there is enormous demand in Yugoslavia. Since no previous attempts had been made to raise capital from the society at large, the sale of these bonds, which, it is claimed, were sold overnight, represented a breakthrough.[17]

The law for encouragement of foreign capital was in itself an ideological innovation. For years, Communism considered foreign capital a vehicle of exploitation to be avoided. Foreign capital was discouraged because of a fear of dependency on foreign interests. Yugoslavia experienced this dependency before the war, and claimed it was disadvantageous. The country's arrival at the conclusion that competition in foreign markets needs foreign know-how and foreign capital, and the subsequent decision based on this analysis, are interesting developments worth noting.

Centripetal Forces Counter-Balancing Centrifugal Decentralization Pressures

The reform of 1965 affected both the economic and the social functions within the companies. The economic effect may be seen in the decentralization of the economic powers on the macro- and the micro-levels. Decentralization occurred not only in the government's relationship to the enterprise, but also in the relationship between the central decision-making bodies within a company and the various Economic Units and beyond to the immediate producer.

---

17. *The Economist* (London), January 6, 1968, p. 22.

The social effect of the 1965 reform reflected the economic aspect. Under decentralization, the individual workers were expected to find greater freedom and, eventually, greater self-respect through the realization that they were the vital force responsible for the success or failure of the company. Further pressure to decentralize on the micro-level, resulting in the establishment of subsystems, was created by the political bodies. They requested the establishment of separate Economic Units within each company, appropriately controlled in order to measure the value of each Unit's contribution to the company as a whole. They also suggested that each Unit should have the power to make those decisions which would maximize the profits of the individual Unit. In essence, the desired end result was profit decentralization—self-management style (that is, in self-management, the delegation process refers to a group of people rather than to an individual).

The political pressure to decentralize on the micro-level was so great that the process occurred even in those companies where it was inefficient. For instance, some service companies could not be expected to establish effective Economic Units; in these cases, the whole company was too dependent on the interaction and cooperation of all the Units. Further, there could be no adequate means of measuring each Unit's separate contribution to the whole as a method of determining objective distribution of income. Thus, friction among Economic Units resulted from "unfair" distribution, and the companies were paralyzed. Competition over a fixed amount of income will lead, by definition, to conflict, and such was the result of the pressure exerted by the political bodies. This situation occurred at the most inappropriate time as well—at a point when the companies were desperately attempting to reconcile and adapt their activities to the new demands of a competitive system.

Even though the Party officially had withdrawn its power of influence over the actions of Yugoslav companies, as noted previously, it continued to impose a *moral* obligation upon its members to fight for the continued use and advancement of the self-management ideology. The Party workers were urged to promote the Communist doctrine; they considered themselves the most conscientious members of the organization, since, in their view, they carried full responsibility for the success or failure of the self-management system.

Members of the Party were frequently asked by Party organs outside the companies, such as the leaders of various communes or city groups, whether the resolutions of the Sixth Plenum of the Communist Party were being enforced in their companies, i.e., whether the decentralization was being pursued. No one really knew the purpose or effect of these questions, that is, whether they were solely for information or to be considered as orders. Many Directors, both Party members and nonmembers, were approached by Party activists, and—preferring to be on the safe side—they complied with this informative questioning as if it had been ordered. Only those Directors who possessed either a high degree of professional knowledge or strong party backing dared to oppose the pressures of the Party.[18] Opposition was relatively easy to express; because of the increase in freedom to dissent and because of Party factionalism, the Director merely had to base his dissent on ideological or technical grounds.

Thus, the companies affected most adversely by the decentralization process on the micro-level were those controlled either politically or professionally by weak Directors. Such companies found themselves struggling to cope in the competitive market, frustrated by a disintegrated and ineffectual decision-making system. They had yielded by mistake to the decentralization pressures for political reasons and not because of their economic needs.

---

18. It should be understood that the Party itself is composed of many factions; thus, a person could be politically strong and still oppose the "Party." Stankovic, p. 12—as we have already mentioned—reports that Tito officially admittted the existence of two opposing groups for the first time in November, 1959. He called the first the "Economists," and the other the "Communists" (whom we call in this book the "Syndicalists"), the latter being greatly outnumbered. Stankovic got his data from *Komunist,* November 26, 1959.

A comparison of the two companies observed by the researcher will illustrate this political phenomenon. In ABC, the Director was strong politically, and, therefore, he could afford to oppose inquiries. He was able not only to oppose further internal decentralization in his company, but also to deliver speeches on the radio urging decentralization only when the technological constraints had been taken into account. XYZ, which had the *same* technological processes as ABC, decentralized its decision-making powers (for instance, decisions on annual plans) to the Economic Units. XYZ was facing great difficulties as a result of this decentralization, but could not reverse the process, because its Director did not have enough backing to take a firm stand of opposition.

Despite the fact that the decision-making machinery of the organization had been fragmented, the economic situation still required action. The informal organization found its own way to surmount the formal organizational barriers imposed by this decentralization by establishing a degree of congruity in the decision-making process. Three informal groups emerged with a definite function to perform in the system: the *Politikal Aktive,* the *Extended Collegium,* and the Company's Central Party Committee.

It became accepted practice to subject any significant decision to these three groups for discussion before formally offering it for discussion or voting. The decision was sent down to the Economic Units only after the cooperation of these groups had been secured. In essence, these informal groups exerted a centripetal force which counterbalanced the centrifugal forces introduced by decentralization. It was the researcher's impression, confirmed by many of those interviewed, that the stronger the decentralization, as measured by the powers delegated, the more frequent were the meetings of these three groups. Informally, they would smooth conflicts and produce solutions accepted by the influential, which were then offered to the Workers' Council for a vote.

In essence, these institutions created a ripple effect. In the center were the Workers' Council and the executive branch; at the outskirts, competing among themselves, were the Economic

Units with their various delegated powers. The center was not able to coordinate effectively and to solve the conflicts because it was divided into executive and governing bodies. The split in responsibilities and authorities diminished central power, which presumably was needed to resolve these conflicts. The Central Party Committee, the *Extended Collegium,* and the *Politikal Aktive* informally united these two branches of management by serving as intermediary bodies and bridging the gap between the Units and the center. They were able to perform this function not only because they united governing and execution into one body, but also because their own members were drawn from both the center and the peripheries of the organizational bodies.[19]

Further signs of a centripetal reaction can be noted from the tendencies to eliminate the Governing Board, to prolong the mandate of the Council for five years, thus enabling prolonged cooperation with the executive branch, and to legitimitize the *Extended Collegium* by assigning it some formal authority which it did not have.

All of these tendencies indicate that the trend in Yugoslavia appears to be to strengthen the executive branch by adding to its authority and power, and to establish workers' dominancy more through "management by exception" than by direct decision-making, i.e., a less participative structure than the existent one. If this is true, then it might be concluded that there is a direct relationship between organizational structures (i.e., how much participation) and the structure of the economy within which the organizations operate.

If this conclusion is accepted, we might further speculate that the reverse reasoning might be true as well: if we want to make organizations more participative in the United States, the environment will have to be less competitive, and more regulated as well, if we want to see these organizations operate efficiently.

---

19. "Organizational peripheries" may be an unfortunate term, but it seems to be the most adequate for purposes of describing a *process* of decentralization which has the centrifugal forces delegating powers to organizational subsystems further and further from the center.

8.

Balancing Environmental Requirements and Personal Needs Through an Organizational Structure

A trend of contemporary management theory is to expound the advantages of increased participation by subordinates in organizational decision-making processes.[1] This trend suggests altering organizational structure for decision-making from the vertical type of structure toward the horizontal type of structure.[2]

It has been theorized that increased participation and responsibility in decision-making on the part of the general workers tend to yield organizational loyalty, confidence, trust, favorable attitudes toward superiors, low abstenteeism, high productivity, etc.[3] Increased participation diminishes behavior which is detrimental to the organization or to its members' behavior classified as dysfunctional. In addition, it has been claimed that "democracy . . . is the only system which can successfully cope with the changing demands of contemporary civilization.[4]

---

1. McGregor's "Y" theory, Bennis' democratic value system, Argyris' mix model, and Likert's participative management are the best known illustrations of this trend.

2. For definitions, see Chapter 1 and a discussion following.

3. See the graphical representation in R. Likert, *The Human Organization* (New York: McGraw-Hill, 1967), p. 137.

4. W. Bennis, *Changing Organizations* (New York: McGraw-Hill, 1966), p. 17.

A question, therefore, arises as to whether there is a limit, a point of diminishing returns, to the amount of authority in the decision-making process which can be placed upon the shoulders of the general membership, i.e., a limit to the character and magnitude of democracy in industrial organizations. In more general terms, what is a desirable organizational structure? In order to answer this question, an analysis must be made of the external (environmental) and internal (personal needs) constraints which an organizational structure has to satisfy.

The holistic and behavioristic approaches to organizational design differ primarily in the amount of importance they give to external and internal constraints. The holistic approach views organizations as a goal-fulfilling system, and, through departmentalization and specialization, designs the structure for efficient realization of given goals. Membership's personal needs are considered mainly as a means to be manipulated toward the achievement of the goal which is influenced by environmental forces.

The behavioristic approach focuses on behavior primarily within the organization. Through job enlargement and participative structures, the realization of membership needs is sought. External environmental pressures are considered, but, for the most part, only in terms of how they affect the behavior of the participants.[5]

In answering the above question on the desirable organizational structure, the researcher intends to consider an optimal structure as a goal in itself. For this purpose, a third approach is taken: an organization is viewed as a social boundary mechanism which encompasses resources and operates within an environment. In order to answer the question of what kind of structure is necessary for this mechanism to work, both the environment within which an organization operates and the personal needs of the participants who are bound by the organization must be analyzed. An organizational structure is viewed, then, as a mechanism which buffers

---

5. C. Argyris in his early writing, *Personality and Organization* (New York: Harper & Row, 1957), took this approach.

and balances between external and internal pressures, a structure which optimizes between the conflicting requirements rather than a structure which maximizes any one of them separately.

This chapter analyzes the manner in which both the environment *and* the psychological needs of the participants in the Yugoslav companies observed affected organizational behavior and change in the organizational structure. In addition, a comparison is made of these changes in relationship to those taking place in American companies. From this comparison of environments and structures, some insights are derived, which should answer the question of how much democracy is feasible in an industrial organization.

The chapter is organized in the following manner: first, a distinction is made between the peripheries of the spectrum of vertical-horizontal organizational structures and the changes taking place in those structures in both the United States and Yugoslavia; second, the relationship of the changes in the environment to the changes in organizations is analyzed; third, personal needs as satisfied in both structures are discussed. In summary, then, this chapter presents an approach to organizational design which takes into account the needs of both the environment and the participants.

Organizational Structures

THE VERTICAL MODEL AT WORK

The vertical structure and its related organizational structures are found throughout the American industrial organization scene. The general structure is usually a pyramidal formation, with authority, power, and financial rewards increasing as the pyramid is ascended. Legislative and executive directives are formulated at higher levels in the pyramidal structure, and are received and carried out at its lower levels. Thus, major decisions, including those

234

concerned with tenure, hiring, firing, modernization, or relocation of the firm, as well as the power to veto such decisions, are made within certain constraints in the higher levels of the organization.

THE HORIZONTAL MODEL AT WORK

In terms of structure, the assumption upon which the Yugoslav organizational theory is built is that all the members of the organization have equal voice and authority in the determination of plans, rewards, and operations of the company.

Since the total membership has all the legislative authority, while executives have only the authority derived from their professional expertise or specifically assigned to them to implement these decisions; and since the general membership makes decisions on selection, tenure, and dismissal; and since the power of the veto is rendered to the general membership through the referendums, the Yugoslav self-management system qualifies as the horizontal edge of the spectrum of organizational structures.[6]

THE CHANGES IN THE ORGANIZATIONAL STRUCTURE

It has been specified throughout this work that the Yugoslav companies studied by the researcher have adapted their organizational structure to be more hierarchical (vertical) than originally conceived. The strengthening of the executive's function, "contractual management," the functions of the *Politikal Aktive* and the *Extended Collegium*, usurpation of power by executives by acceptance or sufferance, the idea of eliminating the Governing Boards and prolonging the mandate of the Workers' Councils (decrease rotation), and the pressures to emancipate executives from the bonds of self-management, to elevate their status—all may be cited as indicators of this trend.

---

6. For a more detailed discussion of democratic vs. hierarchical structures, see Katz and Kahn, p. 211.

On the other hand, the increase in the United States of profit sharing, participative management programs, which themselves became a fad, and writings supporting industrial democracy seems to indicate that the American hierarchical structure aims to be more permissive. Therefore, it would seem that, in terms of the continuum of structures, both ends of the spectrum are moving toward the middle. What are the environmental changes in both countries which may be affecting this movement?

Environmental Forces and Organizational Adaptation

THE YUGOSLAV ENVIRONMENT

Yugoslavia changed from a centrally planned to a highly regulated economic environment which, lately, has become more competitive. On the political level, the country seemed to move toward more pluralism than was true in its former structure of a tightly knit political elite ruling through a police force.[7]

This change had two main effects: (1) it increased the uncertainty within which a company had to operate, and (2) it altered the goal structure of a company: constraint goals were relaxed and deterministic goals were emphasized.[8] Uncertainty increased since the various alternatives for action in a competitive market increased. Goals became more deterministic since the sociopolitical decentralization allegedly relaxed the processes required for decision-making and allowed organizations to determine their own courses of action. As constraint goals were relaxed and profit maximization became the criterion of a company's survival, deterministic goals were emphasized to a greater degree.

---

7. See Chapter 2.
8. Deterministic goals are goals the company was set to achieve—"do" goals. Constraint goals are those the company decided not to violate—"do not do" goals.

ORGANIZATIONAL ADAPTATION IN YUGOSLAVIA

In hierarchical (vertical) organizations, the higher one ascends in the hierarchy, the greater the reward to the individual in terms of status, power, and financial remuneration. However, it is also true that the higher the level reached on the pyramid, the greater is the magnitude of uncertainty a decision-maker has to absorb. Thus, the hierarchical organization has the equilibrating quality of offering greater inducements in terms of rewards for greater contributions, i.e., larger rewards or stronger punishment for making decisions which have greater commitment and repercussions for the organization.

The self-management system does not have this quality. The differences in rewards do not necessarily represent differences in responsibility. Executives are not allocated significantly higher economic or social rewards. The economic rewards are limited because of egalitarian principles. Status allocation is limited because even though there are pressures to elevate the status of technocrats as mentioned before, the syndicalist stream of thought considers such a trend as a contra-revolutionary phenomenon. Those who formally are required to undertake responsibility, the members of the Workers' Council, are not paid for their membership in the Council, and their rotation does not facilitate the process of decision-making.

As long as the process of decision-making was not directly related to results, there was no need for responsibility to be contained effectively within the organization. Rather, the government at large undertook responsibility and handed down regulations. In a competitive situation, when someone had to account for results and take the lead in making certain decisions, group responsibility seemed to be inadequate since it was difficult to find out who was responsible for decisions.

An organization seeks to replace those of its parts which are not functioning well; however, group responsibility also can constrain such actions. Furthermore, group decisions are vulnerable to emotional factors, and thus are not always predictable, while organizations operating in a competitive environment need a level of predictability, or rationality, in their behavior in order for decisions to have a logical sequence. When an individual feels responsible for his decisions, they are more predictable since the values that affect them are relatively stable. In a leaderless group the decisions change their course as the power structure composing the group changes, and under these circumstances it is more difficult to predict the group's decisions. Predictability of decisions could be achieved in this group decision-making situation if there were a leader who felt responsible for decisions made. But in that case we would be back to our initial query: Why would anyone take responsibility in this situation without commensurate authority and adequate rewards? Moreover, in a competitive market, timing of decisions is crucial, whereas the ponderous development of consensus was time-consuming.

The comparative difficulty of identifying those individuals responsible for decisions, unpredictability of group decisions, lack of a mechanism for allocating higher rewards for gerater risk absorption, and time pressure to make faster decisions are some of the instances where the pure, democratic (horizontal) structure and the competitive environment seemed to conflict. Because of this conflict, pressure was exerted on self-management to become less participative and more hierarchical, although this does not imply development into a pure vertical structure (the American business organizational structure) as defined in this book.

THE AMERICAN ENVIRONMENT COMPARED TO YUGOSLAVIA AND ORGANIZATIONAL ADAPTATION

In analyzing the American environment, different developments may be noted. The economy is becoming more regulated. The comparatively clear goals of profit maximization as measured by financial results are becoming less clearly defined, since ambiguous components such as social responsibility and satisfaction of participants' psychological needs are becoming a part of the "bundle of corporate goals." There are pressures for participation in decision-making because the technology and the handling of information are becoming more complicated. The labor force is encompassing more white collar workers with accentuated personal growth needs. The educational level of the population has increased as well, thereby decreasing the educational gulf between the general membership and the managerial elite. In the United States, economic goals have been achieved by at least part of the society. Now the goal, perhaps, is not "a chicken in every pot," or "two cars in every garage," but *how* a person works, how he feels within an organization—is he involved in decision-making? What these decisions yield is important, but so is the method by which they were reached. It may be an outcome of the economic affluence of American society that economic needs are being satisfied and an escalation to higher needs is taking place.

Yugoslavia, on the other hand, has not achieved the desired level of economic affluence. For ideological reasons, the country first emphasized the process in organizations, putting social needs ahead of economic needs. However, once decentralization took place and a choice was given, it would seem that economic results took precedence over how these results were achieved, and pressure was put on the organization to decrease participation in the short run if increased efficiency would result.

Thus, in juxtaposing the changing environments of Yugoslavia and America, with all the dangers of oversimplifying the issues that are involved, it can be said that the changes in the American environment are leading to more emphasis on process, on participation, rather than on immediate economic results. The replacement of achievement by self-actualization is one illustration of this trend. In contrast, the decentralization policy in Yugoslavia, which thawed the constraints on *process*, offered a choice between *process* and *results*. The outcome was greater attention toward economic results rather than toward the social process by which results were achieved, possibly as a result of the fact that attention is given to process only after the results, relatively speaking, are satisfied. Then the process is brought to attention, and a better balance is achieved. Thus, in the United States, the trade-off is in favor of process since results were emphasized too much. In Yugoslavia, the attention is now on results because the process was both overemphasized and the desired economic results were not yet achieved. Furthermore, using the previous definitions, American environmental changes led to more emphasis on constraint goals as deterministic goals became more ambiguous, while Yugoslav decentralization led to more emphasis on deterministic goals as constraint goals were relaxed.

The increase in uncertainty in Yugoslavia and in the United States (in Yugoslavia resulting partly from decentralization, and in the United States partly from enlarged goal ambiguity) had different effects on organizational behavior. In Yugoslavia, the increase in uncertainty revealed the lack of a mechanism for adequate identification of individual responsibility; the realization of this introduced pressure on the organization to define authority allocation more discriminately. This, however, meant less group decision-making and more individual executive discretion, a factor which is strengthening the hierarchical authority structure.

In the United States, goal ambiguity leads to more participation, since, among other reasons, the existing hierarchical structure is too rigid to enable the handling of information and the securing of commitment for operations whose value could not be assessed so easily because of the goal ambiguity. Furthemore, participative management satisfies the psychological needs of the participants who attach less value to financial rewards *per se*.

How can a change in uncertainty lead on the one hand to a more vertical structure and on the other hand to a more horizontal structure? The answer to this question lies in understanding what a spectrum is—its edges meet in infinity. What one end has in extreme abundance, the other has in extreme shortage. While the horizontal structure is too nebulous, and thus needs more backbone structure to produce predictable output, the hierachical structure has too rigid a backbone; the latter needs more flexibility and less predictability, since what it has to achieve is not clear. Thus, organizational adaptation of both structures was necessary since neither end of the spectrum in its pure form was structured to handle uncertainty. This point needs further clarification since the increase in uncertainty in both environments originated differently.

In Yugoslavia, increased uncertainty resulted from an increase in the number of alternatives opened up by decentralization. In the United States, the increase in uncertainty is not caused by a greater number of alternatives, but primarily by goal ambiguity. In Yugoslavia, the ambiguity lies in the components of the constraints, while in the United States ambiguity lies in the objective function (the last is borrowed from linear programming).

There would seem to be justification in claming that an increase in uncertainty, because of a constraint ambiguity, reinforces a vertical structure, while an increase in uncertainty, because of goal ambiguity, reinforces a horizontal structure. It is the researcher's belief that ambiguity as to which alternative will yield best results requires more professional managerial knowledge than goal identification where judgment is the primary requirement. Thus, in Yugoslavia the managerial group is strentghened in order to identify the best alternative, while in the United States general participation is encouraged, since goal ambiguity requires higher commitment of the general membership for actions taken.[9]

As stated earlier, neither the vertical nor the horizontal structures, in their extreme forms, were designed on erroneous assumptions of a closed system. In their purest form, both structures are based on the assumption that goals are clearly identifiable and agreeable to all participants. Thus, the vertical structure designs departmentalization and fosters specialization to achieve the goal.

---

9. The author realizes that he is dealing with only one variable, goal ambiguity *per se,* and as an outcome of relatively saturated materialistic needs. It is dealt with in terms of its effects on organizational structures. Other important factors are not presented, since they are not significantly relevant in making comparisons with Yugoslavia.

In contrast, the horizontal structure also assumes known goals and, therefore, ignores the possibility of conflict which may make the horizontal system, with its required unanimous consensus, very ponderous and ineffective. Both the pure vertical and horizontal systems are extremely inflexible and, thus, are not designed to handle uncertainty, in which the main characteristic is change.

Conclusions

A horizontal structure may be more welcome in a company operating in an environment which imposes increasing goal ambiguity. In addition, the industry is regulated to the degree that the economic results achieved in the market and necessary for satisfying the company's level of anticipation are not highly affected by the efficiency of decision-making, i.e., the timeliness and the feasibility of identifying individuals accountable for various results. Furthermore, the horizontal structure will be welcome if the society and/or the organization concerned have arrived at some level of affluence (desired economic results, which enables the society or organization to turn its attention to process). Hence, the organization will be free from the pressures for immediate economic gratification to devote itself to activities which may yield postponed results, such as participation in decision-making. (It is assumed that, if participation and economic efficiency correlate, the process will occur within a time lag.[10])

The vertical structure may be desirable in a company which has clearer and more measurable goals, where the economy is less regulated compared to the previous case, and the company is pressed to meet economic results in order to survive. The ability to identify those responsible for results, as well as the timeliness

---

10. On participative management and productivity, and a comment on the time lag consumed in effecting changes in management systems, see Likert, p. 38.

of the process, is crucial for the company's success, since the organization must be able to replace promptly those parts which are not instrumental in achieving the desired immediate results. Economic results in this environment are crucial, because the society from which the organization draws its labor force seeks more affluence than it has, and economic growth in real terms is on the top of the list of society's priorities. Since economic results are the primary goal, shorter perspectives may be developed which discourage activities with a postponed result, such as participation of the total membership in decision-making.[11]

Organizational Structures and the Fulfillment of Individual Needs

The above discussion analyzed environmental pressures and organizational structures; this, however, is only half the answer. A pure hierarchical structure designed because of environmental forces, may be found to be disadvantageous because it may have an adverse effect on the behavior of its participants. It was stated above that a vertical structure will be more welcome in an environment where short-run economic results are desired and the process of achieving them is ignored. What effect such a structure has on its participants is important, since it was claimed at the outset of this chapter that an organization should meet not only environmental constraints but internal personal needs as well.

The following is a brief analysis of the effect extreme vertical organizations (with workers on production line) have on the fulfillment of individual needs. The researcher discusses his experience with the horizontal structure.

---

11. Note that the author constantly distinguishes between participation of the professional elite, which is necessary for economic efficiency in the short run, and participation of the general membership, which is not imperative for the achievement of economic results and has an educational, humanistic flavor.

THE VERTICAL STRUCTURE AND INDIVIDUAL NEEDS

The hierarchical organization with its unity of command, span of control, and emphasis on specialization generates incongruity with personal needs for growth, self-realization, involvement, etc. The point is that people possess complex needs; they desire that sense of "mastery" or "competence" in dealing with the working environment. When the organization thwarts the fulfillment of these needs, the worker often responds with dysfunctional behavior. Along this line of thought, Argyris stated, ". . . the more the rigidity, specialization, tight control, and directive leadership the worker experiences, the more he will tend to create antagonistic adaptive activities."[12] The incongruity between the vertical structure and individual needs is a well-known theory and thus does not need to be repeated in this book. (We refer the reader to Argyris' writings, for example.)

It is interesting to note that the horizontal structure imposes a set of constraints on individuals within the organization which are incongruous with a different set of personal needs. The following section presents this phenomenon by means of an analysis of the organizational constraints imposed on executives by the horizontal structure; of those executive needs which are being constrained and unfulfilled; and of those symptoms of dysfunctional behavior, observed by the researcher, which can point to the above-mentioned incongruity.

THE HORIZONTAL STRUCTURE AND INDIVIDUAL NEEDS

1. The Constraints of the Structure.[13]

a) In group decision-making by workers, risk-taking is not necessarily related to skill.

---

12. C. Argyris, *Integrating the Individual and the Organization* (New York: Wiley, 1964), p. 59.

13. It should be re-emphasized that we are dealing with a pure horizontal structure where self-management is being fully observed.

b) Long-range planning may be constrained because of the rotation of the decision-makers.

c) Executives are in a passive role—a staff position—but are expected to be responsible for the outcome of the decision they formally did not make.

d) Executives are not *formally* making tactical, strategic decisions. Such decisions are left to the governing bodies. Executives have to deal with routine operations.

e) Generally, there is no place for individual responsibility (unless specifically defined as a personal responsibility)—only group responsibility. What an executive is really responsible for is ambiguous.

f) Harder work on the part of the executive does not necessarily mean that the results achieved will be attributed to him, since the major part of his work is in convincing the group to accept a decision. Once the group is convinced, the decision may be considered their achievement rather than his.

g) Role ambiguity and group decision-making reinforce the difficulties of predicting behavior, since they postpone feedback and make this feedback somewhat ambiguous.

Are these constraints congruent with individual needs fulfillment?

2. Executive Needs.

This analysis concentrates only on the executives. The researcher, however, realizes that in dictatorial vertical organizations, management that is one level below the President is as alienated as the workers. And in an anarchistic horizontal organization, workers are as alienated as executives. This analysis, however, concentrates on executives' behavior which can be attributed to constraints imposed *specifically* by the horizontal organizational structure.

One assumption made here is that entrepreneurial needs are similar enough to executive needs to make the forthcoming conclusions valid. An additional and crucial assumption is that, for the purposes of the analysis, it is unimportant that the horizontal system was forced on the executives. The researcher claims that because of the incongruity between organizational structure and executive psychological needs, a pure horizontal structure will always be somewhat forced and never fully accepted voluntarily. (Except if a "New Man" is created, which is a matter of "religious" belief.)

According to McClelland, the executive has a need for "moderate risk-taking as a function of skill."[14] This implies a need to make important, not routine, decisions in the organization. At the same time, McClelland notes the executive need for individual responsibility.[15] The executive gains great satisfaction from initiating successful action,[16] as well as from creating and selecting the plan of action. Another executive need is related to the fact that executives ". . . appear to work harder only when . . . personal efforts will make a difference in the outcome."[17] McClelland also states that the executive performs better when given a concrete feedback on how well he is doing.[18] He states, too, that executives have a need to make long-range plans.[19]

Thus, while the entrepreneurial executive seeks individual responsibility and risk-taking, desires to make strategic, long-range decisions where his personal effort will make a difference in the outcome, and seeks rapid feedback on how well he is doing, he is being constrained by the self-management structure. Furthermore, even though he is forced into a staff position, he is still expected to create results and to be responsible for them. While a good staff person should have the ability to keep away from the center of attention, the good line executive in Yugoslavia has to manifest leadership traits in time of need which may put him in a focal, influential position. This position can be interpreted as power

---

14. D. McClelland, *The Achieving Society* (New York: Free Press, 1961), p. 207.
15. *Ibid.*
16. *Ibid.,* p. 230.
17. *Ibid.,* p. 226.
18. *Ibid.,* p. 231.
19. *Ibid.,* p. 237.

rather than mere influence, and power is condemned as an abuse of one's position.

The Yugoslav executive thus was required by the post-reform conditions and organizational structure to be unnoticed, yet able to lead. He was expected to be responsible voluntarily, yet he was not given any large differential in rewards as an inducement. A decision made by the Workers' Council did not necessarily represent the risk he was willing to absorb. He will lead the way to strategic decisions, but he was restrained legally and socially from forcing the decisions or making them himself. His personal efforts would make a difference in the outcome but only after the decision had filtered through numerous group decision-making processes until it was impossible to identify the executive with the outcome. He did not receive rapid feedback on how well he was doing, since what he was supposed to be doing or what results might be attributed to him was not clear.

Incongruity between personal needs and organizational demands leads to dysfunctional behavior which is analyzed in the following section.

Dysfunctional Behavior

Dysfunctional behavior in vertical organizations has been researched extensively.[20] Some of this research will be repeated here, since the dysfunctional behavior displayed by the executives in horizontal structures is similar although not identical.

BEHAVIORAL RESPONSES: VERTICAL STRUCTURES

According to Argyris, dysfunctional behavior may take many forms. An initial form is caused by a sense of conflict. It can be resolved if the worker is "to leave the conflict situation," which

---

20. Argyris, *Personality and Organization,* chap. IV, summarizes major findings.

he may do either physically or mentally. Physically, he may transfer or quit, or otherwise remove himself from the situation. Mentally, in order to leave the situation, the individual ". . . may decrease the psychological importance of one set of factors (the organization or the individual)."[21] This mode of adaptation enables the individual to decide that he is capable of working only in the present job situation, or he may decide that the job means very little to him. According to Argyris, the result of conflict, in terms of dysfunctional behavior, is "apathy, lack of interest, decreased involvement, and lessened loyalty toward the set of factors rejected."[22]

The conflict between organizational demands and workers' personal needs may also yield frustration for the worker. Of the many responses to frustrations, one of the most common is aggression which manifests itself variously as absenteeism, turnover, quota restrictions, rate setting, goldbricking, slowdown, stealing, cheating (on production records), causing waste, and making errors which reduce the quality of the work. Also, singularly or in combination, the individual may react by:

1. Regressing, i.e., becoming less mature and less efficient.

2. Giving up and leaving the situation.

3. Becoming aggressive and attacking what is frustrating him; developing a tendency to blame others.

4. Remaining frustrated by doing nothing. This choice leads to still more tensions.[23]

BEHAVIORAL RESPONSES: HORIZONTAL STRUCTURES

Unfortunately, there are no extensive research findings on the dysfunctional behavior that pure horizontal organizational constraints impose on executives. In the following statements, the researcher has utilized only his own observations.

---

21. *Ibid.,* p. 78.
22. *Ibid.*
23. *Ibid.*

One pattern of behavioral response is characterized by the individual's leaving the conflict situation either physically or mentally. In terms of a physical withdrawal, it is a known fact that many organizations in Yugoslavia find it difficult to locate candidates for executive positions.[24] As a consequence, some companies have been forced to operate without a top executive. Along the lines of adaptation by physical withdrawal was absenteeism. Participation in Workers' Council meetings was considered a necessary evil by many executives; consequently, they tried to avoid them. There was also a desire to quit, which was manifested by wishful waiting for retirement age. Those who do not physically leave the conflict situation display apathy toward the self-management system, and they abhor even discussing it. In such cases, the executives have decreased their personal involvement to a minimum.

Leaving the situation mentally if not physically was another observed phenomenon. Daydreaming was common behavior, though leaving the situation mentally was done in other ways as well. For instance, in one company, the Diretcor made loud phone calls during all sessions of the Governing Board, thereby obstructing the work of the Board; he also wrote letters, and seldom participated in the discussion. In another company, the Director came to the meetings to suggest topics for discussion, but then would leave once his presence had been noted.

The Finance Director of one company provides an illustration of dysfunctional behavior resulting from the prevention of personal executive action. He was always late to work and tried to avoid meetings. When he was finally forced to attend a meeting, he would make a sincere attempt to explain his suggestions. When his highly sophisticated financial arguments were not accepted because apparently they were not understood, his response to the frustration was to turn inward, or to converse with other executives, and then to lose interest in the discussion.

Responses to frustration created by the system also appeared

24. Many of the top executives the researcher interviewed confessed to him that if offered the position of a Director, they would not accept it.

as what Berelson and Steiner classify as "displaced aggression,"[25] typified by the individual's hitting the table, clapping his hands in anger, and generally being fidgety. This type of aggression was displayed also when executives repeated the same idea, same sentence, or same word several times at a meeting. And further, the frustration seemed to cause the individual to regress, to revert to less mature modes of coping with his frustration.

This conflict between executives' needs and the horizontal organization also caused some executives to act as if they had lost their self-confidence. Thus, when a worker questioned them on their suggestions, they would react by saying, "I really don't know; I have only suggested; just tell me what you want and I will carry it through." In addition, the tendency to blame others in times of business difficulty is not an unknown phenomenon in Yugoslav organizational behavior. For instance, in one compay, production quality fell for almost fifteen months, but discussions at the meetings still concentrated on blaming each other for the situation, rather than identifying and attacking the source of the problem.

The outcome of executive dysfunctional behavior was the creation of informal groups—"kitchen cabinets"—where decisions were made on which the Workers' Council was then asked to vote. As the workers would "get back at the system" by slowdowns in production in the hierarchical organizations, the frustrated Yugoslav executives seemed to get back at the system by not making the decisions which were within their authority, or by slowing down communications, not answering letters, confusing data, etc. The red tape that evolved from this behavior was a major crisis with which the Yugoslav system had to cope.

Thus, at both ends of the continuum—the *pure* vertical or horizontal structures—certain organizational demands placed upon member individuals conflict with their needs. The result, on both ends of the continuum, is dysfunctional behavior.[26]

25. B. Berelson and G. Steiner, *Human Behavior* (New York: Harcourt, Brace & World, 1964), p. 267.

26. One may wonder why horizontal (democratic) structures in their statewide

In comparing the two companies observed in this study, it can be noted that ABC was closer to the vertical end of the spectrum even though both it and XYZ were within the horizontal structure. Participants of the two companies behaved differently. While at XYZ, the researcher heard numerous complaints and observed much dysfunctional behavior among executives and little among workers (Chapter 6), in ABC, the situation was reversed. The reversal, however, was not of a magnitude to make ABC comparable to the pure vertical structure, since, even in ABC, executives displayed symptomatic dysfunctional behavior which can be attributed to the organizational constraint of a horizontal structure.

Balancing Individual Needs and Environmental Requirements

The first conclusion to be derived from the above analysis is that there is no linear relationship between need fulfillment and organizational structure, i.e., that the more horizontal a structure is, the more satisfied the individuals within it will be. There is a point of diminishing returns. Moving away from the extremely

---

political formations seemingly do not create the dysfunctional phenomena for executives which appear in the industrial democracy. The answer may be that in its statewide context, a democratic "organization," if a state can be called an "organization," is of a size that real authority by acceptance is meaningless. The ability of a citizen to affect executive activities is quite limited compared to an enterprise where 500 or 1,000 workers meet the director or foreman daily, and, thus, where there is role ambiguity. That is, within the organization, problems arise because individuals are in frequent contact with one another, but fulfill roles which are inconsistent in terms of their inherent power. On a statewide basis, on the other hand, because of the organizational distance between the executive and the subordinate, the rules of hierarchical organizations hold in terms of power structure, rather than the rules of democratic organizations as they have been defined here. However, we take the freedom to speculate that the large organizational size creates the information, communication, and credibility gaps that we discussed in Chapter 6. These gaps ignite the strikes in Yugoslavia and may possibly be one of the causes of the sit-ins in the United States.

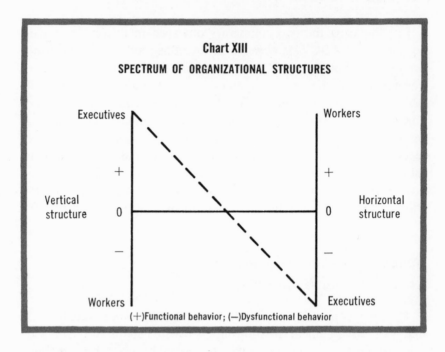

Chart XIII

SPECTRUM OF ORGANIZATIONAL STRUCTURES

(+)Functional behavior; (—)Dysfunctional behavior

vertical structure improves need fulfillment of workers up to a certain point. Then it becomes a constraint for the executives. Similarly, moving away from the extreme horizontal structure improves need fulfillment of executives, but after a certain point it begins to affect the workers adversely.

The extreme cases are not only disadvantageous in terms of need fulfillment but also in terms of satisfying environmental requirements. As shown above, both structures tend to move toward the middle of the spectrum, because neither is designed to handle uncertainty whether it is a result of constraint or goal ambiguity. Both extreme structures are based on closed system assumptions, which have been shown to be typical of the Yugoslav system and which are commonly known in the pure hierarchical structure.[27]

Therefore, one wonders where the region which is most condu-

27. See J. D. Thompson, *Organizations in Action* (New York: McGraw-Hill, 1967), pp. 5-6.

cive to economic efficiency and functional behavior of its participants is located on the continuum of organizational structures.
Below is an *approach* to a solution (the researcher does not pretend
to have found a solution).

Participative management theories, as promulgated by Likert and
Bennis, provide the shading between the two edges of the spectrum previously presented. These theories do not advocate the
pure horizontal structure. They maintain the vertical structure
while making it more permissive. They attempt to orient the
executive toward more participation rather than to change the
organizational structure and to request participation through a
formal allocation of legal authority as is done in the Yugoslav
system. On each hierarchical level of participative management,
Likert states, ". . . the superior is accountable for all decisions, for
their execution, and for their results."[28] Thus, Likert, like Bennis
and McGregor, never eliminated personal responsibility, a factor
necessary for a solution.

Another basic approach which can be fitted into the continuum
is the "mix" model presented by Chris Argyris. In *Integrating the
Individual and the Organization,* he describes what was also a
continuum of organizational structures. Derived from the mix
model, his conclusion is that, depending on the *type of decisions
needed,* organizations can employ the compatible structure.[29]
Therefore, better command of decision typology is necessary in
order to enable more participative organizational structures.

Bennis'[30] theory on a system of values is a necessary, although
not a sufficient, component of a solution, because, unlike Argyris'
theory, it does not elaborate which decisions should be dealt with
in a participative manner and which should not. Not allocating
authority for participation for different decisions may cause minute
as well as crucial decisions to be treated the same way, which may
not lead to efficient decision-making. However, an adequate system

---

28. Likert, p. 51. (Italics in original.)
29. Argyris, *Integrating the Individual and the Organization,* p. 211.
30. Bennis, p. 19.

of values is necessary, since its absence may make the participative structure impotent.

The researcher's contribution to organizational design, derived from this study, is to take into account also the factor of the absorption of uncertainty generated by the environment, and to allocate appropriate rewards for this absorption. In other words, environmental pressures have to be considered in order to design an authority structure which will buffer and respond to these pressures adequately. For that purpose, a system of rewards has to be designed which will make this absorption feasible. Therefore, in the model: Authority = Responsibility = Duties = Rewards, Authority is the legal right to make a decision; Responsibility is an obligation to absorb the uncertainty involved in making the decision which will lead to the achievement of the assigned Duty. In order for this process to take place, an appropriate Reward has to be allocated.

If this equation is maintained, and if decisions are well classified so that group responsibility can be distinguished from personal responsibility (depending on the type of decision to be made), and if management will be participation-oriented (if it wants to survive) and this orientation will be reinforced by a system of values that fosters openness and interaction, then the horizontal organizational structure, the desired medium range between the undesirable extremes or organizational structure, will be approached.

Conclusions

Taking into account the environment, we note that both horizontal and vertical structures in their pure form are inappropriate, since they are not designed for effective absorption of uncertainty and, thus, are based on the erroneous assumption of a closed system.

From the researcher's study of internal organizational behavior, it appears that the continuum of organizational structures, ranging from the vertical to the horizontal structure, has a circular and inverse effect upon organizational behavior. That is, the effect is circular in that dysfunctional behavior, which plagues the vertical structure, decreases in magnitude with increased worker participation in the decision-making process, but then reappears to plague the horizontal structure. The effect is inverse in that the dysfunctional behavior found in the vertical organization is displayed by the workers, while similar, though not identical, dysfunctional behavior in the horizontal organization is displayed by the executives.[31]

It is suggested that the dysfunctional behavior on either end of the spectrum stems from the fact that organizational demands which are rigid, constrictive, and beyond the control of the recipients tend to elicit dysfunctional behavior on the part of the recipients themselves. The vertically structured organization imposes rigidity and constrictiveness on the worker and the horizontally structured organization imposes both factors on the executive.

Thus, while an organizational structure may be designed functionally to meet environmental constraints, this structure may be rigid and dysfunctional to some of its participants. And conversely, if the structure is changed to fully meet individual needs, it may be inadequate to meet environmental requirements. The suggested approach to organizational design is one that enables sufficient flexibility in duty assignment, authority distribution, and allocated rewards, i.e., organizational structure, to meet both the changes in the environment and the psychological needs of its participants. The organization should allocate authority for uncertainty absorption and proportionate to this assignment, allocate rewards. Therefore, the "three-legged stool," where all legs must be equal in size, turns

---

31. This effect in itself is not surprising because the duality effect tends to appear when a phenomenon under study is pushed to the ends of a spectrum.

out to be a "four-legged stool": authority, duty, responsibility, *and* reward. All four components have to be well balanced in order to achieve an effectively operating organization.

To avoid the extremes of organizational structures, the use of Likert's approach—the participative and responsible manager—with Argyris' mix model approach for determining which decisions should be made participatively, together with Bennis' value system to make the structure operate with minimum coercion, is recommended.

Appendix A

Notes on Methodology

This appendix deals with the open systems approach utilized in this study—its limitations, the reasons behind it, and the factors kept constant in choosing the companies for the study—and elaborates on the process of collecting data, which was mentioned in Chapter 1.

The Approach and Its Limitations

The industrial organization was viewed in this book as an open system[1] whereby the interaction between the environmental changes affecting the industrial organization and the performance of the organization, which in turn affects various aspects of the environment itself, were analyzed.

As environmental forces change, new requirements are imposed on the micro-system, including organizational adaptation. The results originally anticipated are not longer satisfactory under the new conditions, and latent dysfunctional phenomena[2] emerge be-

---

1. For a discussion of the approach, see Katz and Kahn, chap. 2.
2. See R. K. Merton, *Social Theory and Social Structure*, rev. ed. (New York: Free Press, 1957).

cause the organization is not yet oriented to the new environment. The organization will achieve equilibrium through interacting with the environment. In this interaction the organizational structure changes: status shifts from one group to another, new organizational parts are added, some old ones are discarded, formal authority is reallocated, and in some cases organizational replenishment is effected whereby some persons are fired and others hired.

The performance of the organization and the process by which it achieves results affect the socio-economic political structure, in turn affecting the environment to change, and both the macro- and micro-systems finally approach an approximate state of equilibrium. A final equilibrium is never really achieved. This equilibrium can happen if no new inputs occur so that the interaction between subsystems can lead to the steady state, i.e., if at some point the source of turbulence stops functioning and no new changes occur that require adaptation. But no environment operates without changes in some of its facets at some point of time;

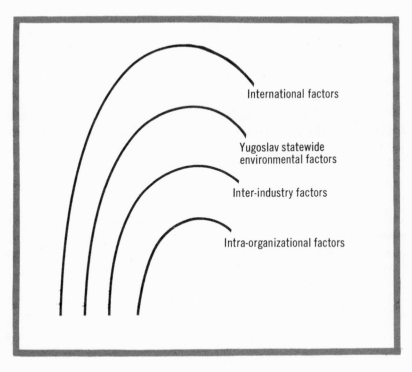

International factors

Yugoslav statewide environmental factors

Inter-industry factors

Intra-organizational factors

either technological, economic, or legal environment's constantly change. Thus, no analysis of an organization at a point of equilibrium can be made. Therefore, the organizations mentioned in this research were studied as they were, in a state of adaptation.

In explaining organizational adaptation to the changes occurring in the Yugoslav system, ideally the research would have to deal with all four layers and with the interaction among them as depicted in the illustration. This was beyond the scope of this study. Therefore, the research emphasized the first three layers, the inter- and intra-organizational behavior, and the changing environment.

This study mentioned the effect the international input had on the changes of the statewide environmental forces and, from there on, the effect of the industrial organization. This description discussed only a one-way effect since, within the scope of this study, the reciprocal influence, i.e., the Yugoslav development and its effect on the international scene, could not be discussed.[3]

Viewing an industrial organization as an open system which receives its input from the environment and strives through throughputs to meet environmental demands and among them legal constraints leads to the following consideration.

As the Yugoslav scene was, and still is, very dynamic, where the environment has been changing at a rather accelerated rate, the requirements imposed on the industrial organization necessitated constant change and readaptation. Since participative observations encompass only one small segment of the activities within the organizations and those between the organization and the various external pressures, this study may appear to have limited value for predictive purposes. However, on the basis of what is known to have happened, as well as from what seems to be the general trend of the Yugoslav economic and political conditions, we may speculate on the direction the process will take. This, however, remains a speculation because historical developments can hardly

---

3. One of them will be the spread of the Yugoslav self-management ideology to developing countries and the function that it serves as an epicenter to the decentralization process in the Communist bloc.

be used for predictions in countries undergoing such dynamic internal change and operating under political constraints which are for the most part unpredictable.

What was observed in the research is the *process* of adaptation. We were fortunate to have available such a dynamic environment, where in four months, change could be observed, the magnitude of which in other countries would have taken years of observation. We had the opportunity of observing the process, but the above-mentioned advantages of rapid change contained methodological limitations for making comparative studies. In order to make the most reliable comparative studies of organizations, we had to compare them at a point of relative equilibrium. This becomes almost impossible when the organizations are undergoing extremely turbulent change. To compare efficiency, or any measurement of output, and to identify its causes is meaningless. The organizations are not the same at any two close points in time, and the output measurements may be a result of the uncontrollable changes rather than of the causal factors which were measured.

Although comparative studies of dynamic organizations impose methodological difficulties, the comparative advantage offered to the researcher was the opportunity to compare the *differences* in organizational adaptations to environmental changes.

The study was complicated as mentioned above by the pendulum effect existent in Yugoslavia; no final equilibrium is really achieved, only a quasi-equilibrium where an adjustment in one direction is countered by movement in the opposite direction. By taking a "snapshot" of this system, a difficulty arose in identifying the direction of the pendulum: is it up (to centralization) or down (to decentralization)? The difficulty in predicting the movement of the pendulum was accentuated in this case because of the universality of the Yugoslav policies—decentralization on one organizational level should mean decentralization on all levels and vice versa. Decentralization of government regulations usually meant decentralization of company decision-making, etc. This universality in approach imposed difficulties because what is dysfunctional on one organizational level may be functional on another. Thus, there are different pendulums for different organizational levels. For instance, while decentralization of central government power seems to be welcomed and yields positive results,[4] forced decentralization on the enterprise level seems to be dysfunctional and to yield observable symptomatic industrial unrest.[5] Therefore, there may be pressure to continue decentralization on the macro-level with pressure to centralize on the micro-level. The ideology of self-management still makes this impossible because of the dogma of the withering away of the state—management and government and any other hierarchical power should be disappearing on all levels.[6] Having two different pressures without knowing where the major force will strike (the political body after Tito's death) makes predictions very speculative.

As it is an open system, the Yugoslav managerial system has an infinite number of ways of adapting itself to the environmental alterations. Thus, the equifinality[7] of the open system comes into play. Even though the system may seem to be very rigid through the very definite and detailed legislation as to the normative state of affairs of decision-making in Yugoslav enterprises, practice has shown that there are many alternative ways of adaptation.[8] Having a limited sample makes this study look inconclusive because of this infinity of practices of adaptation. This sample, however, does not claim to represent the whole array of ongoing

---

4. See S. Pejovich, *The Market Planned Economy of Yugoslavia* (Minneapolis: University of Minnesota Press, 1966).

5. See Chapters 4 to 7 above.

6. See Dušan Bilandzić, *Self-Government* (Belgrade: Medunarodna Politika, 1966), and Radosavljevic, *Samoupravljanje Sustina Pojam* (Belgrade: Rad, 1965).

7. Defined as the variety of ways in which a system achieves equilibrium. See Katz and Kahn, p. 25.

8. K. Kilibarda, in *Produktivnost,* Federal Institute of Productivity (Belgrade: February, 1966), p. 151, claims that the industrial system sometimes takes in reality the form of anarchy or dictatorship.

processes in all companies. Choosing two different companies with an independent variable enabled the researcher to identify certain processes of organizational behavior and to make some generalizations as to the process taking place in other companies where the same variables exist; in other words, this is an explorative study.

Factors Kept Constant in Choosing the "Black Boxes"

The following factors were kept constant: technology, size, geographic dispersion of plants, labor force's cultural basin, ratio of females to males on the labor force, markets, external economic governmental regulations, legal acts affecting the companies' age and organizational structure. The factor kept variable was the leadership style of the Director.

1. Technology:

Several studies, among which the most pre-eminent was Joan Woodward's,[9] indicate the close relationship among technology, the process of management, and the various output measurements. In order to make comparisons as to the process of decision-making, as well as its effectiveness, this variable had to be kept constant.

2. Size and Geographical Dispersion:

Both factors can affect the decision-making process through an intermediate variable, the pattern of communication, which is highly affected by size and the geographical distance between decision-makers. This variable was also controlled by choosing similar organizations.[10]

9. J. Woodward, *Industrial Organization, Theory and Practice* (London: Oxford University Press, 1965).
10. Katz and Kahn, p. 64.

3. Cultural Basin:

"Folkways," to use Katz and Kahn's terminology,[11] have an effect on participation in decision-making. This is especially crucial in a country like Yugoslavia where the multiplicity in national characteristics could have significantly biased the findings if the researcher had not chosen companies located in the same region and which drew their workers from almost identical villages.

4. Ratio of Female/Male Workers:

It was anticipated that an organization with a proportionately higher female labor force might have a different pattern of decision-making than one with a predominantly male labor force. The study deals with Yugoslavian management, where every member of the organization is supposed to participate in decision-making. Females, with homes to take care of, working as supplemental contributors to the family income, may be less involved in company endeavors than males who must support families. Males' interest will be higher, as the quality of their decision-making may affect the results of the company and, in turn, their wages. In order to avoid a bias in patterns of decision-making due to this difference, the ratio of female/male workers was kept constant.

5. Similar Markets:

Joan Woodward's[12] study indicates that market requirements lead to different decision-making patterns in organizations. The potential bias of this factor was nullified by having both the markets and, conceptually, the channels of distribution similar.

---

11. *Ibid.,* p. 65.
12. Woodward, chap. 8.

6. External Economic Policies and Corporation Laws:

These two factors are of importance in dealing with a mixed economy like that of Yugoslavia. Different government bonuses, subsidies, and interest rates could significantly affect the economic performance of the companies under study and also could shape the decision-making pattern of the companies. External laws, which deal with the manner in which organizations should be managed (structured), differ with size, industry, and in a minor manner with the republic. Both economic instruments and laws were neutralized by choosing companies similar in these respects.

7. Age of the Company:

Organizations have memories.[13] It could be anticipated that a new company which did not struggle through the changing Yugoslav environment will behave differently from one established before World War II which still remembers the way things were done during the capitalistic phase. "Organizational memories" are especially significant where companies have workers who have been there for thirty or forty years. The mobility of the labor force has been comparatively low and thus a company's age could be of significance in analyzing its organizational behavior. The effect different organizational memories might have on decision-making was nullified by choosing two companies of the same age.

8. Organizational Structure and the Composition of the Self-Managerial Bodies:

Organizational structure affects the pattern of communication and thus the decision-making process. The composition of the decision-making bodies is significant because with education, training, and job content, participation may differ.[14] Both factors were kept constant in this study.

---

13. Katz and Kahn, chap. 2.

14. Frank Reisman, "Workers' Attitude Towards Participation and Leadership," (Ph.D. thesis, unpublished, Columbia University, 1955).

Procedures for Collecting Data

The researcher arrived at the company with the workers at 6:00 A.M., when the working day started for the first shift, and usually stayed during the second shift which concluded at 10:00 P.M. He located himself in Company ABC in the legal department and in the planning-analytical department of Company XYZ.

There were several reasons for choosing these locations. Because of the highly complicated legal constraints imposed on the decision-making process in Yugoslavia, most decisions had to go through the legal department. In hiring, firing, and disciplining workers, and in following the self-management decisions, the legal department had concurrent authority to see that all decisions were made according to the law. Thus, an excellent observation of the process of decision-making could be achieved by being present there. The whole department, seven people, was in one small room, so there was no need to move from room to room to observe all the discussions.

The planning department is another crucial decision-making body in the organization, because of its connections with the "outside." The pressure of making adaptations between external needs and internal constraints lies with the planning department. By locating himself there, the researcher could witness all the frustrations and difficulties encountered in the numerous attempts of the planners to match needs with resources within the given political and internal organizational constraints.

The researcher had a desk in each place where he would join the officers of the department each morning. His "job" was to go through the minutes from the meetings of the various decision-making bodies, conducting a content analysis of what these groups had covered in their meetings. While conducting this analysis, he was able to witness all the activities going on around him and to record them inconspicuously so as not to affect the behavior of the observed.

The researcher alternated between the companies every ten to twelve days, in order to avoid overextending his presence to the

2 6 5

point of being a nuisance. These discontinuances did not prove to have any dysfunctional repercussions on the attitude of the observed toward the researcher. The absences did not regenerate doubts as to the purpose of his stay in the company; on the contrary, they generated a feeling of "being missed" and, thus, he was always welcomed back and could start "quizzing" everyone again.

There was no specific schedule or allocation of time. Usually, most of the time during one shift was spent in these departments making observations and analyzing the minutes. The researcher spent the rest of his time interviewing or visiting the production facilities to observe the workers on the job. Interviews were scheduled ahead of time but were unstructured in the sense that the researcher tried not to restrict the interviewed to specific topics but rather tried to give them freedom to elaborate on subjects they felt competent and willing to discuss. This lack of "narrowness" to the structure of the interview was designed to avoid an impression of interrogation. This approach generated a vast amount of data with emotional content in a rather disorganized framework, but the researcher found that following the patterns of emotional response had value for his attempts to understand the system at work.

Because of the character of production facilities, the noise of weaving mills, it was impossible to conduct any interviews in the shops. The workers seldom conversed while working because of this. The researcher, however, has had some firsthand observations of the interaction of workers on their job sites. He visited the shops about thirty times for half an hour at a time. These visits were made at random during all hours of the day and night, and no specific subject was followed in making the observations.

The researcher ate his meals with varied groups of people in an effort to avoid raising the image of a partisan management man or "spy" or "workers' man." During the meals, unsolicited interviews were conducted, which provided spontaneous data on the attitudes of rank and file workers toward operations and management process in the company. The manner of attire worn by individuals proved quite helpful to the researcher in directing and evaluating these discussions. The management (executive function and the *"Politikal Aktive"*) personnel were always in suits or sport jackets with ties, whereas the workers in ABC wore overalls and in XYZ they dressed in "street" clothes.

The researcher participated personally in all the meetings of both companies during these four months. Included were six Workers' Council meetings (two of which were emergency meetings), twenty meetings of the Executive Board, six meetiongs of the Councils of the Economic Units, ten meetings of the Disciplinary Committee, four meetings of the *"Politikal Aktive,"* four meetings of the *Extended Collegium,* two meetings of the Communist Party Cell, four meetings of the Trade Union, several election meetings, and six meetings of the *Collegium.* The meetings ranged from *one* to *eight hours each* in length. No meeting of any decision-making group, whether executive or governing, was missed, except for meetings of the *Collegium.* This was the only meeting to which he was not always admitted. The *Collegium* is the highest *executive body* in the organization, *implementing* decisions in the company, while the Workers' Council deals with *decision-making.* As it is difficult to make a rigid distinction between the decision-making function and the executive function, the *Collegium* may have ventured into decision-making not constitutionally permitted it. Exposing such a breach was undesirable, and they were naturally reluctant to let the researcher obtain firsthand observations which could incriminate them. The researcher obtained data about these meetings from interviews.

Researcher's Involvement

The practices of the anthropological approach of participative observation were followed except for the following alterations that the researcher felt were necessary in the circumstances. As already indicated, there was always the chance that the researcher could be asked to leave if the company decided that his presence was undesirable. This could have happened if he gave the impression of being a "spy," or if the company felt that he could incriminate certain individuals by his findings. In addition, the atmosphere was not very conducive to conducting such research because of the political reasons stated in Chapter 1.

In order to minimize the possibility of being asked to leave, a departure from the classical participative observation method of maintaining noninvolvement and remaining inconspicuous became necessary.

1. The researcher made all his notes in Serbo-Croatian and spread them on the table so that anyone could see them. To the best of his knowledge, no one ever looked into them.

2. The researcher engaged in private discussions on the subjects discussed by the organization and expressed his opinions whenever asked. He never volunteered to express them, but, if asked, he offered his best professional knowledge as well as the data that he had acquired in the company. In one case, the researcher was questioned on the company's decision to install a computer. When asked how he thought this would affect the company's self-management system, he gave his opinion which indicated the difficulties the system might encounter as a result of this change. To the best of his knowledge, his opinions were in no way crucial to any of the decisions made; thus, the disadvantage of being active in private discussions was minimal. The advantage was that the researcher was accepted as "one of the crowd." No exceptional efforts were made to conceal things from him. The researcher's overt criticism of certain facets of the self-management system, together with a defense of others, removed him from any disagreeable stereotype of dogmatism. Many times when a person in the organization came to the researcher to discuss politics, economics, etc., the discussion proved to be a useful, unsolicited interview.

During the meetings he attended, the researcher never spoke, nor was he asked to. He chose to sit in different places at each meeting so that he could not have been associated with any particular group. He always sat with someone he had become acquainted with, so that "inside information" as to what was "behind" the discussion could be gleaned. This "subjective interpretation" was used later as a springboard for future interviewing. Once the interviewed determined how much the researcher knew, they felt less inhibited in contributing more from their knowledge. Toward the end of his stay, the researcher was referred to as "the person who knows more than we do."

Minimizing the possibility of suspicion of his intentions in the company, becoming active and participative, expressing his candid opinions, offering his data for review and not concealing his findings—all contributed to the establishment of trust and resulted in eventually unlimited freedom to interview the companies and to stay as long as he wished. (As the 1967 Israeli war started, the researcher considered it prudent to leave Yugoslavia.)

Appendix B

Suggested Organizational Charts

The Yugoslav Institute of Productivity recommends presenting the self-management organizational structure in one chart, as shown on Chart XIV (this does not include the socio-political bodies). The elements of the chart are:

1. The whole organization, i.e., the collective.
2. The Workers' Council of the company.
3. The Governing Board of the company.
4. Committees and various other advisory groups of the Workers' Council.
5. Economic Units.
6. Governing bodies of the Economic Units.
7. The Economic Unit for organization and economics. This Economic Unit offers services and prepares the material for decision-making of the governing bodies and the executive bodies on company level and offers services of similar character to the Economic Units.
8. Governing body, Council of the Economic Unit for Organization and Economics.
9. The Director, the chief organizer of the company, and the *Collegium*.
10. Leaders of the Economic Units, i.e., foremen.
11. Direct interdependency between the Economic Units and Workers' Council of the company.

Chart XIV

**ORGANIZATIONAL CHART OF A COMPANY
WITH ECONOMIC UNITS WHICH ARE NOT
UNITED INTO PLANTS**

SOURCE: Problemi organizacije ekonomskih jedinica i unutrasnje
raspodele u. proizvodnim preduzecima (Belgrade: Jugoslovenski
Zavod za Produktivnost Rada, 1964), p. 110.

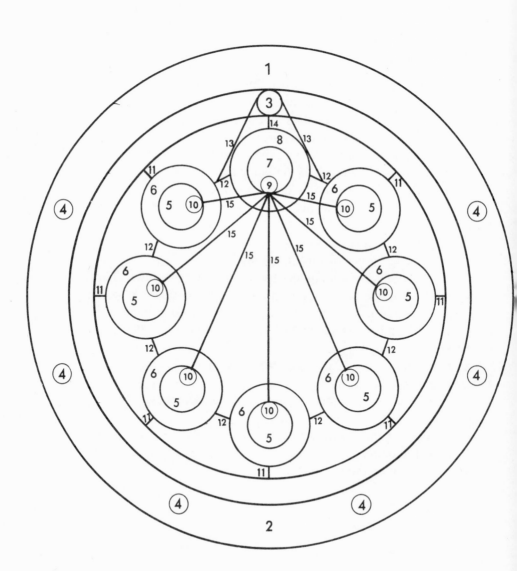

12. Economic and technological interdependency between the Economic Units.

13. The ties between the Economic Units and the Governing Board.

14. Direct connection between the Director, the Professional Collegium, and the Economic Unit for Administration with the Governing Board and the Workers' Council.

15. The ties between the Director, the *Collegium,* and the leaders, i.e., foremen of the Economic Units—and the Economic Units themselves.

A more startling organizational scheme arises when there is an organization containing several plants and independent Economic Units. The elements of this chart are:

1. The whole organization, i.e., the working collective.

2. The Workers' Council of the company.

3. Governing Board.

4. Committees and other consulting groups of the Workers' Council.

5. Plant.

6. Workers' Council of the Plant.

7. Economic Unit which does not belong to any plant.

8. Governing bodies of the Economic Unit.

9. Economic Unit for Economics and Organization.

10. Governing bodies of the Economic Unit for economics and organization.

11. The Director and the *Collegium.*

12. A group for organization and coordination of work in the plant (the Director of the plant belongs to this group).

13. The foremen of the Economic Units, i.e., the leaders.

14. The governing bodies of the Economic Unit in a plant.

15. Direct link between Economic Units and the Central Workers' Council.

16. Ties between the Workers' Council of the plant and the Central Workers' Council.

Chart XV

ORGANIZATIONAL CHART OF A COMPANY
WITH INDEPENDENT ECONOMIC UNITS
AND ECONOMIC UNITS WHICH ARE
UNITED INTO PLANTS

SOURCE: Problemi organizacije ekonomskih jedinica i unutrasnje
raspodele u proizvodnim preduzecima (Belgrade: Jugoslovenski
Zavod za Produktivnost Rada, 1964), p. 111.

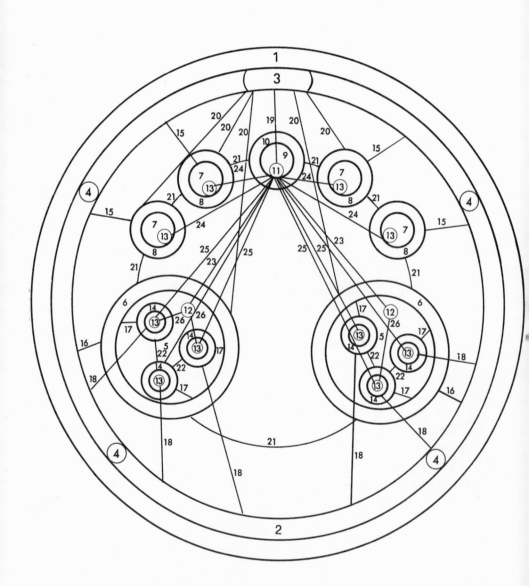

17. Ties between the Economic Unit in the plant with the Workers' Council of the plant.

18. Direct link between the Economic Unit in the plant and the Central Workers' Council.

19. Direct link between the Director, the *Collegium,* and the Economic Unit for organization and economics with the Governing Board and the Workers' Council.

20. Link between the Governing Board and the Workers' Council with the Economic Unit and the plants.

21. Economic and technological linkage between the Economic Units and the plants.

22. The economic and technological interrelationship between the Economic Units in the plants.

23. The link between the Director and the *Collegium* with the leaders, i.e., Directors of each plant, and the unit for organization and coordination of the plants.

24. The link between the Director and the *Collegium* with the leaders of the Economic Units, i.e., the foremen of each Unit.

25. The ties between the Director and the *Collegium* with the leaders, i.e., the foremen of the Economic Units which are within each plant.

26. The ties (links) between the leaders of the plants and the group for Organization and Economics of the plant.

In the organizational chart of the smallest organizational entity, the Economic Unit has the following elements:

1. This line symbolizes the boundary lines which isolate the Economic Unit from other Economic Units as a technological, economic, and social unit.

2. The governing bodies of the Economic Unit. This is usually the assembly of all the workers of the Economic Unit, the *Zbor.*

3. Governing Board of the Economic Units, which is usually the Workers' Council of the Economic Unit. In addition to this governing body, the convention, the *Zbor* of the whole Economic

Chart XVI

ORGANIZATIONAL CHART OF AN ECONOMIC UNIT

Note: No one can tell from any of these charts who is in charge
of whom. Furthermore, no one can identify who is responsible for what. The charts represent the "wholeness" and
equality of the Yugoslav company. SOURCE: Problemi
organizacije ekonomskih jedinica i unutrasnje raspodele u
proizvodnim preduzecima (Belgrade: Jugoslovenski Zavod za
Produktivnost Rada, 1964), p. 112.

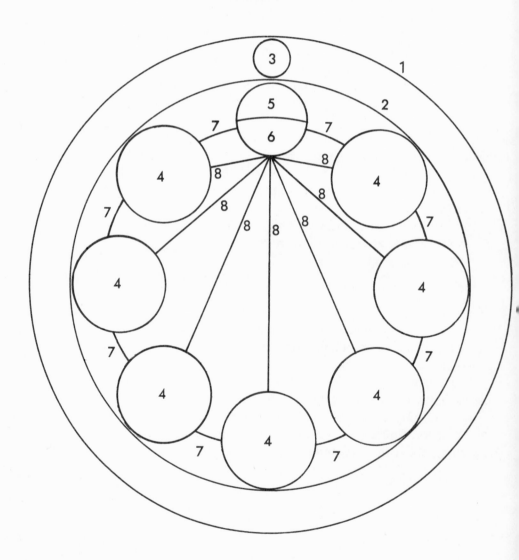

Unit, can decide and establish other committees and groups for decision-making in the Economic Unit.

4. Working places, which can be either different jobs or different groups of workers which perform certain technological processes.

5. The group for organization and coordination of the Economic Unit.

6. The leader, i.e., the organizer of work of the Economic Unit; according to our terminology, it will be the foreman.

7. The technological and economic interrelationships between the working places or working groups.

8. The links between the leader, i.e., the foreman and the Economic Unit for organization and coordination with the working places and working groups.

Bibliography

Public Documents

Belgrade. *Decree to Promulgate a Basic Act Representing Employment Relationship.* (Translated by the International Labor Office, Geneva.) Službeni List, No. 17, April 7, 1965.

Belgrade. *Osnovni Zakon o Poduzećima.* Službeni List. S.F.R.J., 1965.

Skupština Grada Beograda. *Statistički Godišnjak Beograda.* Savezni Zavod za Statistiku, May, 1965.

Books

Aktuelni Problemi Borbe Saveza Komunista Jugoslavije za Sprovodenje Reforme. Belgrade: Komunist, 1966.

Argyris, C. *Personality and Organization.* New York: Harper & Row, 1957.

————. *Integrating the Individual and the Organization.* New York: Wiley, 1967.

Bennis, W. *Changing Organizations.* New York: McGraw-Hill, 1968.

Berelson, B., and Steiner, G. *Human Behavior.* New York: Harcourt, Brace & World, 1964.

Bilandžić, D. *Social Self-Government.* Belgrade: Medunarodna Politika, 1965.

Braut, R., Jaeger, A., and Novak, M. *Priručnik o Organizaciji Poduzeća.* Zagreb: Informator, 1966.

Carzo, R., and Yanouzas, J. *Formal Organization, A Systems Approach.* Homewood, Ill.: Richard D. Irwin and Dorsey Press, 1967.

Drutter, I., and Novak, M. *Poduzeće u Reformi.* Zagreb: Informator, 1968.

Džeba, K., and Beslać, M. *Privredna Reforma.* Zagreb: Stvarnost, 1965.

Etzioni, A. *Modern Organizations.* Englewood Cliffs, N.J.: Prentice-Hall, 1967.

Katz, D., and Kahn, R. *The Social Psychology of Organizations.* New York: Wiley, 1967.

Kolaja, J. *Workers' Councils, The Yugoslav Experience.* London: Tavistock Publications. 1964.

279

Kolaja, J. *A Polish Factory, A Case Study of Workers' Participation in Decision-Making.* Lexington: University of Kentucky Press, 1960.

Kratina, H. I. *Položaj Direktora U Sistemu Samoupravljanja.* Belgrade: Institut Društvenih Nauka, 1965.

Likert, R. *The Human Organization.* New York: McGraw-Hill, 1967.

Lukić, R. *Društvena Svojina i Samoupravljanje.* Belgrade: Savremena Skola, 1964.

Madge, J. *The Tools of Social Science.* Garden City, N.Y.: Doubleday, 1965.

March, J., and Simon, H. *Organizations.* New York: Wiley, 1958.

McClelland, D. *The Achieving Society.* New York: Free Press, 1961.

Merton, R. K. *Social Theory and Social Structure.* New York: Free Press, 1957.

Metodologija Korišćenja Jedinstvenih Pokazatelja i Uporedivanja Poslovnih Rezultata Privrednih Organizacija. Belgrade: Jugoslovenski Zavod za Produktivnost Rada, Privredni Pregled, 1963.

Newman, W., Summer, C., and Warren, K. *The Process of Management.* Englewood Cliffs, N.J.: Prentice-Hall, 1967.

Novak, M. *Organizacija Poduzeća u Socializmu.* Zagreb: Informator, 1967.

Parkinson, C. N. *Parkinson's Law.* Boston: Houghton Mifflin Co., 1957.

Pejović, S. *The Market Planned Economy of Jugoslavia.* Minneapolis: University of Minnesota Press, 1966.

Perović, M. *Društveno Uredjenje SFRJ.* Belgrade: Zavod Udžbenika SRS, 1964.

Poduzeće u Reformi. Zagreb: Informator, 1968. "Samoupravno Poduzeće i Privredna Reforma," by Drago Gorupić; "Privredna Organizacija u Novim Uvjetima Privredivanja," by Mijo Novak; "Sistem Cijena i Tržisnih Odnosa," by Isak Drutter.

Problemi Organizacija Ekonomskih Jedinica i Unutrašnje Raspodele u Proizvodnim Preduzećima. Belgrade: Jugoslovenski Zavod za Produktivnost Rada, 1964.

Radosavljević, M. *Samoupravljanje-Suština-Pojam.* Belgrade: Rad, 1965.

Sturmthal, A. *Workers' Councils,* Cambridge, Mass.: Harvard University Press, 1964.

Tannenbaum, R., Weschler, I., and Massarik, F. *Leadership and Organization: A Behavioral Science Approach.* New York: McGraw-Hill, 1961.

Thompson, J. *Organizations in Action.* New York: McGraw-Hill, 1967.

Woodward, J. *Industrial Organization Theory and Practice.* London: Oxford University Press, 1965.

Zeković, V., and Novaković, S. *Ekonomika Jugoslavije.* Belgrade: Rad, 1964.

Živkov, T. *The New Systems of Economic Management.* Sofia: Foreign Languages Press, 1966.

————. *Ninth Congress of the Bulgarian Communist Party Report and Concluding Speech.* Sofia: Foreign Languages Press, 1967.

Articles and Periodicals

"Central Planning in a Guided Market Model." *Acta Oeconomica Academiae Scientiarum Hungaricae,* 1, 1966.

"Czechs Welcome Signs of Break With Past." *Christian Science Monitor,* February 5, 1968.

Economist (London), January 6, 1968.

Gamarnikow, M. "Another Step Toward Private Enterprise." *East Europe,* 17, January, 1968, pp. 2-9.

_____. "The End of the Party Hack?" *East Europe,* 14, November, 1965, pp. 3-8.

_____. "The New Role of Private Enterprise," *East Europe,* 16, August, 1967, pp. 2-9.

_____. "New Tasks for Trade Unions." *East Europe,* 16, April, 1967, pp. 18-26.

Jukić, I. "Tito's Last Battle," *East Europe,* 16, April, 1967, pp. 2-11.

Kavčić, B. "O Protestnim Obustavama Rada," *Gledista* (Belgrade), February, 1966.

Kilibarda, K. [Title not available.] *Produktivnost* (Belgrade), February, 1966.

"Ko i Zašto Napušta SKJ." *Nin,* April 7, 1968.

"Legal Status of Enterprises in Hungary's New Economic Mechanism Defined." *Figgelo* (Budapest), May 24, 1967.

"New Leaf, Hungary Ushers in Profit Basis." *Christian Science Monitor,* January 2, 1968.

"Pebble in Water, Freedom in Yugoslavia Makes Waves for East Bloc." *Christian Science Monitor,* November 18, 1967.

Politika Express. March 31, 1967.

"Profit Plan." *Christian Science Monitor,* February 2, 1968.

"Rumania Decentralizes." *Christian Science Monitor,* January 20, 1968.

"Rumania Promises Consumer Gains." *Christian Science Monitor,* January 10, 1968.

Stanković, S. "Yugoslavia's Critical Year." *East Europe,* 16, April, 1967, pp. 12-17.

"Stymied Soviets." *The Wall Street Journal,* December 27, 1967.

Triska, J. F. "The Party Apparatchiks at Bay." *East Europe,* 16, December, 1967, pp. 2-8.

Reports

Richman, B. *Empirical Testing of a Comparative and International Management Research Model.* From the Proceedings of the 27th Annual Meeting of the Academy of Management. December 27-29, 1967.

Trist, E. *Urban North America, The Challenge of the Next Thirty Years: A Social Psychological Viewpoint,* Keynote Address to the Annual Meeting and Conference of the Town Planning Institute of Canada, Minaki, Ontario: June 26-28, 1968.

Sindjić, M. M. "Sistem Informacija i Privredno Upravljanje." *Referat Sa I Savetovanja o Složenim Sistemima u Privredi*: Belgrade, 1966.

Tekariv an Muhemet El—Wafd El Arabi Fi Zeyara—tehy Li Yugoslavija. Reports on the Mission of the Arab Delegation on its visit to Yugoslavia. Ministry of

Planning, Permanent Secretariat of the two Permanent Committees for Technical Staff and Manpowers. Cairo, Egypt: 1966.

Unpublished Material

Adizes, I. "The Effect of Decentralization on Organizational Behavior, An Exploratory Study of the Yugoslav Self-Management System." Ph.D. dissertation, Columbia University, 1968.

"Aktuelni Razgovori." TV, Belgrade. February, 1967.

Drašković, Petrović, Subotić, "Funkcije Statuta u Privrednim Organizacijama Yugoslavije." Unpublished study, School of Law, University of Belgrade, 1965.

Reisman, F. "Workers' Attitude Towards Participation and Leadership." Unpublished Ph.D. thesis, Columbia University, 1955.

Supplementary Bibliography

Books

Cerić, Z. *Samoupravljanje i Pravni Propisi: Položaj Pogonskih, Poslovnih i Ekonomskih Jedinica Privrednih Organizacija Prema Vazećim Propisima.* Belgrade: Centar za Radničko Samoupravljanje, 1963.

Desić, V. *Metode Naučne Organizacije Rada.* Belgrade: Naučna Knjiga, 1966.

Direktor u Samoupravnim Odnosima. Zagreb: Informator, 1967. "Analiza Distribucije Osobnih Dohodaka Direktora," by Elvira Vulić; "Analiza Reizbornosti Direktora," by Jovo Brekić; "Director Ismedu Tehnologije i Društvenih Odnosa," by Duško Vojvodić; "Direktor i Suvremeni Metodi Upravljanja Procesima," by Miloš Sindić; "Funkcija Direktora s Obzirom na Tržiste i Cjene," by Marijan Korošić; "Integracija i Funkcija Direktora," by Dražen Kalodera; "Motivacioni Aspekti Regrutiranja Stručnjaka za Funkciju Direktora Radnih Organizacija," by Josip Županov; "Nosioci Stručno-Rukovodećih Funkcija i Društveno-Političke Organizacije u Poduzećima," by Ivan Perić; "Ocjenjivanje Uspešnosti Direktora," by Jovo Brekić; "Odnosi Izmedu Radničkog Savjeta i Direktora u Poduzeću," by Duško Bilandzić; "Odraz Ekonomske Politke na Funkciju Direktora," by Ante Lešaja; "Organizacioni Aspekti Funkcije i Uloge Direktora u Samoupravnim Odnosima," by Jovo Brekić; "Pravna Odgovornost Direktora i Rukovodilaca Sektora Poduzeća," by Husein Kratina; "Procjena Profila Direktora Snimanjem Strukture Radnog Vremena," by Božo Jušić; "Razvoj Rukovodenja i njegove Relacije u Samoupravljanju," by Josip Anić; "Sociološki Aspekt Odgovornosti Rukovodilaca," by Veljko Rus; "Socijalno-

Ekonomske Determinante Položaja i Uloge Direktora Radnih Organizacija," by Zoran Vidaković; "Tendencije u Razvoju Radničkog Samoupravljanja U Jugoslaviji," by Drago Gorupić.

Djordević, J. *Socijalizam i Demokratija*. Belgrade: Saremena Administracija, 1962.

Dordević, M. *Problem Formiranja i Raspodele Dohortka na Nivou Ekonomskih Jedinica u Preduzeću*. Belgrade: Centar za Strućno Osposobljavanje Rukovodećih Kadrova u Privredi, 1966.

Džinić, F. *Samoupravljanje u Oblasti Zajedničke Potrošnje*. Belgrade: Institut Društvenih Nauka, 1964.

Hadžistević, V., Kratina, H., and Džinić, F. *Tendencije i Praksa Neposrednog Upravljanja Radnika u Ekonomskim Jedinicama*. Belgrade: Institut Društvenih Nauka i Visoka Skola Političkih Nauka, 1963.

Jaeger, A. *Problemi Rukovodjenja u Privrednim Preduzećima*. Zagreb: Informator, 1961.

Jovanović, A. *Komercijalno Poslovanje Preduzeća*. Belgrade: Savremena Administracija, 1967.

Kilibarda, K. *Samoupravljanje i Savez Komunista*. Belgrade: Sociološki Institut, 1966.

Knežević, F. (ed.). *Priručnik o Organizaciji Poduzeća*. Zagreb: Novinsko-Izdavački-Stamparski Zavod, 1966.

Kostić, Ž. *Osnovi Organizacije Preduzeca*. Belgrade: Savremena Administracija, 1966.

Kostić, Ž., and Kukoleća, S. *Raspodela Dohotka u Preduzeću*. Zagreb: Novinsko-Izdavački-Štamparski i Birotehnićki Zavod, 1967.

Kratina, H. *Proces Donošenja Pravilnika Preduzeća*. Belgrade: Institut Društvenih Nauka, 1963.

Kukoleća, S. *Osnove Ekonomije i Organizacije Preduzeća*. Zagreb: Informator, 1962.

Laković, M., Tomić, T., and Bujić, S. *Priručnik za Primenu Osnovnog Zakona o Radnim Odnosima*. Belgrade: Izdavačko-Stamparsko Preduzeće, Savremena Administracija, 1967.

Marjanović, S. *Analiza Donošenja Odluka*. Belgrade: Centar za Stručno Osposobljanajne Rukovodećih Kadrova u Privredi, 1963.

————. *Organizacija i Poslovanje Industrijskih Preduzeća*. Belgrade: Savremena Administracija, 1966.

Matić, S. Paček, M., and Bosanac, G. *Aktivnost Radnih Ljudi u Samoupravljanju Radnom Organizacijom*. Jedan pokušaj istraživanja na području komune Varaždin. Zagreb: Institut za Društveno Upravljanje, 1962.

Matović, J. *Raspodela Dohotka i Organizacija Ekonomskih Jedinica u Preduzećima Unutrasnje i Spoljne Trgovine*. Belgrade: Savremena Administracija, 1966.

Sirotković, J. *Planiranje u Sistemu Samoupravljanja*. Zagreb: Novinsko-Izdavački-Stamparski i Birotechnićki Zavod, 1966.

Stojanović, P. *Industry: Worker Management in Practice*. Belgrade: Export Press (no year).

Tanič, Ž. *Društveni Procesi, Odnosi i Strukture u Industrijskoj Organizaciji.* Belgrade: Institut Društvenih Nauka, 1966.
Tanić, Ž. (ed) *Redničko Samoupravljanje: Razvoj i Problemi 1950-1960.* Belgrade: Institut Društvenih Nauka, 1963.

Articles and Periodicals

Adizes, I. "Odnosi Izmedu Organa Samoupravljanja i Organa Rukovodenja." *Gledista,* 4, April, 1969, pp. 535-550.
Adizes, I., and Županov, J. "A Discussion on: 'Odnosi Izmedu Organa Samoupravljanja i Organa Rukovodenja.'" *Gledišta,* 5, May, 1969, pp. 804-810.
Balog, N. "Bitne Promene Osnovnog Zakona o Preduzećima." *Savremena Praksa,* 203, December 2, 1968, p. 1.
Bezdanov, S. "Društvena i Privredna Reforma Zahtevaju Afirmaciju Stručnosti." *Gledišta,* April, 1967, p. 507.
Bijalić, S. "Aktuelna Pitanja Samoupravljanja i Reforme." *Naše Teme,* April, 1968, p. 548.
Bilandžić, D. "Pretpostavke Daljeg Razvitka Radničkog Samoupravljanja," *Gledišta,* 3, March, 1965, p. 325.
————. "Problemi Materijalne Osnove Samoupravljanja u Radnim Organizacijama." *Socijalizam. Časopis Saveza Komunista Jugoslavije.* VII, 3 (Belgrade), 1964, pp. 332-352.
————. "Problemi Samoupravljanja Danas." *Naše Teme,* 5, May, 1968, pp. 714-723.
Bolčić, S. "Direktor u Samoupravnim Osnosima," *Gledišta,* 1, January, 1968, pp. 102-111.
Dordan, Š. "Reformu Provesti Bez Kompromisa." *Naše Teme,* 5, May, 1968, pp. 765-773.
Dragičević, A. "Tko i Što Ugrožava Privrednu i Društvenu Reformu." *Naše Teme,* 5, May, 1968, pp. 795-801.
Fazlibegović, A. "Principi Organizacije i Oblici Unutrašnih Jedinica u Preduzeću." *Ekonomika Preduzeća,* 10, October, 1967, p. 649.
Fiamengo, A. "Informisanost Proizvodjaća o Radu Organa Samoupravljanja." *Pregled,* XVI (LIV), I, 4 (Sarajevo), 1964, pp. 325-348.
Gamarnikow, M. "Can They Decentralize?" *East Europe,* 15, July, 1966, pp. 16-23.
————. "The Costs of Reform." *East Europe,* 15, August, 1966, pp. 15-21.
————. "Political Patterns and Economic Reforms." *Problems of Communism,* 18, March-April, 1969, pp. 11-23.
————. "The Reforms." *East Europe,* 15, January, 1966, pp. 13-23.
Gorupić, D. "Donošenje Odluke i Poslovna Politika Preduzeća." *Izobrazba Rukovodilaca.* (Zagreb), VII, 2, 1962.

Hostanski, R. "Uskladivanje Organizacije Preduzeća Sa Novim Propisima." *Savremena Praksa,* 219, March 24, 1969, p. 6.

Ibrahimagić, O. "O Nekim Pitanjima Metoda Rada Organa Radničkog Samoupravljanja, Donošenja i Izvršavanja Odluka." *Narodna Uprava,* XIII, 9-10 (Sarajevo), 1962, pp. 392-394.

Ivošević, Z. "Imenovanje Vršioca Dužnosti Direktora Radne Organizacije." *Savremena Praksa,* 231, June 16, 1969, p. 3.

Jerovšek, J. "Zašto Visokokvalifikovan Kadrov ne Kaže Direktorskim Položajima." *Sociolosko Istraživanje Komune,* 5 (Belgrade), November, 1964.

Jončić, M. "Radni i Drugi Odnosi u Organima Uprave." *Savremena Praksa,* 207, December 30, 1968, p. 2.

Jovanov, N. "Neka Opšta Pitanja Protestnih Obustava Rada." *Gledišta,* February, 1967, p. 187.

Kamušić, M., "Učešće Proizvodjaća u Upravljanju Preduzećem." *Produktivnost,* IV, 6 (Belgrade), 1962, pp. 367-374.

Kilibarda, K. "Neke Pojave Nesklada u Odnosima u Radnim Organizacijama." *Socijalizam,* VII, 6 (Belgrade), 1964, pp. 849-854.

_____. "Odnos Radnih Ljudi Prema Samoupravljanju u Radnoj Organizaciji i Komuni." *Komuna,* XI, 8 (Belgrade), 1964, pp. 14-17.

Kostić, M. "Raspodjela i Samoupravni Odnosi u Ekonomskim Jedinicama." *Ekonomska Jedinica,* 2, February, 1968, p. 2088.

Kraiger, S. "Aktuelni Problemi Razvoja Samoupravnih Odnosa." *Gledišta,* May, 1967, p. 661.

Marković, D., Mimica, M., and Ristović, L. "Fabrike Radnicima." *Privredni Pregled,* 1964.

Nikolić, T. "Predlog Koncepcije Organizacije Planiranja u Preduzeću." *Planiranje i Analiza Poslovanja,* 1, 1968, p. 9.

Pokorni-Salabov, V. "Neki Psiho-Sociološki Problemi u Procesu Decentralizacije Radničkog Samoupravljanja." *Produktivnost,* VI, 4 (Belgrade), 1964, pp. 277-283.

Popović, M. "Uoći Primene Principa Reizbornosti Direktora." *Gledišta,* January, 1966, p. 98.

Radosavljević, M. "Iskustva iz Prakse Neposrednog Samoupravljanja u Radnim Jedinicama." *Socializam,* VII, 3 (Belgrade), 1964, p. 381-393.

R. Lj. "Neka Pitanja Imenovanja Direktora." *Savremena Praksa,* 225, May 5, 1969, p. 1.

Sekulović, A. "Kako Ostvariti Delegatski Odnos Izmedu Članova Organa Upravljanja i Radne Zajednice." *Savremena Praksa,* 211, January 27, 1969.

Škrbić, M. "Dezintegracija Radničke Klase—Uzrok Neuspjeha u Provodenju Reforme." *Naše Teme,* (May, 1968), p. 795.

Škrbić, S. "Osnovni Zadatci Planiranja u Uslovima Neposrednog Samoupravljanja u Poduzećima." *Ekonomika Preduzeča,* 9, September, 1967, p. 599.

Stankov, J. "Analiza Efikasnosti Organizacije Rada." *Ekonomska Jedinica,* 2, February, 1968, pp. 5068-5078.

Starčević, D. "Prilog Problemu Daljeg Razvitka Neposrednog Samoupravljanja." *Ekonomika Preduzeća*, 9, September, 1967, p. 607.

Subotić, N. "Normativni Akti Privrednih Organizacija." *Organizacija Rada* (Belgrade), XIV, 2, 1964, pp. 379-382.

Šuvar, S. "Ne Odgadati Otvorenu i Odlučnu Bitku za Samoupravljanje," *Naše Teme*, 5, May, 1968, pp. 756-764.

Vasović, V. "Izborni Sistem u Uslovima Samoupravljanja." *Gledišta*, December, 1966, p. 1534.

Vidaković, Z. "Odnos Programa Reforme i Opčeg Komunističkog Programa." *Naše Teme*, 5, May, 1968, pp. 724-747.

————. "Dva Prilaza Protestnim Obustavama Rada." *Gledišta*, 1, January, 1968, pp. 29-45.

Vojinović, J. "Usklađivanje Statuta Sa Novim Propisima." *Savremena Praksa*, 219, March 24, 1969, p. 7.

Vukadinović, V. "Koja Pitanja Treba Regulisati Statutima i Drugim Opštim Aktima." *Savremena Praksa*, 209, January, 1969.

Z. I. [Proper name not available.] "Direktor Kao Zakonski Zastupnik Radne Organizacije." *Savremena Praksa*, 203, December, 1968, p. 3.

Županov, J., and Marjanović, I. "Problemi Autonomije Ekonomskih Jedinica." *Organizacija Rada*, XII, 11 (Belgrade), 1962, pp. 250-254.

Županov, J. "Radni Kolektiv i Ekonomska Jedinica U Svijetlu Organizacione Teorije." *Ekonomski Pregled*, XIII, 2-3 (Zagreb), 1962, pp. 143-167.

————. "Strukturalne Reforme Poduzeća." *Naše Teme*, VIII, 3 (Zagreb), 1964, pp. 319-338.

————. "Poduzeće i Asocijacija—Stvarna i Iluzorna Dilema." *Sociologija*, 3-4, 1967.

————. "Tri Pristupa Samoupravnoj Organizaciji." *Gledišta*, 2, 1965, p. 165.

Reports

Institut za Organizaciju Rada i Automatizaciju Poslovanja. *Savetovanje o Raspodeli Dohotka na Nivou Pojedinaca na Bazi Individualne Proizvodnosti Rada.* Belgrade, 1966.

Komisija za Družbeno Samoupravljanje. *Delovna Razmerja v Statutih in Pravnih o Delovnih Razmerjih.* Report of the Komisija za Družbeno Samoupravljanje pri RS ZSS. Ljubljana: May, 1967.

Radosavljević, M. *O Nekim Pitanjima Samoupravljanja U Radnim Jedinicama Preduzeća.* Belgrade: Centar za Radničko Samoupravljanje Republičkog Veća SSJ za Srbiju, 1964.

Zagrebaćko Sveučilište. *Obračun i Raspodjela Dohotka i Osobnih Dohodaka u Radnim Jedinicama Poduzeća.* Simpozij Visoke Privredne Skole Sveučilišta. Vols. I, II, III. Opatija: March, 1967.

Unpublished Material

Kavčić, B., and Polak, F. "Zaključno Poroćilo o Reelekiji Direktorjev v SR Sloveniji." Material from the discussion of the "Komisija za Družbeno Samoupravljanje pri RS ZSS." Ljubljana: October, 1966.

Krajne-Čuk, A. "Grupne Karakteristike in Formiranje Delovnih Grup." A Study for the Institut za Sociologio in Filozofijo Pri Univerzi v Ljubljani. Ljubljana, 1967.

Milisavljević, M. "Planiranje i Poslovna Politika Poduzeća." Vols. I and II. Belgrade: Udruženje Saveza Studenata Ekonomskog Fakulteta, 1965-1967.

Poček-Matić, M., Bosanac, G., and Ugljen, S. "Samoupravljanje i Integracija u Privredi," A Study for the Institut za Društveno Upravljanje SRH. Zagreb, 1964.

Index